STRAIGHT UP!

By A.G. TERRILL

STRAIGHT UP!

Copyright © 2014, 2013 by A.G. TERRILL
All rights reserved.
ISBN: 978-1-312-14540-5
Published by Lulu.com

"Scripture taken from the NEW AMERICAN STANDARD BIBLE®, *NASB®*,
© Copyright 1960, 1962, 1963, 1968, 1971, 1972, 1973, 1975, 1977, 1995 by The Lockman Foundation
All rights reserved. Used by permission. (www.Lockman.org)

Scripture quotations marked (NLT) are taken from the *Holy Bible,* New Living Translation, copyright © 1996, 2004, 2007 by Tyndale House Foundation. Used by permission of Tyndale House Publishers, Inc., Carol Stream, Illinois 60188. All rights reserved.

Unless otherwise indicated, all Scripture quotations are taken from the *Holy Bible,* New Living Translation, copyright © 1996, 2004, 2007 by Tyndale House Foundation. Used by permission of Tyndale House Publishers, Inc., Carol Stream, Illinois 60188. All rights reserved.

Scripture taken from the Holy Bible, NEW INTERNATIONAL VERSION®. Copyright © 1973, 1978, 1984, 2011 by Biblica, Inc. All rights reserved worldwide. Used by permission.

NEW INTERNATIONAL VERSION® and NIV® are registered trademarks of Biblica, Inc. Use of either trademark for the offering of goods or services requires the prior written consent of Biblica US, Inc.

Definitions taken from Dictionary.com. LLC. Copyright © 2012. All rights reserved.

American Psychological Association (APA):

sin. (n.d.). *Dictionary.com Unabridged.*. Retrieved December 03, 2012, from Dictionary.com website: http://dictionary.reference.com/browse/sin

Chicago Manual Style (CMS):

sin. Dictionary.com. Dictionary.com Unabridged. Random House, Inc. http://dictionary.reference.com/browse/sin (accessed: December 03, 2012).

Modern Language Association (MLA):

"sin." *Dictionary.com Unabridged.* Random House, Inc. 03 Dec. 2012. <Dictionary.com http://dictionary.reference.com/browse/sin>.

Institute of Electrical and Electronics Engineers (IEEE):

Dictionary.com, "sin," in *Dictionary.com Unabridged.* Source location: Random House Inc. http://dictionary.reference.com/browse/sin. Available: http://dictionary.reference.com. Accessed: December 03, 2012.

BibTeX Bibliography Style (BibTeX)

```
@article {Dictionary.com2012,
    title = {Dictionary.com Unabridged},
    month = {Dec},day = {03},year = {2012},
    url = {http://dictionary.reference.com/browse/sin},}
```

Definitions taken from WEBSTER'S ENCYCLOPEDIC UNABRIDGED DICTIONARY of the ENGLISH LANGUAGE

Acknowledgments and Permissions

The "A Dictionary of the English Language" portion of *Webster's Encyclopedic Unabridged Dictionary* is based on the second edition of *The Random House Dictionary of the English Language, the Unabridged Edition*, copyright © 1993,1987

Copyright © 1996 by Random House Value Publishing, Inc.

All rights reserved under International and Pan-American Copyright Conventions.

The 1996 edition is published by Gramercy Books, a division of Random House Value Publishing Inc.

For my family

May the information contained in this book make it easier for you to walk the straight path with God.

Acknowledgments

Thanks to my Mother, her Mother, her Grandfather and my Mother's brothers and sisters. They are a true example of a family having a close relationship with God. Without whom I would not have been prepared to follow The Holy Spirit's guidance to write this book.

Table of Contents:

Introduction Page 1

Chapter One: What is SIN anyway? Page 15

Chapter Two: Don't Know Jesus? Page 25

Chapter Three: WHAT ARE THE TEN COMMANDMENTS ANYWAY? Page 63

Chapter Four: The Commandments of Jesus Page 89

Chapter Five: Is Drinking or doing Drugs wrong? Page 107

Chapter Six: Is Abortion Murder? Page 125

Chapter Seven: Is it alright for my boyfriend and I to have sex, if we love each other? Page 141

Chapter Eight: Forbidden Sexual Practices: Page 157

Chapter Nine: What is Adultery? Page 173

Chapter Ten: IS HOMOSEXUALITY A SIN? Page 189

Chapter Eleven: Is Marriage only supposed to be between a Man and a Woman? Page 203

Chapter Twelve: BEWARE the Supernatural? Page 209

Chapter Thirteen: **Are these the END TIMES, the END OF DAYS?** Page 245

Chapter Fourteen: Why should I go to Church? Page 261

Chapter Fifteen Other Questions and Sundry Commandments... Page 267

Introduction:

Let me start out honestly by saying that:
I am not a Pastor or Minister or anything like that.
I have no doctorate or degree in Theology.
I am not a Teacher or Bible Study Leader either.

I think of myself as just a normal Christian person.
I go to church fairly regularly.
I read my Bible fairly regularly.
I am an assistant in the children's Sunday school classes when needed, and have taken a few Sunday school/Bible study classes myself.
I've learned about my Spiritual Gifts, Abilities, etc. and how I might be called to help the church or such. Nothing a lot of Christian's haven't done.
So as you can see… I am nothing special.

BUT, I think that is exactly why the Holy Spirit has directed and guided me to write this book.
Because if "I" can find the answers to these questions… and more….

THEN YOU CAN TOO!

GOD is showing YOU that you don't have to be "Called", trained, have a degree or anything else to understand HIS word, and to find out HIS WILL… you just have to WANT TO.
And GOD LOVES it when you want to spend time getting to know HIM and his WILL.

Matthew 7:7-8

"Ask, and it will be given to you; seek, and you will find; knock and it will be opened to you.
For everyone who asks receives, and he who seeks finds, and to him who knocks it will be opened." NASB

"Keep on asking, and you will be given what you ask for. Keep on looking, and you will find. Keep on knocking, and the door will be opened.

For everyone who asks, receives. Everyone who seeks, finds, And the door is opened to everyone who knocks." NLT

So how did I do it? How can you do it too?

I would recommend that first you decide on what you really want to know; making a list might help.

Then you should start by reading the entire Bible all the way through (*Especially* if you have never done this before), start to finish, Genesis to Revelation. Making notes of all the scriptures that mention the items on your list for further research later.

I have been told you can read through the entire Bible in a year just by reading only 15-20 minutes a day.

I don't know that myself as I read Parallel Bibles (the ones with several versions of the Bible in it) so my time is way off.

But I must confess that one of the easiest ways of finding what I need... is by letting the Holy Spirit guide me.

You probably won't believe how many times I have simply "thought" about what I was looking for and "asked" the Holy Spirit for guidance... only to close my eyes and let my hand touch the Bible and open it to a scripture that had to do with exactly what I was asking for!

YES! People, The Holy Spirit really is there to help you... just give him a chance.

And Praying!

Simply meditating on God's Word and Praying for the answers you are seeking will often lead you to new scriptures you hadn't even thought dealt with your question until you REALLY read it again. Or you may have a dream or just a wild thought about where to look or such. LISTEN! That thought is for YOU... from The Holy Spirit, Jesus or even The Heavenly Father.

HAVE FAITH!

Now I will admit that my Spiritual Gift is FAITH, and I come from a family where my great grandfather, grandmother and mother have all had close relationships with, and spoken to, God (the Heavenly Father, Holy Spirit, and Jesus)... and the conversations went both ways.

They prayed and things happened. It takes more than one hand to count the number of major miracles God has worked in my family...so that lets me TRUST God better than some.

BUT ANYONE can still learn to Trust God and find Faith.

And ANYONE can find the answers they need in THE SCRIPTURES of God's Word.

We just have to ask, seek... and find, so pay attention when you read.

Sometimes checking out the internet will also lead you to scriptures about what you are looking for... but make sure you read them for yourself out of YOUR OWN Bible to make sure they are REALLY Bible scriptures.

You can also try reading different Bible versions, Bible based books, etc. And be ready to go back to your Bible and previous styles of research that may have already worked for you.

Psalm 111:7-8

"All he does is just and good,
and **all his commandments are trustworthy.**
They are forever true,
to be obeyed faithfully and with integrity. NLT

The works of his hands are verity and judgment;
All his commandments are sure.
They stand fast for ever and ever,
And are done in truth and uprightness. KJV

Note: For this book the initials KJV will stand for the King James Version of the Bible, ASV will stand for American Standard Version of the Bible, NLT will stand for the New Living Translation of the Bible, NASB will stand for the New American Standard Bible, and NIV will stand for the New International Version of the Bible.

Now let's go to the real introduction...

THE REAL INTRODUCTION....

Between Television, Movies, Books, Newspapers, the Internet and even the person next door... today's Christian moral values have been compromised to the extent that, for most people, they no longer agree with God's values and God's Laws. But many Christian's do not realize this...

Because, in today's society many people are too busy, too tired, or just don't think to look for answers to some of their important moral questions in the Bible.

A lot of "Christians" have never read the Bible all the way through... even once, and many more don't even go to church or read the bible AT ALL.

Others read the Bible but have trouble understanding what they are reading or simply finding what they are looking for.

Then there are those that simply choose which scriptures they will believe and obey and which scriptures they will ignore or absolutely deny, never understanding the problems this will cause.

Add in the fact that so many people today are overly concerned with being "politically correct" and "not offending anyone" that they see SIN all around them and say or do nothing.

So others then see the sin, and since nothing is being said about how it is wrong... **a SIN...** the others come to believe that the SIN is "acceptable", even "normal" behavior.

These are some of the reasons I wrote this book.

In this book I will attempt to list many of today's most confusing and bothersome moral questions, using only one chapter on each, so the answers will be quick and easy to find.

Then I will list biblical scriptures that pertain to that question. I will use several different Bible versions for this so that the reader may compare and contrast them to get a better understanding of their meanings.

For example: King James Version of the Bible, NASB, NLT, etc.

For many questions there will be too many scriptures to print them all in this... quick reference... book, but I will list some of them so that anyone curious about them can go and look them up in their own Bible at their leisure.

I will put most comments in a passage that deals directly with the chapter question in a **"Bold"** font or larger letters for speed and ease of finding the information... but please make sure you read the entire passage to gain true understanding. Sometimes even the verses before and after if applicable.

I may make a few comments throughout the book, but for the most part I let the scripture's do all the talking, so to speak, and most of the comments are simply about the scripture.

I hope this book is easy to read and understand as it offers quick and concise answers to some of your important questions, using God's word... the scriptures.

Now let's get back to the issue at hand...

God's Laws, His Commandments, **are meant to help people live better lives**, not to put unreasonable constraints on them for no reason.

Not following God's commandments leads to sinning and the degradation of our Christian Moral Values.

The decay can start in small ways, like people not going to church or reading the Bible so they can learn the scriptures and find out about God's commandments in the first place.

Or people who learn about the scriptures and commandments and then selectively choose which scriptures they will believe and obey and which scriptures they will ignore or absolutely deny, never understanding that this can lead to sin and moral decay.

They give many reasons for not following God's word:

They "no longer" apply: either due to the fact that **it is in the "Old Testament" but not in the "New Testament".**

Or

Because something else of that same area of scripture is old and seemingly out of date (as 'do not mix two types of cloth."-- It was probably very important back before we had synthetics and machines that are better at sewing, etc. But under the same or similar circumstances; perhaps third world countries, then that scripture would still be pertinent.). **Therefore whatever scriptural command they don't want to follow must also be "old and out of date."**

Note: If a scripture does not specifically state that the command no longer applies (like no longer making sacrifices, restrictions on food, etc.), and you know that God is the same now as he was then... then shouldn't you believe that **the command still applies today?**

"For verily I say unto you, Till heaven and earth pass away, one jot or one tittle shall in no wise pass away from the law, till all things be accomplished. Whosoever therefore shall break one of these least commandments, and shall teach men so, shall be called least in the kingdom of heaven: but whosoever shall do and teach them, he shall be called great in the kingdom of heaven" Matthew 5:18-19, ASV

Others choose to believe that **"A Loving God" would not have made such a commandment**, or "has changed his mind" about that command.

What they are unable to see (because they are not God) is how that command, in relation to millions of people and generations of sliding morals, might save people from losing their souls. And the LORD does not change.

And the list goes on… (And needs clarifying for many).

Here are a few Scriptures that talk about how such "reasons" are inaccurate.

Malachi 3:6

For I am the LORD, I change not; therefore ye sons of Jacob are not consumed. KJV

"I am the LORD, and I do not change. That is why you descendents of Jacob are not already completely destroyed." NLT

Hebrew 13:8

Jesus Christ the same yesterday, and to day, and for ever. KJV

Jesus Christ is the same yesterday, today, and forever. NLT

Matthew 5:17-18

"Don't misunderstand why I have come. I did not come to abolish the law of Moses or the writings of the prophets. No, I came to fulfill them. I assure you, until heaven and earth disappear, even the smallest detail of God's law will remain until its purpose is achieved. NLT

And not one iota of the law has been abolished...... Think not that I am come to destroy the law, or the prophets: I am not come to destroy, but to fulfil. For verily I say unto you, Till heaven and earth pass, one jot or one tittle shall in no wise pass from the law, till all be fulfilled. KJV

<u>And when our Christian Moral Values degrade... bad things happen.</u>

Promiscuity, Homosexuality, Adultery and Divorce...often preceded, accompanied, or followed by... drug use or alcohol abuse, are the main reasons for the fall of the "traditional family" (Father, Mother, and Kids) and Christian moral values.

And when the "traditional family" falls apart statistics show that you have countless single parents, usually mothers; who either work one or even two jobs to support the "modern family" or who are on some kind of welfare or other monetary assistance program... that most "traditional families" are taxed into paying for.

But that is not the worst. Read any number of news articles, or watch the documentaries; the kids from those "modern families" are who suffer.

Kids, who have less, if any, time with valuable parental role models.

Kids who have no one around to help with homework, or important questions about sex, drugs, bullying, or other life changing events or decisions.

Kids who spend more time alone and unsupervised, allowing for problem behaviors to develop.

Kids who feel alone, or even abandoned, but who are not taken to church to learn of God's Love, or Jesus' Sacrifice for them. Or the comfort the Holy Spirit can provide and the fact that with God... they are NOT ALONE... and someone DOES CARE.

Kids who go out into the world in search of the acceptance, love and companionship that they don't feel they get at home.

Kids who join gangs, become promiscuous, or take to using alcohol or drugs… or even worse…all to make them feel like they matter to someone… or just to escape the fact that they believe no one cares.

But this isn't just about the "single parent". Some apparently "traditional families" are rampant with adultery, homosexuality, alcohol or drug abuse…or worse.

The kids are not stupid. They see, they hear, and they grow up to believe all of these things are "acceptable" behavior. So they grow up like this, and usually get even worse than their parents… then they have children… and the cycle continues.

Who is really happy here? Who is even really content?

Just think… seriously think… consider… how much better life could be for everyone if people actually "Loved God with all their heart, mind, body and strength" and "Loved their neighbor as themselves". If everyone tried to follow God's Commandments and avoid Sin?

And there are even more reasons than those I just listed. Can you think of any?

As you can see, if you let sin slide… it only gets worse. And between the modern media who are more concerned about sensationalism and making money, and the "politically correct" people who refuse to say anything against anything (except those people who ARE trying to save our values), very few people are trying to stop the slow slide of modern morality which leads to the disintegration of the "traditional family".

That leaves it mainly up to the Churches.

But unfortunately, so many of today's churches are ALSO too worried about being "politically correct" or afraid of offending someone that they are no longer doing their job and teaching the things God truly feels are right and wrong, especially when those teachings might keep people from doing wrong and possibly losing their souls.

Or worse, some Churches are actively teaching non-Christian morals and breaking God's commandments (allowing openly homosexual ministers… which actively condone the breaking of several of God's commandments, and other "False Teachings" that the Bible warns about.)

So of course there would be mass confusion about what God really wants from his children… and what he DOES NOT want.

Just another reason I wrote this book for today's Christian.

The book is for Christians?

What is a Christian?

For the person looking into this book that hasn't a clue what a Christian really is…

A Christian is a person who believes and acknowledges that Jesus Christ is the son of God, that he was born of a virgin woman, lived a sin-free life and died on a cross to save us from all of our sins... and three days later rose again (came back to life).

Acknowledged acceptance of Jesus Christ, what he has done for you, and asking his forgiveness for your sins, is the only way to get to his Father (our Heavenly Father) and into heaven. All who do not know and accept him… will be cast into the lake of fire at the time of Judgment.

Again this is all from scripture, as you will see as you read further.

<u>If you are not a Christian or would like more information about Jesus, please see the chapter: DON'T KNOW JESUS? (He loves for people to get to know him better). And please,</u>

continue to read and learn even more about Him… or look for answers to questions you might have.

Proverbs 2:1-11

My son, **if thou wilt receive my words, And lay up my commandments with thee**; So as to incline thine ear unto wisdom, And apply thy heart to understanding; Yea, **if thou cry after discernment, And lift up thy voice for understanding; If thou seek her as silver, And search for her as for hid treasures: Then shalt thou understand the fear of Jehovah, And find the knowledge of God. For Jehovah giveth wisdom; Out of his mouth cometh knowledge and understanding:** He layeth up sound wisdom for the upright; He is a shield to them that walk in integrity; **That he may guard the paths of justice, And preserve the way of his saints. Then shalt thou understand righteousness and justice, And equity, yea, every good path. For wisdom shall enter into thy heart**, **And knowledge shall be pleasant unto thy soul; Discretion shall watch over thee; Understanding shall keep thee**: ASV

My son, if thou wilt receive my words, And hide my commandments with thee;

So that thou incline thine ear unto wisdom, And apply thine heart to understanding;

Yea, if thou criest after knowledge, And liftest up thy voice for understanding;

If thou seekest her as silver, And searchest for her as for hid treasures;

Then shalt thou understand the fear of the LORD, And find the knowledge of God.

For the LORD giveth wisdom:

Out of his mouth cometh knowledge and understanding.

He layeth up sound wisdom for the righteous:

He is a buckler to them that walk uprightly. He keepeth the paths of judgment,

And preserveth the way of his saints.

Then shalt thou understand righteousness, and judgment, And equity; yea, every good path.

When wisdom entereth into thine heart,
And knowledge is pleasant unto thy soul;
Discretion shall preserve thee, Understanding shall keep thee" KJV

Psalm 119:1-7

Blessed are they that are perfect in the way, Who walk in the law of Jehovah.
Blessed are they that keep his testimonies, That seek him with the whole heart.
Yea, they do no unrighteousness; They walk in his ways.
Thou hast commanded us thy precepts, That we should observe them diligently.
Oh that my ways were established to observe thy statutes!
Then shall I not be put to shame, When I have respect unto all thy commandments.
I will give thanks unto thee with uprightness of heart, When I learn thy righteous judgments. ASV

Blessed are the undefiled in the way, who walk in the law of the LORD. Blessed are they that keep his testimonies, and that seek him with the whole heart. They also do no iniquity: they walk in his ways. Thou hast commanded us to keep thy precepts diligently. O that my ways were directed to keep thy statutes! Then shall I not be ashamed, when I have respect unto all thy commandments. I will praise thee with uprightness of heart, when I shall have learned thy righteous judgments. KJV

And YES, there are a lot of Commandments, Laws, statutes, etc. that make it pretty impossible to stay sin-free (which is why we need Jesus Christ).

BUT there is the OOPS, I made a mistake… I'm sorry; please forgive me, kind of sin.

And then there is the continual, habitual, "I don't care what God thinks, I'm doing what I want" kind of sin that is willfully and continually defying God and his commandments.

This is the type of sin that can put your very soul in peril. Because if you are not Obeying the commandments... on purpose... it is like rejecting God along with his laws.

See the chapter: Other Questions and Sundry Commandments... (Can I lose my Salvation?)

This is the type of sin (and the kinds of sinful behaviors/beliefs that promote this type of sin) that I primarily try to cover in this book.

1 Corinthians 2:9

Eye hath not seen, nor ear heard, neither have entered into the heart of man, the things which God hath prepared for them that love him. KJV

Chapter One

WHAT IS SIN ANYWAY?

According to Dictionary.com, Sin is…

Sin [sin] - noun

1. **Transgression of divine law: *the sin of Adam.***
2. **Any act regarded as such a transgression, esp. a willful or deliberate violation of some religious or moral principle.**
3. **Any reprehensible or regrettable action, behavior, lapse, etc.; great fault or offense: *It's a sin to waste time.***

According to WEBSTER'S ENCYCLOPEDIC UNABRIDGED DICTIONARY of the ENGLISH LANGUAGE the definition of Sin is,

1. Transgression of divine law; *the sin of Adam.*
2. Any act regarded as such a transgression, esp. a willful or deliberate violation of some religious or moral principle.
3. Any reprehensible action, behavior, etc.; serious fault or offense.
4. To commit a sinful act.
5. To offend against a principle, standard, etc.
6. To commit or perform sinfully: *He sinned his crimes without compunction.*
7. To bring, drive, etc., by sinning: *He sinned his soul to perdition.*

-Syn. 1. Trespass, violation. 2. wrong, wickedness. 3. transgress, trespass.

Now you know the definition of sin… but how does Sin affect our relationship and interactions with God?

SIN... *SEPARATES* us from GOD.

God's very nature is so PURE and HOLY, that just looking at Sin causes him great sorrow. He cannot look upon SIN with any type of tolerance or acceptance.

That is not to say that God can't look at SIN, but, He HATES it so strongly He usually feels compelled to punish, so he looks away... *stays separate from us.*

Habakkuk 1:13

Thou art of purer eyes than to behold evil,
And canst not look on iniquity; KJV

Your eyes are too pure to approve evil,
And **You can not look on wickedness with favor.** NASB

Isaiah 59:2

But your iniquities have separated you from your God; your sins have hidden his face from you, so that he will not hear. NIV

But your iniquities have made a separation between you and your God,
And your sins have hidden His face from you so that He does not hear. NASB

But your iniquities have separated between you and your God, and your sins have hid his face from you, that he will not hear. KJV

Now you have the definition of SIN, and you know how Sin affects God, but a lot of people are not aware that...

You may be sinning and not even realize it!

So this book tries to explain many of today's most common sins that really bother God, so you will then know and be able to stop doing them.

Don't forget; you can always ask God for help, he loves to hear from you.

Proverbs 14:12

"There is a way that seems right to a man, but in the end it leads to death." NIV

There is a way which seemeth right unto a man, but the End thereof are the ways of death. KJV

Jeremiah 9:12-13

Who is the wise man, that may understand this? And who is he to whom the mouth of the LORD hath spoken, that he may declare it, for what the land perisheth and is burnt up like a wilderness, that none passeth through?
And the LORD saith, **Because they have forsaken my law which I set before them, and have not obeyed my voice, neither walked therein.** KJV

What man is wise enough to understand this? Who has been instructed by the LORD and can explain it? Why has the land been ruined and laid waste like a desert that no one can cross?
The LORD said, **"It is because they have forsaken my law, which I set before them; they have not obeyed me or followed my law.** NIV

Isaiah 59

Behold, the LORD's hand is not shortened, that it cannot save; neither his ear heavy, that it cannot hear: **But your iniquities have separated between you and your God, and your sins have hid his face from you, that he will not hear.** For your hands are defiled with blood, and your fingers with iniquity; your lips have spoken lies, your tongue hath muttered perverseness.

None calleth for justice, nor any pleadeth for truth: they trust in vanity, and speak lies; they conceive mischief, and bring forth iniquity. They hatch cockatrice' eggs, and weave the spider's web: he that eateth of their eggs dieth, and that which is crushed breaketh out into a viper. Their webs shall not become garments, neither shall they cover themselves with their works: their works are works of iniquity, and the act of violence is in their hands. **Their feet run to evil, and they make haste to shed innocent blood: their thoughts are thoughts of iniquity; wasting and destruction are in their paths**. The way of peace they know not; and there is no judgment in their goings: they have made them crooked paths: whosoever goeth therein shall not know peace. Therefore is judgment far from us, neither doth justice overtake us: we wait for light, but behold obscurity; for brightness, but we walk in darkness. We grope for the wall like the blind, and we grope as if we had no eyes: we stumble at noonday as in the night; we are in desolate places as dead men. We roar all like bears, and the act of violence is in their hands. and mourn sore like doves: we look for judgment, but there is none; for salvation, but it is far off from us. For our transgressions are multiplied before thee, and our sins testify against us: for our transgressions are with us; and as for our iniquities, we know them; In transgressing and lying against the LORD, and departing away from our God, speaking oppression and revolt, conceiving and uttering from the heart words of falsehood. And judgment is turned away backward, and justice standeth afar off: for truth is fallen in the street, and equity cannot enter. Yea, truth faileth; and he that departeth from evil maketh himself a prey: and **the LORD saw it, and it displeased him that there was no judgment.** And he saw that there was no man, and wondered that there was no intercessor: therefore his arm brought salvation unto him; and his righteousness, it sustained him. For he put on righteousness as a breastplate, and an helmet of salvation upon his head; and he put on the garments of vengeance for clothing, and was clad with zeal as a cloke. **According to their deeds, accordingly he will repay, fury to his adversaries, recompense to his enemies; to the islands he will repay recompense**. So shall they fear the name of the LORD from the west, and his glory from the rising of the sun. When the enemy shall come in like a flood, the Spirit of the LORD shall lift up a standard against him. **And the Redeemer shall come to Zion, and unto them that turn from transgression** in Jacob, saith the LORD. As for me, this is my covenant with them, saith the LORD; My spirit that is upon thee, and my words which I have put in thy mouth, shall not depart out of thy mouth, nor out of the mouth of thy seed, nor out of the mouth of thy seed's seed, saith the LORD, from henceforth and for ever. KJV

Behold, Jehovah's hand is not shortened, that it cannot save; neither his ear heavy, that it cannot hear: **but your iniquities have separated between you and your God, and your sins have hid his face from you, so that he will not hear.** For your hands are defiled with blood, and your fingers with iniquity; your lips have spoken lies, your tongue muttereth wickedness. None sueth in righteousness, and none pleadeth in truth: they trust in vanity, and speak lies; they conceive mischief, and bring forth iniquity. They hatch adders' eggs, and weave the spider's web: he that eateth of their eggs dieth; and that which is crushed breaketh out into a viper. Their webs shall not become garments, neither shall they cover themselves with their works: their works are works of iniquity, and the act of violence is in their hands. **Their feet run to evil, and they make haste to shed innocent blood: their thoughts are thoughts of iniquity; desolation and destruction are in their paths.** The way of peace they know not; and there is no justice in their goings: they have made them crooked paths; whosoever goeth therein doth not know peace.

Therefore is justice far from us, neither doth righteousness overtake us: we look for light, but, behold, darkness; for brightness, but we walk in obscurity. We grope for the wall like the blind; yea, we grope as they that have no eyes: we stumble at noonday as in the twilight; among them that are lusty we are as dead men. We roar all like bears, and moan sore like doves: **we look for justice, but there is none; for salvation, but it is far off from us. For our transgressions are multiplied before thee, and our sins testify against us; for our transgressions are with us, and as for our iniquities, we know them**: transgressing and denying Jehovah, and turning away from following our God, speaking oppression and revolt, conceiving and uttering from the heart words of falsehood. And justice is turned away backward, and righteousness standeth afar off; for truth is fallen in the street, and uprightness cannot enter. Yea, truth is lacking; and he that departeth from evil maketh himself a prey. And **Jehovah saw it, and it displeased him that there was no justice.**

And he saw that there was no man, and wondered that there was no intercessor: therefore his own arm brought salvation unto him; and his righteousness, it upheld him. And he put on righteousness as a breastplate, and a helmet of salvation upon his head; and he put on garments of vengeance for clothing, and was clad with zeal as a mantle. **According to their deeds, accordingly he will repay, wrath to his adversaries, recompense to his enemies;** to the islands he will repay recompense. So shall they fear the name of Jehovah from the west, and his glory from the rising of the sun; for he will come as a rushing stream, which the breath of Jehovah driveth.

And a Redeemer will come to Zion, and unto them that turn from transgression in Jacob, saith Jehovah. And as for me, this is my covenant with them, saith Jehovah: my Spirit that is upon thee, and my words which I have put in thy mouth, shall not depart out of thy mouth, nor out of the mouth of thy seed, nor out of the mouth of thy seed's seed, saith Jehovah, from henceforth and for ever. ASV

Matthew 4:17

"**Turn from your sins and turn to God**, because the Kingdom of Heaven is near." NLT

"**Repent:** for the kingdom of heaven is at hand." KJV

Psalm 1:1-6

Blessed is the man **that walketh not in the counsel of the ungodly, nor standeth in the way of sinners, nor sitteth in the seat of the scornful.** But his delight is in the law of the LORD; and in his law doth he meditate day and night. And he shall be like a tree planted by the rivers of water, that bringeth forth his fruit in his season; his leaf also shall not wither; and whatsoever he doeth shall prosper. **The ungodly are not so: but are like the chaff which the wind driveth away. Therefore the ungodly shall not stand in the judgment, nor sinners in the congregation of the righteous.** For the LORD knoweth the way of the righteous: **but the way of the ungodly shall perish**. KJV

How blessed is the man **who does not walk in the counsel of the wicked,**

Nor stand in the path of sinners,

Nor sit in the seat of scoffers!
But his delight is in the law of the LORD,
And in His law he meditates day and night.
He will be like a tree firmly planted by streams of water,
Which yields its fruit in its season
And its leaf does not wither;
And in whatever he does, he prospers.
The wicked are not so,
But they are like chaff which the wind drives away.
Therefore the wicked will not stand in the judgment,
Nor sinners in the assembly of the righteous.
For the LORD knows the way of the righteous,
But the way of the wicked will perish. NASB

Revelation 2:5

"**Repent and do the things you did at first. If you do not repent,** I will come to you and remove your lampstand from its place." NIV

Remember therefore from whence thou art fallen, and repent, and do the first works; or else I will come unto thee quickly, and will remove thy candlestick out of his place, **except thou repent.** KJV

John 8:11

Jesus declared. **"Go now and leave your life of sin."** NIV

And Jesus said, **"Go. From now on sin no more."** NASB

Romans 3:23

"For all have sinned and fall short of the glory of God."
NIV and NASB

For all have sinned; all fall short of God's glorious standard. NLT

No human being is, or was ever, Perfect (Never Sinned), except

Jesus Christ.

So, whatever the sin you may have done, or may even still be doing... You can still be saved (forgiven your sins) and enter into the Family of God.

But you must Repent (Tell God you are sorry for sinning against Him and his laws, and ask forgiveness)... and mean it, and truly try not to sin again.

Now that may be really hard, and you may stumble and fall many times... but if you are SINCERELY trying to stop the sin... that is what God wants from you.

But NOT SINNING, or asking forgiveness for your sins ALONE is not going to please God, save you from HELL or get you into HEAVEN.

For THAT you still need one VERY IMPORTANT Thing...

JESUS CHRIST

You must accept and acknowledge that Jesus Christ is the son of God. That he was born of a virgin woman, lived a sin-free life but willingly died on a cross (a sinners death) to save all who trust in him from their sins... and three days later he rose again (came back to life).

For then God, through the cleansing blood of his SON and our mediator Jesus Christ, is then able to turn back toward us sinners, and SEE us as Pure and spotless...being WITHOUT SIN. And HE can welcome us.

Timothy 2:5

"For there is one God and one mediator between God and men, the man **Christ Jesus."** KJV and NIV

"For there is one God, and one mediator also between God and men, the man Christ Jesus." NASB

Romans 5:8

"But God demonstrates his own love for us in this: While we were still sinners, Christ died for us." NIV

But God commendeth his love toward us, in that, while we were yet sinners, Christ died for us. KJV

1 Peter 3:18

For **Christ also died for sins once for all, the just and the unjust, so that He might bring us to God.** NASB

Christ also suffered when he died for our sins once for all time. He never sinned, but he died for sinners that he might bring us safely home to God NLT

Don't know about Jesus Christ?

See Don't know Jesus?

the very next chapter.

You **do** know Jesus but need help to stop sinning as much as is humanly possible and live a life more pleasing to God?

Romans 8:6

For the mind set on the flesh is death, **but the mind set on the Spirit is life and peace**. NASB

The mind of sinful man is death, **but the mind controlled by the Spirit is life and peace;** NIV

Romans 12:2

Don't copy the behavior and customs of this world, but let God transform you into a new person by changing the way you think. NLT

And be not conformed to this world: but be ye transformed by the renewing of your mind, that ye may prove what is that good, and acceptable, and perfect will of God.
KJV

Need to read more scriptures about sin?

Here are just a few of the many examples; Genesis 9:9, Genesis 42:22, Leviticus 4:20, 2 Kings 21:11, Leviticus 9:3, 2 Kings 17:21, Isaiah 59:2, 2 Chronicles 6:27, John 5:14, John 16:8, Romans 8:2

For Lots more... check your local Bible.

Isaiah 55:6-7

Seek ye the LORD while He may be found,
Call ye upon him while he is near:
Let the wicked forsake his way,
And the unrighteous man his thoughts:
And let him return unto the LORD,
and he will have mercy upon him;
And to our God, for he will abundantly pardon.
KJV

Chapter Two

Don't know Jesus?

Let us take a look at a life full of love and compassion. And a death and resurrection that is the only thing that can save your very soul… if you believe.

John 14:6

Jesus answered **"I am the way and the truth and the life. No one comes to the Father except through me."** NIV

Jesus saith unto him, **I am the way, the truth, and the life: no man cometh unto the Father, but by me.** KJV

1John 5:12-13

"He who has the Son has life; he who does not have the Son of God does not have life. I write these things to **you who believe in the name of the Son of God so that you may know that you have eternal life."** NIV

He who has the Son has the life; he who does not have the Son of God does not have the life.

These things **I have written to you who believe in the name of the Son of God, so that you may know that you have eternal life.** NASB

Romans 5:8-11

But God commendeth his love toward us, in that, **while we were yet sinners, Christ died for us.** Much more then, **being now justified by his blood, we shall be saved from wrath through him.** For if, when we were **much more, being reconciled, we shall be saved by his life.** And not only so, but we also joy in God through **our Lord Jesus Christ, by whom we have now received the atonement.** KJV

But God commendeth his own love toward us, in that, while we were yet sinners, Christ died for us. Much more then, being now justified by his blood, shall we be saved from the wrath of God through him. For if, while we were enemies, we were reconciled to God through the death of his Son, much more, being reconciled, shall we be saved by his life; and not only so, but we also rejoice in God through our Lord Jesus Christ, through whom we have now received the reconciliation. ASV

Romans 10:8-10

Salvation that comes from trusting Christ-which is the message we preach-is already within easy reach. In fact, the Scriptures say, "The message is close at hand; it is on your lips and in your heart."

For if you confess with your mouth that Jesus is Lord and believe in your heart that God raised him from the dead, you will be saved. For **it is by believing in your heart that you are made right with God, and it is by confessing with your mouth that you are saved.** NLT

But what does it say? "The word is near you; it is in your mouth and in your heart," that is, the word of faith we are proclaiming: **That if you confess with your mouth, "Jesus is Lord," and believe in your heart that God raised him from the dead, you will be saved.** For **it is with your heart that you believe and are justified, and it is with your mouth that you confess and are saved.** NIV

Romans 10:13

"WHOEVER WILL CALL ON THE NAME OF THE LORD WILL BE SAVED." NASB

"Everyone who calls on the name of the Lord will be saved." NIV

1 Peter 1:18-20

For you know that **God paid a ransom to save you** from the empty life you inherited from your ancestors. And the ransom he paid was not mere gold or silver. **He paid for you with the precious lifeblood of Christ, the sinless, spotless Lamb of God.**

God chose him for this purpose long before the world began, but now in these final days, he was sent to the earth for all to see. **And he did this for you.** NLT

Forasmuch as ye know that **ye were not redeemed with corruptible things**, as silver and gold, from your vain conversation received by tradition from your fathers; **but with the precious blood of Christ, as of a lamb without blemish and without spot:** who verily was foreordained before the foundation of the world, **but was manifest in these last times for you.** KJV

How did this all come about?

THE HOPE AND BIRTH

Luke 1:26-38

Now in the sixth month the angel Gabriel was sent from God unto a city of Galilee, named Nazareth, to a virgin betrothed to a man whose name was Joseph, of the house of David; and the virgin's name was Mary. And he came in unto her, and said, Hail, thou that art highly favored, the Lord is with thee. But she was greatly troubled at the saying, and cast in her mind what manner of salutation this might be. **And the angel said unto her, Fear not, Mary: for thou hast found favor with God. And behold, thou shalt conceive in thy womb, and bring forth a son, and shalt call his name JESUS. He shall be great, and shall be called the Son of the Most High: and the Lord God shall give unto him the throne of his father David: and he shall reign over the house of Jacob for ever; and of his kingdom there shall be no end.** And Mary said unto the angel, How shall this be, seeing I know not a man? **And the angel answered and said unto her, The Holy Spirit shall come upon thee, and the power of the Most High shall overshadow thee: wherefore also the holy thing which is begotten shall be called the Son of God.** And behold, Elisabeth thy kinswoman, she also hath conceived a son in her old age; and this is the sixth month with her that was called barren. For no word from God shall be void of power. **And Mary said, Behold, the handmaid of the Lord; be it unto me according to thy word**. And the angel departed from her. ASV

The angel Gabriel was sent from God unto a city of Galilee, named Nazareth, to a virgin espoused to a man whose name was Joseph, of the house of David; and the virgin's name was Mary. And the angel came in unto her, and said, Hail, thou that art highly favoured, the Lord is with thee: blessed art thou among women. And when she saw him, she was troubled at his saying, and cast in her mind what manner of salutation this should be. And the angel said unto her, **Fear not, Mary: for thou hast found favour with God. And behold, thou shalt conceive in thy womb, and bring forth a son, and shalt call his name JESUS. He shall be great, and shall be called the Son of the Highest: and the Lord God shall give unto him the throne of his father David: and he shall reign over the house of Jacob for ever; and of his kingdom there shall be no end.** Then said Mary unto the angel, How shall this be, seeing I know not a man? And the angel answered and said unto her, **The Holy Ghost shall come upon thee, and the power of the Highest shall overshadow thee: therefore also that holy thing which shall be born of thee shall be called the Son of God.** And behold, thy cousin Elisabeth, she hath also conceived a son in her old age: and this is the sixth month with her, who was called barren. For with God nothing shall be unpossible.

And Mary said, Behold the handmaid of the Lord; be it unto me according to thy word. And the angel departed from her. KJV

Matthew 1:18-24

Now the birth of Jesus Christ was as follows: when His mother Mary had been betrothed to Joseph, **before they came together she was found to be with child by the Holy Spirit.** And Joseph her husband, being a righteous man and not wanting to disgrace her, planned to send her away secretly. But when he had considered this, behold, **an angel of the Lord appeared to him in a dream, saying, "Joseph, son of David, do not be afraid to take Mary as your wife; for the Child who has been conceived in her is of the Holy Spirit. She will bear a Son; and you shall call His name Jesus, for He will save His people from their sins."** Now all this took place to fulfill what was spoken by the Lord through the prophet: "BEHOLD, THE VIRGIN SHALL BE WITH CHILD AND SHALL BEAR A SON, AND THEY SHALL CALL HIS NAME IMMANUEL," which translated means, "GOD WITH US." **And Joseph awoke from his sleep and did as the angel of the Lord commanded him,** and **took Mary as his wife, but kept her a virgin until she gave birth to a Son; and he called His name Jesus.** NASB

Now the birth of Jesus Christ was on this wise: When as his mother Mary was espoused to Joseph, before they came together, **she was found with child of the Holy Ghost.** Then Joseph her husband, being a just man, and not willing to make her a public example, was minded to put her away privily. But while he thought on these things, **behold, the angel of the Lord appeared unto him in a dream, saying, Joseph, thou son of David, fear not to take unto thee Mary thy wife: for that which is conceived in her is of the Holy Ghost. And she shall bring forth a son, and thou shalt call his name Jesus: for he shall save his people from their sins.** Now all this was done, that it **might be fulfilled which was spoken of the Lord by the prophet, saying, Behold, a virgin shall be with child, and shall bring forth a son, and they shall call his name Emmanuel, which being interpreted is, God with us.** Then **Joseph being raised from sleep did as the angel of the Lord had bidden him, and took unto him his wife: And knew her not till she had brought forth her firstborn son: and he called his name Jesus.** KJV

THE MIRACLES, TEACHINGS AND LIFE

Matthew 3:13-17

Then cometh Jesus from Galilee to the Jordan unto John, to be baptized of him. But John would have hindered him, saying, **I have need to be baptized of thee,** and comest thou to me? But Jesus answering said unto him, **Suffer it now: for thus it becometh us to fulfil all righteousness.** Then he suffereth him. And **Jesus when he was baptized, went up straightway from the water: and lo, the heavens were opened unto him, and he saw the Spirit of God descending as a dove, and coming upon him; and lo, a voice out of the heavens, saying, This is my beloved Son, in whom I am well pleased**. ASV

Then Jesus came from Galilee to the Jordan to be baptized by John. But John tried to deter him, saying, **"I need to be baptized by you,** and do you come to me?"

Jesus replied, **"Let it be so now; it is proper for us to do this to fulfill all righteousness."** Then John consented.

As soon as Jesus was baptized, he went up out of the water. **At that moment heaven was opened, and he saw the Spirit of God descending like a dove** and lighting on him.

And a voice from heaven said, "This is my Son, whom I love; with him I am well pleased." NIV

Luke 8:22-25

Now it came to pass on a certain day, that he went into a ship with his disciples: and he said unto them, Let us go over unto the other side of the lake. And they launched forth. But as they sailed he fell asleep: and there came down a storm of wind on the lake; and they were filled with water, and were in jeopardy. And they came to him, and awoke him, saying, Master, master, we perish. **Then he rose, and rebuked the wind and the raging of the**

water: and they ceased, and there was a calm. And he said unto them, Where is your faith? And they being afraid wondered, saying one to another, **What manner of man is this? For he commandeth even the winds and water, and they obey him.** KJV

One day Jesus said to his disciples, "Let's cross over to the other side of the lake." So they got into a boat and started out. On the way across, Jesus lay down for a nap, and while he was sleeping the wind began to rise. A fierce storm developed that threatened to swamp them, and they were in real danger.

The disciples woke him up, shouting, "Master, Master, we're going to drown!"

So Jesus rebuked the wind and the raging waves. The storm stopped and it was calm! Then he asked them, "Where is your faith?"

And they were filled with awe and amazement. They said to one another, "Who is this man, that even the winds and waves obey him?" NLT

Luke 9:10-17

And the apostles, when they were returned, declared unto him what things they had done. And he took them, and withdrew apart to a city called Bethsaida. But the multitudes perceiving it followed him: and **he welcomed them, and spake to them of the kingdom of God, and them that had need of healing he cured.** And the day began to wear away; and the twelve came, and said unto him, Send the multitude away, that they may go into the villages and country round about, and lodge, and get provisions: for we are here in a desert place. But **he said unto them, Give ye them to eat. And they said, We have no more than five loaves and two fishes; except we should go and buy food for all this people. For they were about five thousand men.** And he said unto his disciples, Make them sit down in companies, about fifty each. And they did so, and made them all sit down. And **he took the five loaves and the two fishes, and looking up to heaven, he blessed them, and brake; and gave to the disciples to set before the multitude. And they ate, and were all filled: and there was taken up that which**

remained over to them of broken pieces, twelve baskets. ASV

Taking them with Him, He withdrew by Himself to a city called Bethsaida. But the crowds were aware of this and followed Him; and **welcoming them, He began speaking to them about the kingdom of God and curing those who had need of healing.**

Now the day was ending, and the twelve came and said to Him, "Send the crowd away, that they may go into the surrounding villages and countryside and find lodging and get something to eat; for here we are in a desolate place." But **He said to them, "You give them something to eat!"** And they said, "We have no more than five loaves and two fish, unless perhaps we go and buy food for all these people." (For there were about five thousand men.) And He said to His disciples, "Have them sit down to eat in groups of about fifty each." They did so, and had them all sit down. Then **He took the five loaves and the two fish, and looking up to heaven, He blessed them, and broke them, and kept giving them to the disciples to set before the people. And they all ate and were satisfied; and the broken pieces which they had left over were picked up, twelve baskets full.** NASB

Luke 9:18-27

And it came to pass, as he was praying apart, the disciples were with him: and he asked them, saying, **Who do the multitudes say that I am?** And they answering said, John the Baptist; but others say, Elijah; and others, that one of the old prophets is risen again. And he said unto them, **But who say ye that I am? And Peter answering said, The Christ of God.** But he charged them, and commanded them to tell this to no man; saying, **The Son of man must suffer many things, and be rejected of the elders and chief priests and scribes, and be killed, and the third day be raised up.**

And he said unto all, **If any man would come after me, let him deny himself, and take up his cross daily, and follow me.** For whosoever would save his life shall lose it; but whosoever shall lose his life for my sake, the same shall save it. For **what is a man profited, if he gain the whole world, and lose or forfeit his own self?** For **whosoever shall be ashamed of me and of my words, of him shall the Son of man be ashamed, when he cometh in his own glory, and the glory of the Father, and of the holy angels**. But I tell you of a truth, There are some of them that stand here, who shall in no wise taste of death, till they see the kingdom of God. ASV

And it came to pass, as he was alone praying, his disciples were with him: and **he asked them, saying, Whom say the people that I am?** They answering said, John the Baptist; but some say, Elias; and others say, that one of the old prophets is risen again. **He said unto them, But whom say ye that I am? Peter answering said, The Christ of God.**

And he straitly charged them, and commanded them to tell no man that thing; **saying, The Son of man must suffer many things, and be rejected of the elders and chief priests and scribes, and be slain, and be raised the third day.** And he said to them all, **If any man will come after me, let him deny himself, and take up his cross daily, and follow me.** For whosoever will save his life shall lose it: but whosoever will lose his life for my sake, the same shall save it. ***For what is a man advantaged, if he gain the whole world, and lose himself, or be cast away?*** **For whosoever shall be ashamed of me and of my words, of him shall the Son of man be ashamed, when he shall come in his own glory, and in his Father's, and of the holy angels.**

But I tell you of a truth, there be some standing here, which shall not taste of death, till they see the kingdom of God. KJV

Luke 22:1-7

Now the feast of unleavened bread drew nigh, which is called the Passover. And **the chief priests and the scribes sought how they might put him to death**; for they feared the people.

And Satan entered into Judas who was called Iscariot, being of the number of the twelve. And he went away, and communed with the chief priests and captains, how he might deliver him unto them. And they were glad, and covenanted to give him money. And he consented, and sought opportunity to deliver him unto them in the absence of the multitude.

And the day of unleavened bread came, on which **the passover must be sacrificed.** ASV

Now the Feast of Unleavened Bread, which is called the Passover, was approaching. **The chief priests and the scribes were seeking how they might put Him to death;** for they were afraid of the people.

And Satan entered into Judas who was called Iscariot, belonging to the number of the twelve. And he went away and discussed with the chief priests and officers how he might betray Him to them. They were glad and agreed to give him money. So he consented, and began seeking a good opportunity to betray Him to them apart from the crowd.

Then came the first day of Unleavened Bread on which **the Passover lamb had to be sacrificed.** NASB

Luke 22:14-38

And when the hour was come, he sat down, and the apostles with him. And he said unto them, **With desire I have desired to eat this passover with you before I suffer:** for I say unto you, **I shall not eat it again, until it be fulfilled in the kingdom of God.** And he received a cup, and when he had given thanks, he said, **Take this, and divide it among yourselves: for I say unto you, I shall not drink from henceforth of the fruit of the vine, until the kingdom of God shall come.**

And he took bread, and when he had given thanks, he brake it, and gave to them, saying, **This is my body which is given for you: this do in remembrance of me.** And the cup in like manner after supper, saying, **This cup is the new covenant in my blood, even that which is poured out for you.**

But behold, the hand of him that betrayeth me is with me on the table. For the Son of man indeed goeth, as it hath been determined: **but woe unto that man through whom he is**

betrayed! And they began to question among themselves, which of them it was that should do this thing.

And there arose also a contention among them, which of them was accounted to be greatest. And he said unto them, The kings of the Gentiles have lordship over them; and they that have authority over them are called Benefactors. But ye shall not be so: but he that is the greater among you, let him become as the younger; and he that is chief, as he that doth serve. For which is greater, he that sitteth at meat, or he that serveth? is not he that sitteth at meat? but I am in the midst of you as he that serveth. **But ye are they that have continued with me in my temptations; and I appoint unto you a kingdom, even as my Father appointed unto me, that ye may eat and drink at my table in my kingdom; and ye shall sit on thrones judging the twelve tribes of Israel.**

Simon, **Simon, behold, Satan asked to have you, that he might sift you as wheat: but I made supplication for thee, that thy faith fail not; and do thou, when once thou hast turned again, establish thy brethren**. And he said unto him, Lord, with thee I am ready to go both to prison and to death. And he said, **I tell thee, Peter, the cock shall not crow this day, until thou shalt thrice deny that thou knowest me**. And he said unto them, When I sent you forth without purse, and wallet, and shoes, lacked ye anything? And they said, Nothing. And he said unto them, But now, he that hath a purse, let him take it, and likewise a wallet; and he that hath none, let him sell his cloak, and buy a sword. For I say unto you, **that this which is written must be fulfilled in me, And he was reckoned with transgressors: for that which concerneth me hath fulfilment**. And they said, Lord, behold, here are two swords. And he said unto them, It is enough. ASV

And when the hour was come, he sat down, and the twelve apostles with him. And he said unto them, **With desire I have desired to eat this passover with you before I suffer:** For I say unto you, **I will not any more eat thereof, until it be fulfilled in the kingdom of God**. And he took the cup, and gave thanks, and said, Take this, and divide it among yourselves: For I say unto you, I will not drink of the fruit of the vine, until the kingdom of God shall come.

And he took bread, and gave thanks, and brake it, and gave unto them, saying, This is my body which is given for you: this do in remembrance of me. Likewise also the cup after supper, saying, **This cup is the new testament in my blood, which is shed for you.**

But, behold, the hand of him that betrayeth me is with me on the table. And truly the Son of man goeth, as it was determined: **but woe unto that man by whom he is betrayed**! And they began to enquire among themselves, which of them it was that should do this thing.

And there was also a strife among them, which of them should be accounted the greatest. And he said unto them, The kings of the Gentiles exercise lordship over them; and they that exercise authority upon them are called benefactors. But ye shall not be so: but he that is greatest among you, let him be as the younger; and he that is chief, as he that doth serve. For whether is greater, he that sitteth at meat, or he that serveth? is not he that sitteth at meat? but I am among you as he that serveth. **Ye are they which have continued with me in my temptations. And I appoint unto you a kingdom, as my Father hath appointed unto me; That ye may eat and drink at my table in my kingdom, and sit on thrones judging the twelve tribes of Israel.**

And the Lord said, Simon, **Simon, behold, Satan hath desired to have you, that he may sift you as wheat: But I have prayed for thee, that thy faith fail not: and when thou art converted, strengthen thy brethren.** And he said unto him, Lord, I am ready to go with thee, both into prison, and to death. And he said**, I tell thee, Peter, the cock shall not crow this day, before that thou shalt thrice deny that thou knowest me.** And he said unto them, When I sent you without purse, and scrip, and shoes, lacked ye any thing? And they said, Nothing. Then said he unto them, But now, he that hath a purse, let him take it, and likewise his scrip: and he that hath no sword, let him sell his garment, and buy one. **For I say unto you, that this that is written must yet be accomplished in me, And he was reckoned among the transgressors: for the things concerning me have an end**. And they said, Lord, behold, here are two swords. And he said unto them, It is enough. KJV

THE SACRIFICE AND DEATH

Mark 10:32-34

They were on the road going up to Jerusalem, and **Jesus was walking** on ahead of them; and they were amazed, and those who followed were fearful. And again **He took the twelve aside and began to tell them what was going to happen to Him, saying,**

"Behold, we are going up to Jerusalem, and the Son of Man will be delivered to the chief priests and the scribes; and they will condemn Him to death and will hand Him over to the Gentiles.

They will mock Him and spit on Him, and scourge Him and kill Him, and three days later He will rise again." NASB

They were on their way up to Jerusalem, with Jesus leading the way, and the disciples were astonished, while those who followed were afraid. **Again he took the Twelve aside and told them what was going to happen to him.**

"We are going up to Jerusalem," he said, "and the Son of Man will be betrayed to the chief priests and teachers of the law. They will condemn him to death and will hand him over to the Gentiles, who will mock him and spit on him, flog him and kill him. Three days later he will rise." NIV

Matthew 26:36-54

Then cometh **Jesus with them unto a place called Gethsemane,** and saith unto his disciples, Sit ye here, while I go yonder and pray. And he took with him Peter and the two sons of Zebedee, **and began to be sorrowful and sore troubled. Then saith he unto them, My soul is exceeding sorrowful, even unto death: abide ye here, and watch with me.** And he went forward a little, and **fell on his face, and prayed,**

saying, My Father, if it be possible, let this cup pass away from me: nevertheless, not as I will, but as thou wilt. And he cometh unto the disciples, and findeth them sleeping, and saith unto Peter, What, could ye not watch with me one hour? Watch and pray, that ye enter not into temptation: the spirit indeed is willing, but the flesh is weak. Again **a second time he went away, and prayed, saying, My Father, if this cannot pass away, except I drink it, thy will be done.** And he came again and found them sleeping, for their eyes were heavy. And **he left them again, and went away, and prayed a third time, saying again the same words.** Then cometh he to the disciples, and saith unto them, Sleep on now, and take your rest: **behold, the hour is at hand, and the Son of man is betrayed into the hands of sinners. Arise, let us be going: behold, he is at hand that betrayeth me.**

And while he yet spake, lo, **Judas, one of the twelve**, came, and with him a great multitude with swords and staves, from the chief priest and elders of the people. **Now he that betrayed him gave them a sign, saying, Whomsoever I shall kiss, that is he: take him. And straightway he came to Jesus, and said, Hail, Rabbi; and kissed him. And Jesus said unto him, Friend, do that for which thou art come. Then they came and laid hands on Jesus, and took him.** And behold, one of them that were with Jesus stretched out his hand, and drew his sword, and smote the servant of the high priest, and struck off his ear. Then saith **Jesus unto him**, Put up again thy sword into its place: for all they that take the sword shall perish with the sword. Or **thinkest thou that I cannot beseech my Father, and he shall even now send me more than twelve legions of angels? How then should the scriptures be fulfilled that thus it must be?**

ASV

Then cometh Jesus with them unto a place called Gethsemane, and saith unto the disciples, Sit ye here, while I go and pray yonder. And he took with him Peter and the two sons of Zebedee, **and began to be sorrowful and very heavy. Then saith he unto them, My soul is exceeding sorrowful, even unto death: tarry ye here, and watch with me. And he went a little further, and fell on his face, and prayed,**

saying, O my Father, if it be possible, let this cup pass from me: nevertheless not as I will, but as thou wilt.

And he cometh unto the disciples, and findeth them asleep, and saith unto Peter, **What, could ye not watch with me one hour?** Watch and pray, that ye enter not into temptation: the spirit indeed is willing, but the flesh is weak. **He went away again the second time, and prayed, saying, O my Father, if this cup may not pass away from me, except I drink it, thy will be done.** And he came and found them asleep again: for their eyes were heavy. And **he left them, and went away again, and prayed the third time, saying the same words.** Then cometh he to his disciples, and saith unto them, Sleep on now, and take your rest: **behold, the hour is at hand, and the Son of man is betrayed into the hands of sinners. Rise, let us be going: behold, he is at hand that doth betray me.**

And **while he yet spake, lo, Judas, one of the twelve, came,** and with him a great multitude with swords and staves, from the chief priests and elders of the people.

Now he that betrayed him gave them a sign, saying, Whomsoever I shall kiss, that same is he: hold him fast.

And forthwith he came to Jesus, and said, Hail, master; and kissed him. And Jesus said unto him, Friend, wherefore are thou come? Then came they, and laid hands on Jesus, and took him. And behold, one of them which were with Jesus stretched out his hand, and drew his sword, and stroke a servant of the he high priests', an smote off his ear. Then said Jesus unto him, Put up again thy sword into his place: for all they that take the sword shall perish with the sword. **Thinkest thou that I cannot now pray to my Father, and he shall presently give me more than twelve legions of angels? But how then shall the scriptures be fulfilled, that thus it must be?** KJV

Mark 14:53-65

They led Jesus away to the high priest; and all the chief priests and the elders and the scribes gathered together. Peter had followed Him at a distance, right into the courtyard of the high priest; and he was sitting with the officers and warming himself at the fire. Now the chief priests and **the whole Council kept trying to obtain testimony against Jesus to put Him to death**, and they were not finding any. For many were giving false testimony against Him, but their testimony was not consistent.

Some stood up and began to give false testimony against Him, saying, **"We heard Him say, 'I will destroy this temple made with hands, and in three days I will build another made without hands.'"**

Not even in this respect was their testimony consistent. The high priest stood up and came forward and questioned Jesus, saying, “Do You not answer? What is it that these men are testifying against You?” But He kept silent and did not answer.

Again **the high priest was questioning Him, and saying to Him, “Are You the Christ, the Son of the Blessed One?”**

And Jesus said, “I am; and you shall see THE SON OF MAN SITTING AT THE RIGHT HAND OF POWER, and COMING WITH THE CLOUDS OF HEAVEN.” Tearing his clothes, the high priest said, “What further need do we have of witnesses? You have heard the blasphemy; how does it seem to you?” **And they all condemned Him to be deserving of death. Some began to spit at Him, and to blindfold Him, and to beat Him with their fists, and to say to Him, “Prophesy!” And the officers received Him with slaps in the face.** NASB

And they led Jesus away to the high priest: and with him were assembled all the chief priests and the elders and the scribes. And Peter followed him afar off, even into the palace of the high priest: and he sat with the servants, and warmed himself at the fire. And **the chief priests and all the council sought for witness against Jesus to put him to death; and found none**. For **many bare false witness against him, but their witness agreed not together. And there arose certain, and bare false witness against him, saying, We heard him say, I will destroy this temple that is made with hands, and within three days I will build another made without hands. But neither so did their witness agree together.** And the high priest stood up in the midst, and asked Jesus, saying, Answerest thou nothing? what is it which these witness against thee? **But he held his peace, and answered nothing.** Again the high priest asked him, and said unto him, **Art thou the Christ, the Son of the Blessed? And Jesus said, I am: and ye shall see the Son of man sitting on the right hand of power, and coming in the clouds of heaven**. Then the high priest rent his clothes, and saith, What need we any further witnesses? Ye have heard the blasphemy: what think ye? **And they all condemned him to be guilty of death. And some began to spit on him, and to cover his face, and to buffet him, and to say unto him, Prophesy: and the servants did strike him with the palms of their hands.** KJV

Mark 15:1-5

And straightway in the morning **the chief priests held a consultation with the elders and scribes and the whole council, and bound Jesus, and carried him away, and delivered him to Pilate.** And **Pilate asked him, Art thou the King of the Jews? And he answering said unto him, Thou sayest it.** And the chief priests accused him of many things: but he answered nothing. And Pilate asked him again, saying, Answerest thou nothing? Behold how many things they witness against thee. **But Jesus yet answered nothing; so that Pilate marveled.** KJV

Very early in the morning, **the chief priests, with the elders, the teachers of the law and the whole Sanhedrin, reached a decision. They bound Jesus, led him away and handed him over to Pilate.**

"Are you the king of the Jews?" asked Pilate.

"Yes, it is as you say," Jesus replied.

The chief priests accused him of many things. So again Pilate asked him, "Aren't you going to answer? See how many things they are accusing you of."

But Jesus still made no reply, and Pilate was amazed. NIV

John 19:1-24

Then Pilate therefore took Jesus, and scourged him. And the soldiers platted a crown of thorns, and put it on his head, and they put on him a purple robe, And said, Hail, King of the Jews! and they smote him with their hands. Pilate therefore went forth again, and saith unto them, **Behold, I bring him forth to you, that ye may know that I find no fault in him**. Then came Jesus forth, wearing the crown of thorns, and the purple robe. And Pilate saith unto them, Behold the man! **When the chief priests therefore and officers saw him, they cried out, saying, Crucify him, crucify him. Pilate saith unto them, Take ye him, and crucify him: for I find no fault in him.** The Jews answered him, **We have a law, and by our law he ought to die, because he made himself the Son of God.**

When Pilate therefore heard that saying, he was the more afraid; And went again into the judgment hall, and saith unto Jesus, **Whence**

art thou? But Jesus gave him no answer. Then saith Pilate unto him, Speakest thou not unto me? **knowest thou not that I have power to crucify thee, and have power to release thee? Jesus answered, Thou couldest have no power at all against me, except it were given thee from above: therefore he that delivered me unto thee hath the greater sin.** And from **thenceforth Pilate sought to release him:** but the Jews cried out, saying, If thou let this man go, thou art not Caesar's friend: whosoever maketh himself a king speaketh against Caesar.

When Pilate therefore heard that saying, he brought Jesus forth, and sat down in the judgment seat in a place that is called the Pavement, but in the Hebrew, Gabbatha. And it was the preparation of the passover, and about the sixth hour: and he saith unto the Jews, Behold your King! **But they cried out, Away with him, away with him, crucify him. Pilate saith unto them, Shall I crucify your King? The chief priests answered, We have no king but Caesar. Then delivered he him therefore unto them to be crucified**. And they took Jesus, and led him away. And **he bearing his cross went forth** into a place called the place of a skull, which is called in the Hebrew Golgotha: **Where they crucified him,** and two other with him, on either side one, and Jesus in the midst.

And **Pilate wrote a title, and put it on the cross. And the writing was, Jesus of Nazareth the King of the Jews.** This title then read many of the Jews: for the place where Jesus was crucified was nigh to the city: and it was written in Hebrew, and Greek, and Latin. Then said the chief priests of the Jews to Pilate, Write not, The King of the Jews; but that he said, I am King of the Jews. **Pilate answered, What I have written I have written.**

Then the soldiers, when they had crucified Jesus, took his garments, and made four parts, to every soldier a part; and also his coat: now the coat was without seam, woven from the top throughout. They said therefore among themselves, Let us not rend it, but cast lots for it, whose it shall be: **that the scripture might be fulfilled, which saith, They parted my raiment among them, and for my vesture they did cast lots.** These things therefore the soldiers did. KJV

Then **Pilate therefore took Jesus, and scourged him**. And **the soldiers platted a crown of thorns, and put it on his head, and arrayed him in a purple garment; and they came unto him, and said, Hail, King of the Jews! and they struck him with their**

hands. And Pilate went out again, and saith unto them, Behold, I bring him out to you, that ye may know **that I find no crime in him**. Jesus therefore came out, wearing the crown of thorns and the purple garment. And Pilate saith unto them, Behold, the man! When therefore **the chief priests and the officers saw him, they cried out, saying, Crucify him, crucify him!** Pilate saith unto them, **Take him yourselves, and crucify him: for I find no crime in him.** The Jews answered him, **We have a law, and by that law he ought to die, because he made himself the Son of God.**

When Pilate therefore heard this saying, **he was the more afraid;** and he entered into the Praetorium again, **and saith unto Jesus, Whence art thou? But Jesus gave him no answer. Pilate therefore saith unto him, Speakest thou not unto me? Knowest thou not that I have power to release thee, and have power to crucify thee? Jesus answered him, Thou wouldest have no power against me, except it were given thee from above: therefore he that delivered me unto thee hath greater sin.** Upon this **Pilate sought to release him**: but the Jews cried out, saying, If thou release this man, thou art not Caesar's friend: every one that maketh himself a king speaketh against Caesar.

When Pilate therefore heard these words, he brought Jesus out, and sat down on the judgment-seat at a place called The Pavement, but in Hebrew, Gabbatha. Now it was the Preparation of the passover: it was about the sixth hour. And he saith unto the Jews, **Behold, your King! They therefore cried out, Away with him, away with him, crucify him! Pilate saith unto them, Shall I crucify your King? The chief priests answered, We have no king but Caesar. Then therefore he delivered him unto them to be crucified.** They took **Jesus** therefore: and he went out, **bearing the cross for himself, unto the place called The place of a skull, which is called in Hebrew, Golgotha: where they crucified him**, and with him two others, on either side one, and Jesus in the midst.

And Pilate wrote a title also, and put it on the cross. And there was written, **JESUS OF NAZARETH, THE KING OF THE JEWS**. This title therefore read many of the Jews, for the place where Jesus was crucified was nigh to the city; and it was written in Hebrew, and in Latin, and in Greek. **The chief priests of the Jews therefore said to Pilate, Write not, The King of the Jews; but that he said, I am King of the Jews. Pilate answered, What I have written I have written.**

The soldiers therefore, when they had crucified Jesus, took his garments and made four parts, to every soldier a part; and also the coat: now the coat was without seam, woven from the top throughout. They said therefore one to another, Let us not rend it, but cast lots for it, whose it shall be: **that the scripture might be fulfilled, which saith, They parted my garments among them, And upon my vesture did they cast lots.** ASV

Mark 15:33-39

At the sixth hour darkness came over the whole land until the ninth hour. And at the ninth hour **Jesus cried out in a loud voice, "Eloi, Eloi, lama sabachthani?"-which means, "My God, my God, why have you forsaken me?"**

When some of those standing near heard this, they said, "Listen, he's calling Elijah."

One man ran, filled a sponge with wine vinegar, put it on a stick, and offered it to Jesus to drink. "Now leave him alone. Let's see if Elijah comes to take him down." He said.

With a loud cry, Jesus breathed his last.

The curtain of the temple was torn in two from top to bottom. And when **the centurion**, who stood there in front of Jesus, heard his cry and saw how he died, he **said, "Surely this man was the Son of God!"** NIV

And when the sixth hour was come, there was darkness over the whole land until the ninth hour. **And at the ninth hour Jesus cried with a loud voice, Eloi, Eloi, lama sabachthani? which is, being interpreted, My God, my God, why hast thou forsaken me?** And some of them that stood by, when they heard it, said, Behold, he calleth Elijah. And one ran, and filling a sponge full of vinegar, put it on a reed, and gave him to drink, saying, Let be; let us see whether Elijah cometh to take him down. **And Jesus uttered a loud voice, and gave up the ghost. And the veil of the temple was rent in two from the top to the bottom.**

And when the centurion, who stood by over against him, saw that he so gave up the ghost, he said, Truly this man was the Son of God. ASV

THE RESURRECTION, AND SALVATION FOR ALL WHO BELIEVE

Matthew 27:57-66

And when even was come, there came a rich man from Arimathaea, named Joseph, who also himself was Jesus' disciple: **this man went to Pilate, and asked for the body of Jesus.** Then Pilate commanded it to be given up. And **Joseph took the body, and wrapped it in a clean linen cloth, and laid it in his own new tomb, which he had hewn out in the rock: and he rolled a great stone to the door of the tomb, and departed.** And Mary Magdalene was there, and the other Mary, sitting over against the sepulchre.

Now on the morrow, which is the day after the Preparation, the chief priests and the **Pharisees were gathered together unto Pilate, saying, Sir, we remember that that deceiver said while he was yet alive, After three days I rise again. Command therefore that the sepulchre be made sure until the third day,** lest haply his disciples come and steal him away, and say unto the people, He is risen from the dead: and the last error will be worse than the first. Pilate said unto them, Ye have a guard: go, make it as sure as ye can. **So they went, and made the sepulchre sure, sealing the stone, the guard being with them.** ASV

When the even was come, there came a rich man of Arimathea, named Joseph, who also himself was Jesus' disciple: he went to Pilate, and begged the body of Jesus. Then **Pilate commanded the body to be delivered. And when Joseph had taken the body, he wrapped it in a clean linen cloth, and laid it in his own new tomb, which he had hewn out in the rock: and he rolled a great stone to the door of the sepulcher, and departed.** And there was Mary Magdalene, and the other Mary, sitting over against the sepulcher.

Now the next day, that followed the day of the preparation, **the chief priests and Pharisees came together unto Pilate, Saying, Sir, we remember that that deceiver said, while he was yet alive, After three days I will rise again.**

Command therefore that the sepulcher be made sure until the third day, lest his disciples come by night, and steal him away, and say unto the people, His is risen from the dead: so the last error shall be worse than the first. Pilate said unto them. Ye have a watch: go your way, make it as sure as you can. **So they went, and made the sepulcher sure, sealing the stone, and setting a watch.** KJV

Matthew 28:1-10

In the end of the sabbath, as it began to dawn toward the first day of the week, came Mary Magdalene and the other Mary to see the sepulchre. And, behold**, there was a great earthquake: for the angel of the Lord descended from heaven, and came and rolled back the stone from the door, and sat upon it. His countenance was like lightning, and his raiment white as snow**: **And for fear of him the keepers did shake, and became as dead men**. And **the angel answered** and said unto the women, **Fear not ye: for I know that ye seek Jesus, which was crucified. He is not here: for he is risen, as he said. Come, see the place where the Lord lay. And go quickly, and tell his disciples that he is risen from the dead; and, behold, he goeth before you into Galilee; there shall ye see him: lo, I have told you**. And they departed quickly from the sepulchre with fear and great joy; and did run to bring his disciples word.

And as they went to tell his disciples, **behold, Jesus met them, saying, All hail. And they came and held him by the feet, and worshipped him. Then said Jesus unto them, Be not afraid: go tell my brethren that they go into Galilee, and there shall they see me**. KJV

Now **late on the sabbath day, as it began to dawn toward the first day of the week**, came Mary Magdalene and the other Mary to see the sepulchre. And behold, **there was a great earthquake; for an angel of the Lord descended from heaven, and came and rolled away the stone, and sat upon it. His**

appearance was as lightning, and his raiment white as snow: and for fear of him the watchers did quake, and became as dead men. And the angel answered and said unto the women, Fear not ye; for I know that **ye seek Jesus, who hath been crucified. He is not here; for he is risen, even as he said. Come, see the place where the Lord lay. And go quickly, and tell his disciples, He is risen from the dead; and lo, he goeth before you into Galilee; there shall ye see him: lo, I have told you**. And they departed quickly from the tomb with fear and great joy, and ran to bring his disciples word.

And **behold, Jesus met them, saying, All hail. And they came and took hold of his feet, and worshipped him. Then saith Jesus unto them, Fear not: go tell my brethren that they depart into Galilee, and there shall they see me**. ASV

Luke 24:44-51

And he said unto them, **These are the words which I spake unto you, while I was yet with you, that all things must be fulfilled, which were written in the law of Moses, and in the prophets, and in the psalms, concerning me.** Then opened he their understanding, that they might understand the scriptures, And said unto them, **Thus it is written, and thus it behoved Christ to suffer, and to rise from the dead the third day: And that repentance and remission of sins should be preached in his name among all nations, beginning at Jerusalem.** And ye are witnesses of these things.

And, **behold, I send the promise of my Father upon you**: but tarry ye in the city of Jerusalem, until ye be endued with power from on high.

And he led them out as far as to Bethany, and he lifted up his hands, and blessed them. And it came to pass, while he blessed them, **he was parted from them, and carried up into heaven.**

KJV

Now He said to them, **"These are My words which I spoke to you while I was still with you, that all things which are written about Me in the Law of Moses and the Prophets and the psalms must be fulfilled."** Then He opened their minds to understand the Scriptures, and He said to them, **"Thus it is written, that the Christ would suffer and rise again from the dead the third day, and that repentance for forgiveness of**

sins would be proclaimed in His name to all the nations, beginning from Jerusalem.

You are witnesses of these things. And **behold, I am sending forth the promise of My Father upon you;** but you are to stay in the city until you are clothed with power from on high."

And He led them out as far as Bethany, and He lifted up His hands and blessed them. While He was blessing them, **He parted from them and was carried up into heaven.** NASB

The Revelation (Revelation) 1:17-18

When I saw Him, I fell at His feet like a dead man. And He placed His right hand on me, saying, "Do not be afraid; I am the first and the last, and the living One; **and I was dead, and behold, I am alive forevermore, and I have the keys of death and of Hades.** NASB

When I saw him, I fell at his feet as dead. But he laid his right hand on me and said, "Don't be afraid! I am the First and the Last. **I am the living one who died. Look, I am alive forever and ever! And I hold the keys of death and the grave"** NLT

So what does all this mean?

1 Peter 1:18-21

For you **know that it was not with perishable things such as silver or gold that you were redeemed** from the empty way of life handed down to you from your forefathers, **but with the precious blood of Christ, a lamb without blemish or defect. He was chosen before the creation of the world, but was revealed in these last times for your sake. Through him you believe in God, who raised him from the dead and glorified him, and so your faith and hope are in God.** NIV

Forasmuch as ye **know that ye were not redeemed with corruptible things, as silver and gold,** from your vain conversation received by tradition from you fathers; **but with the precious blood of Christ, as of a lamb without blemish and without spot: who verily was foreordained before the foundation of the world, but was manifest in these last times for you, who by him do believe in God, that raised him up from the dead, and gave him glory; that your faith and hope might be in God.** KJV

Mark 2:3-12

And they come, bringing unto him a man sick of the palsy, borne of four. And when they could not come nigh unto him for the crowd, they uncovered the roof where he was: and when they had broken it up, they let down the bed whereon the sick of the palsy lay. And **Jesus seeing their faith saith unto the sick of the palsy**, **Son, thy sins are forgiven**. But there were certain of the scribes sitting there, and reasoning in their hearts, Why doth this man thus speak? he blasphemeth: who can forgive sins but one, even God? **And straightway Jesus, perceiving in his spirit that they so reasoned within themselves, saith unto them, Why reason ye these things in your hearts? Which is easier, to say to the sick of the palsy, Thy sins are forgiven; or to say, Arise, and take up thy bed, and walk? But that ye may know that the Son of man hath authority on earth to forgive sins** (he saith to the sick of the palsy)**, I say unto thee, Arise, take up thy bed, and go unto thy house. And he arose, and straightway took up the bed, and went forth before them all; insomuch that they were all amazed, and glorified God**, saying, We never saw it on this fashion. ASV

And they came, bringing to Him a paralytic, carried by four men. Being unable to get to Him because of the crowd, they removed the roof above Him; and when they had dug an opening, they let down the pallet on which the paralytic was lying. **And Jesus seeing their faith said to the paralytic, "Son, your sins are forgiven."** But some of the scribes were sitting there and reasoning in their hearts, "Why does this man speak that way? He is blaspheming; **who can forgive sins but God alone?" Immediately Jesus, aware in His spirit that they were reasoning that way within themselves, said to them, "Why are you reasoning about these things in your hearts? Which is easier, to say to the paralytic, 'Your sins are forgiven'; or to say, 'Get up, and pick**

up your pallet and walk'? But so that you may know that the Son of Man has authority on earth to forgive sins"-He said to the paralytic, "I say to you, get up, pick up your pallet and go home." And **he got up and immediately picked up the pallet and went out in the sight of everyone, so that they were all amazed and were glorifying God, saying, "We have never seen anything like this."** NASB

Mark 2:16-17

When the scribes and Pharisees **saw him eat with publicans and sinners,** they said unto his disciples, How is it that he eateth and drinketh with publicans and sinners? When Jesus heard it, **he saith unto them, They that are whole have no need of the physician, but they that are sick: I came not to call the righteous,** but **sinners to repentance.** KJV

But when some of the teachers of religious law who were Pharisees saw him eating with people like that, **they said to his disciples, "Why does he eat with such scum?"**

When Jesus heard this, he told them, "Healthy people don't need a doctor-sick people do. I have come to call sinners, not those who think they are already good enough."

NLT

Revelation 1:5-6

And from **Jesus Christ,** who is the faithful witness to these things, **the first to rise from the dead, and the commander of all the rulers of the word.**

All praise to him who loves us and has freed us from our sins by shedding his blood for us. He has made us his Kingdom and his priests who serve before God his Father. Give to him everlasting glory! He rules forever and ever! Amen! NLT

And from **Jesus Christ**, the faithful witness, **the firstborn of the dead, and the ruler of the kings of the earth.**

To Him who loves us and released us from our sins by His blood- and He has made us to be a kingdom, priests to His God and Father-to Him be the glory and the dominion forever and ever. Amen. NASB

Acts 4:8-12

Then Peter, filled with the Holy Ghost, said unto them, Ye rulers of the people, and elders of Israel, if we this day be examined of the good deed done to the impotent man, by what means he is made whole; be it known unto you all, and to all the people of Israel, that **by the name of Jesus Christ of Nazareth, whom ye crucified, whom God raised from the dead, even by him doth this man stand here before you whole. This is the stone which was set at nought of you builders, which is become the head of the corner.**

Neither is there salvation in any other: for there is none other name under heaven given among men, whereby we must be saved. KJV

Then Peter, filled with the Holy Spirit, said to them: "Rulers and elders of the people! If we are being called to account today for an act of kindness shown to a cripple and are asked how he was healed, then know this, you and all the people of Israel: **It is by the name of Jesus Christ of Nazareth, whom you crucified but whom God raised from the dead,** that this man stands before you healed. **He (Jesus) is**

'the stone you builders rejected,
Which has become the capstone.'

Salvation is found in no one else, for there is no other name under heaven given to men by which we must be saved." NIV

Matthew 11:27-28

"**All things have been committed to me by my Father**. No one knows the Son except the Father, and no one knows the

Father except the Son and those to whom the Son chooses to reveal him.

Come to me, all you who are weary and burdened, and I will give you rest. Take my yoke upon you and learn from me, for I am gentle and humble in heart, and **you will find rest for your souls**. For my yoke is easy and my burden is light." NIV

All things have been handed over to Me by My Father; and no one knows the Son except the Father; nor does anyone know the Father except the Son, and anyone to whom the Son wills to reveal Him.

"Come to Me, all who are weary and heavy-laden, and I will give you rest. Take My yoke upon you and learn from Me, for I am gentle and humble in heart, and **YOU WILL FIND REST FOR YOUR SOULS.** For My yoke is easy and My burden is light." NASB

Galatians 3:19-29

What then is the law? It was added because of transgressions, till the seed should come to whom the promise hath been made; and it was ordained through angels by the hand of a mediator. Now a mediator is not a mediator of one; but God is one.

Is the law then against the promises of God? God forbid: for if there had been a law given which could make alive, verily righteousness would have been of the law. **But the scriptures shut up all things under sin, that the promise by faith in Jesus Christ might be given to them that believe.** But before faith came, we were kept in ward under the law, shut up unto the faith which should afterwards be revealed. So that the law is become our tutor to bring us unto Christ, that we might be justified by faith. But now faith that is come, we are no longer under a tutor.

For ye are all sons of God, through faith, in Christ Jesus. For as many of you as were baptized into Christ did put on Christ. There can be neither Jew nor Greek, there can be neither bond nor free, there can be no male and female; **for ye all are one man in Christ Jesus. And if ye are Christ's, then are ye Abraham's seed, heirs according to promise**. ASV

Why the Law then**? It was added because of transgressions**, having been ordained through angels by the agency of a mediator, **until the seed would come to whom the promise had been made.** Now a mediator is not for one party only; whereas God is only one. Is the Law then contrary to the promises of God? May it never be! For if a law had been given which was able to impart life, then righteousness would indeed have been based on law.

But the Scripture has shut up everyone under sin, so that the promise by faith in Jesus Christ might be given to those who believe.

But before faith came, we were kept in custody under the law, **being shut up to the faith which was later to be revealed.** Therefore **the Law has become our tutor to lead us to Christ, so that we may be justified by faith**. But now that faith has come, we are no longer under a tutor. **For you are all sons of God through faith in Christ Jesus. For all of you who were baptized into Christ have clothed yourselves with Christ.** There is neither Jew nor Greek, there is neither slave nor free man, there is neither male nor female; **for you are all one in Christ Jesus. And if you belong to Christ, then you are Abraham's descendants, heirs according to promise.** NASB

Revelation 21:3-8

And I heard a great voice out of the throne saying, **Behold, the tabernacle of God is with men, and he shall dwell with them, and they shall be his peoples, and God himself shall be with them, and be their God: and he shall wipe away every tear from their eyes; and death shall be no more; neither shall there be mourning, nor crying, nor pain, any more: the first things are passed away.**

And he that sitteth on the throne said, **Behold, I make all things new**. And he saith, Write: for these words are faithful and true.

And he said unto me, They are come to pass**. I am the Alpha and the Omega, the beginning and the end. I will give unto him that is athirst of the fountain of the water of life freely. He that overcometh shall inherit these things; and I will be his God, and he shall be my son. But for the fearful**, and

unbelieving, and abominable, and murderers, and fornicators, and sorcerers, and idolaters, and all liars, **their part shall be in the lake that burneth with fire and brimstone; which is the second death**. ASV

And I heard a great voice out of heaven saying, Behold, the tabernacle of God is with men, and he will dwell with them, and they **shall be his people, and God himself shall be with them, and be their God. And God shall wipe away all tears from their eyes; and there shall be no more death, neither sorrow, nor crying, neither shall there be any more pain: for the former things are passed away.** And he that sat upon the throne said**, Behold, I make all things new.** And he said unto me, Write: for **these words are true and faithful. And he said unto me, It is done. I am Alpha and Omega, the beginning and the end. I will give unto him that is a thirst of the fountain of the water of life freely. He that overcometh shall inherit all things; and I will be his God, and he shall be my son.**

But the fearful, and unbelieving, and the abominable, and murderers, and whoremongers, and sorcerers, and idolaters, and all liars, **shall have their part in the lake which burneth with fire and brimstone: which is the second death.** KJV

Revelation 22:12-17

"Behold, I am coming soon! My reward is with me, and I will give to everyone according to what he had done. I am the Alpha and the Omega, the First and the Last, the Beginning and the End.

"**Blessed are those who wash their robes, that they may have the right to the tree of life and may go through the gates into the city.**

Outside are the dogs, those who practice magic arts, the sexually immoral, the murderers, the idolaters and everyone who loves and practices falsehood.

"I, Jesus, have sent my angel to give you this testimony for the churches. I am the Root and the Offspring of David, and the bright Morning Star."

The Spirit and the bride say, **"Come!" And let him who hears say, "Come!" Whoever is thirsty, let him come and whoever wishes, let him take the free gift of the water of life.**

NIV

"Behold, I am coming quickly, and My reward is with Me, to render to every man according to what he has done. I am the Alpha and the Omega, the first and the last, the beginning and the end."

Blessed are those who wash their robes, so that they may have the right to the tree of life, and may enter by the gates into the city. Outside are the dogs and the sorcerers and the immoral persons and the murderers and the idolaters, and everyone who loves and practices lying. "I, Jesus, have sent My angel to testify to you these things for the churches. I am the root and the descendant of David, the bright morning star."

The Spirit and the bride say, **"Come." And let the one who hears say, "Come." And let the one who is thirsty come; let the one who wishes take the water of life without cost.**" NASB

Revelations 22:20-21

He which testifieth these things saith, **Surely I come quickly. Amen. Even so, come, Lord Jesus.** The grace of our Lord Jesus Christ be with you all. Amen. KJV

He who testifies to these things says, **"Yes, I am coming soon."**

Amen. Come, Lord Jesus.

The grace of the Lord Jesus be with God's people.
Amen. NIV

So in summary....

1 Peter 1:1-25

Peter, an apostle of Jesus Christ, to the strangers scattered throughout Pontus, Galatia, Cappadocia, Asia, and Bithynia, Elect according to the foreknowledge of God the Father, through sanctification of the Spirit, unto obedience and sprinkling of the blood of Jesus Christ: **Grace unto you, and peace, be multiplied. Blessed be the God and Father of our Lord Jesus Christ, which according to his abundant mercy**

hath begotten us again unto a lively hope by the resurrection of Jesus Christ from the dead, To an inheritance incorruptible, and undefiled, and that fadeth not away, **reserved in heaven for you, Who are kept by the power of God through faith unto salvation ready to be revealed in the last time.** Wherein ye greatly rejoice, though now for a season, if need be**, ye are in heaviness through manifold temptations: That the trial of your faith, being much more precious than of gold** that perisheth, though it be tried with fire, might be found unto praise and honour and glory at the appearing of Jesus Christ: Whom having not seen, ye love; in whom, though now ye see him not, **yet believing, ye rejoice with joy unspeakable and full of glory: Receiving the end of your faith, even the salvation of your souls**. Of which salvation the prophets have enquired and searched diligently, who prophesied of the grace that should come unto you: Searching what, or what manner of time the Spirit of Christ which was in them did signify**, when it testified beforehand the sufferings of Christ, and the glory that should follow.** Unto whom it was revealed, that not unto themselves, but unto us they did minister the things, which are now reported unto you by them that have preached the gospel unto you with the Holy Ghost sent down from heaven; which things the angels desire to look into. Wherefore gird up the loins of your mind, be sober, and hope to the end for the grace that is to be brought unto you at the revelation of Jesus Christ; As obedient children, not fashioning yourselves according to the former lusts in your ignorance: But as he which hath called you is holy, so be ye holy in all manner of conversation; Because it is written, Be ye holy; for I am holy. And if ye call on the Father, who without respect of persons judgeth according to every man's work, pass the time of your sojourning here in fear: **Forasmuch as ye know that ye were not redeemed with corruptible things, as silver and gold, from your vain conversation received by tradition from your fathers; But with the precious blood of Christ, as of a lamb without blemish and without spot: Who verily was foreordained before the foundation of the world,** but was manifest in these last times for you, Who by him do believe in God, that raised him up from the dead, and gave him glory; that your faith and hope might be in God. **Seeing ye have purified your souls in obeying the truth through the Spirit unto unfeigned love of the brethren, see that ye love one another with a pure heart fervently**: Being born again, not of corruptible seed, but of incorruptible, by the word of God, which liveth and abideth for ever. For all flesh is as grass, and all the glory of man as the flower of grass. The grass withereth, and the flower thereof falleth away**: But the word of the Lord endureth for ever. And this is the word which by the gospel is preached unto you.** KJV

Read the following and put your own emphasis as you feel it…

Peter, an apostle of Jesus Christ, to the strangers scattered throughout Pontus, Galatia, Cappadocia, Asia, and Bithynia, Elect according to the foreknowledge of God the Father, through sanctification of the Spirit, unto obedience and sprinkling of the blood of Jesus Christ: Grace unto you, and peace, be multiplied. Blessed be the God and Father of our Lord Jesus Christ, which according to his abundant mercy hath begotten us again unto a lively hope by the resurrection of Jesus Christ from the dead, To an inheritance incorruptible, and undefiled, and that fadeth not away, reserved in heaven for you, Who are kept by the power of God through faith unto salvation ready to be revealed in the last time. Wherein ye greatly rejoice, though now for a season, if need be, ye are in heaviness through manifold temptations: That the trial of your faith, being much more precious than of gold that perisheth, though it be tried with fire, might be found unto praise and honour and glory at the appearing of Jesus Christ: Whom having not seen, ye love; in whom, though now ye see him not, yet believing, ye rejoice with joy unspeakable and full of glory: Receiving the end of your faith, even the salvation of your souls. Of which salvation the prophets have enquired and searched diligently, who prophesied of the grace that should come unto you: Searching what, or what manner of time the Spirit of Christ which was in them did signify, when it testified beforehand the sufferings of Christ, and the glory that should follow. Unto whom it was revealed, that not unto themselves, but unto us they did minister the things, which are now reported unto you by them that have preached the gospel unto you with the Holy Ghost sent down from heaven; which things the angels desire to look into. Wherefore gird up the loins of your mind, be sober, and hope to the end for the grace that is to be brought unto you at the revelation of Jesus Christ; As obedient children, not fashioning yourselves according to the former lusts in your ignorance: But as he which hath called you is holy, so be ye holy in all manner of conversation; Because it is written, Be ye holy; for I am holy. And if ye call on the Father, who without respect of persons judgeth according to every man's work, pass the time of your sojourning here in fear: Forasmuch as ye know that ye were not redeemed with corruptible things, as silver and gold, from your vain conversation received by tradition from your fathers; But with the precious blood of Christ, as of a lamb without blemish and without spot: Who verily was foreordained before the foundation of the world, but was manifest in these last times for you, Who by him do believe in God, that raised him up from the dead, and gave him glory; that your faith and hope might be in God. Seeing ye have purified your souls in obeying the truth through the Spirit unto unfeigned love of the brethren, see that ye love one another with a pure heart fervently: Being born again, not of corruptible seed, but of incorruptible, by the word of God, which liveth and abideth for ever. For all flesh is as grass, and all the glory of man as the flower of grass. The grass withereth, and the flower thereof falleth away: But the word of the Lord endureth for ever. And this is the word which by the gospel is preached unto you. ASV

John 3:16

"For God so loved the world that he gave his one and only Son, that whoever believes in him shall not perish but have eternal life." NIV

For God so loved the world, that he gave his only begotten Son, that whosoever believeth in him should not perish, but have everlasting life. KJV

Revelation 3:20

"Here I am! I stand at the door and knock. If anyone hears my voice and opens the door, I will come in and eat with him, and he with me." NIV

Behold, I stand at the door and knock: if any man hear my voice and open the door, I will come in to him, and will sup with him, and he with me. ASV

How can YOU receive Jesus Christ into your life?

1. You need to admit your sins (confess your sins to the Lord)

2. You need to repent for your sins (be truly sorry for committing them and sincerely be willing to stop sinning)

3. You MUST Believe that Jesus Christ was born the son of God and man (Mary), he lived a SIN-free life but willingly died a sinner's death on the cross... for YOUR salvation, and he rose from the dead (came back to life).

4. You must INVITE Jesus Christ to come into your life as your Lord and Savior. Allowing him control of your life through the Holy Spirit.

Romans 10:9-10

That **if you confess with your mouth Jesus as Lord, and believe in your heart that God raised Him from the dead, you will be saved;** for **with the heart a person believes, resulting in righteousness, and with the mouth he confesses, resulting in salvation.** NASB

That **if you confess with your mouth, "Jesus is Lord," and believe in your heart that God raised him from the dead, you will be saved**. For **it is with your heart that you believe and are justified, and it is with your mouth that you confess and are saved.** NIV

A Simple prayer will do, like the prayers below, or one in your own words.

"Dear Lord Jesus,

I know I am a sinner, and I ask for your forgiveness.

I believe you were born, lived, died on the cross and rose from the dead, to save me from my sins.

I am turning from my sins oh Lord, and ask you to come into my heart and my life.

I want to follow and trust you as my Lord and Savior.

In your name, dear Jesus, Amen.

Or

"Dear Jesus,

I know I am a sinner, please forgive me of my sins.

I believe you died for me and then came back to life.

Please come into my heart and my life and be my Savior and Lord. I ask in your name, Amen"

Romans 10:13

"Anyone who calls on the name of the Lord will be saved." NLT

"Everyone who calls on the name of the Lord will be saved." NIV

Romans 6:23

"For the wages of sin is death, but the gift of God is eternal life in Christ Jesus our Lord." NIV

For the wages of sin is death; but the gift of God is eternal life through Jesus Christ our Lord. KJV

John 1:12-13

"Yet **to all who received him, to those who believed in his name, he gave the right to become children of God**-children born not of natural descent, nor of human decision or a husband's will, but born of God." NIV

But **as many as received him, to them gave he power to become the sons of God,** even to them that believe on his name: which were born, not of blood, nor of the will of the flesh, nor of the will of man, but of God. KJV

But now the work begins....

Matthew 28:16-20

"Then the eleven disciples went to Galilee, to the mountain where Jesus had told them to go. When they saw him, they worshiped him; but some doubted. Then Jesus came to them and said, 'All authority in heaven and on earth has been given to me. Therefore **go and make disciples of all nations, baptizing them in the name of the Father and of the Son and of the Holy Spirit,** and **teaching them to obey everything I have commanded you.** And surely I am with you always, to the very end of the age.'" NIV

Then the eleven disciples left for Galilee, going to the mountain where Jesus had told them to go. When they saw him, they worshiped him-but some of them still doubted!

Jesus came and told his disciples, “I have been given complete authority in heaven and on earth. Therefore, **go and make disciples of all the nations, baptizing them in the name of the Father and the Son and the Holy Spirit. Teach these new disciples to obey all the commands I have given you.** And be sure of this: I am with you always, even to the end of the age.” NLT

Turn to your Bible to Learn more about Jesus.

To give a simple list of Jesus Scriptures is almost impossible since he is referenced SO MANY TIMES in BOTH the Old Testament as well as the New Testament.

I suggest you might start with Matthew, Mark, Luke and John in the New Testament and go from there.

Then you might go on and read the Bible sections preceding and following the “quotes” (when someone is referencing some earlier Bible reference) that are from other books of the Bible; Proverbs, Isaiah, John, Revelation, etc.

And then you might even want to read the entire Bible from cover to cover. You will probably be surprised at where and how Jesus is spoken about.

But here is a very small list of other scriptures about Jesus (or that make references): Isaiah 7:14-16, Isaiah 9:1-7, Isaiah 53 (all of it), Galatians 3:1-7, Colossians 1:11-14, Romans 5:1, John 10:10, Genesis 22:2-18 (Abraham and Isaac), Psalms 22:18

Matthew 7:24-27

Therefore whosoever heareth these sayings of mine, and doeth them, I will liken him unto a wise man, which built his house upon a rock: and the rain descended, and the floods came, and the winds blew, and beat upon that house; and it fell not: for it was founded upon a rock.

And every one that heareth these sayings of mine, and doeth them not, shall be likened unto a foolish man, which built his house upon the sand: and the rain descended and the floods came, and the winds blew, and beat upon that house and it fell: and great was the fall of it. KJV

Chapter Three

WHAT ARE
THE TEN COMMANDMENTS
ANYWAY?

Most Christians know that Moses went up Mount Sinai, and God gave him Ten Commandments on stone tablets. But a lot of Christians do not realize that God, and later Jesus, has given more than 600 Commandments, Laws, Precepts, Ordinances, etc.

Now this book will not attempt to cover, or even relate to you, all of them... but this book will attempt to cover many of today's most frequently asked, or studiously avoided, questions based on the Commandments, Laws, Precepts, etc.

In this book you will find biblical scriptures, straight from several different versions of the Bible that will talk about each question raised.

If you have questions that are not covered in this book... PLEASE, read and search through the Bible yourself, I'm sure God will help you find the answers.

Let's start with the Ten Commandments...

Because, yes, a lot of the scriptures regarding those commandments are very pertinent to some of the questions we'll be looking into.

And as many of today's Christians cannot even name all ten of the Ten Commandments I feel they are definitely worth discussing.

Most people know the "Thou shalt not kill", or "Do not commit adultery", but let's look at them all for a few minutes.

Now I will only mention a few scriptures for each Commandment, but you will be able to find many more as you read your Bible.

THE FIRST COMMANDMENT:

YOU SHALL HAVE NO OTHER GODS BEFORE ME.

Exodus 20:3

Thou shalt have no other gods before me. KJV

You shall have no other gods before me. NIV

Do not worship any other gods besides me. NLT

Let us take a look at some other scriptures that support this scripture....

Exodus 22:20

"He who sacrifices to any god, other than to the LORD alone, shall be utterly destroyed." NASB

"Whoever sacrifices to any god other than the LORD must be destroyed." NIV

Exodus 23:13

Now concerning everything which I have said to you, **be on your guard; and do not mention the name of other gods, nor let them be heard from your mouth.** NASB

"Be careful to do everything I have said to you. **Do not invoke the names of other gods; do not let them be heard on your lips."** NIV

Jeremiah 35:15

Turn now every man from his evil way and amend your deeds, and **do not go after other gods to worship them.** NASB

Each of you must turn from your wicked ways and reform your actions; **do not follow other gods to serve them.** NIV

Something to understand...

When God talks of "other gods" he is not just talking about other deities. A "god" can be anything that is VERY important in your life. Think of it as a type of "idol": an object of worship or devotion that can be anything you spend a lot of time on or focus on to the point that the one true God is no longer a priority in your life... something like; Money, Drugs, Career, even Video Games or other distractions.

Matthew 6:24

"No one can serve two masters; for either he will hate the one and love the other, or he will be devoted to one and despise the other. **You cannot serve God and wealth.**" NASB

No man can serve two masters: for either he will hate the one, and love the other; or else he will hold to the one, and despise the other. **Ye cannot serve God and mammon**. KJV

1 John 5:21

Little Children, **keep yourselves from idols**. Amen. KJV

My little children, **guard yourselves from idols**. ASV

THE SECOND COMMANDMENT:

DO NOT MAKE ANY GRAVEN IMAGE OR LIKENESS.

Exodus 20:4-6

Thou shalt not make unto thee any graven image, or any likeness of any thing that is in heaven above, or that is in the earth beneath, or that is in the water under the earth: **thou shalt not bow down thyself to them, nor serve them**: for I the LORD thy God am a jealous God, visiting the iniquity of the fathers upon the children unto the third and fourth generation of them that hate me; and shewing mercy unto thousands of them that love me, and keep my commandments. KJV

"**Do not make idols of any kind,** whether in the shape of birds or animals or fish. **You must never worship or bow down to them,** for I, the LORD your God, am a jealous God who will not share your affection with any other god! I do not leave unpunished the sins of those who hate me, but I punish the children for the sins of their parents to the third and fourth generations. But I lavish my love on those who love me and obey my commands, even for a thousand generations." NLT

"You shall not make for yourself an idol in the form of anything in heaven above or on the earth beneath or in the waters below. **You shall not bow down to them or worship them;** for I, the LORD your God, am a jealous God, punishing the children for the sin of the fathers to the third and fourth generation of those who hate me, but showing love to a thousand generations of those who love me and keep my commandments." NIV

Let us take a look at some other scriptures that support this scripture....

Exodus 20:23

"**You shall not make other gods besides Me**; **gods of silver or gods of gold, you shall not make for yourselves."** NASB

"You shall not make with me gods of silver, neither shall ye make unto you gods of gold." KJV

Deuteronomy 4:15-24

Take ye therefore good heed unto yourselves; for ye saw no manner of form on the day that Jehovah spake unto you in Horeb out of the midst of the fire. Lest ye corrupt yourselves, and make you a graven image in the form of any figure, the likeness of male or female, the likeness of any beast that is on the earth, the likeness of any winged bird that flieth in the heavens, the likeness of anything that creepeth on the ground, the likeness of any fish that is in the water under the earth; **and lest thou lift up thine eyes unto heaven, and when thou seest the sun and the moon and the stars, even all the host of heaven, thou be drawn away and worship them, and serve them,** which Jehovah thy God hath allotted unto all the peoples under the whole heaven. But Jehovah hath taken you, and brought you forth out of the iron furnace, out of Egypt, to be unto him a people of inheritance, as at this day. Furthermore Jehovah was angry with me for your sakes, and sware that I should not go over the Jordan, and that I should not go in unto that good land, which Jehovah thy God giveth thee for an inheritance: but I must die in this land, I must not go over the Jordan; but ye shall go over, and possess that good land. **Take heed unto yourselves, lest ye forget the covenant of Jehovah your God, which he made with you, and make you a graven image in the form of anything which Jehovah thy God hath forbidden thee. For Jehovah thy God is a devouring fire, a jealous God.** ASV

Take ye therefore good heed unto yourselves; for ye saw no manner of similitude on the day that the Lord spake unto you in Horeb out of the midst of the fire**: Lest ye corrupt yourselves, and make you a graven image**, the similitude of any figure, the likeness of male or female, The likeness of any beast that is on the earth, the likeness of any winged fowl that flieth in the air, The likeness of any thing that creepeth on the ground, the likeness of any fish that is in the waters beneath the earth: **And lest thou lift up thine eyes unto heaven, and when thou seest the sun, and the moon, and the stars, even all the host of heaven, shouldest be driven to worship them, and serve them**, which the Lord thy God hath divided unto all nations under the whole heaven. But the Lord hath taken you, and brought you forth out of the iron furnace, even out of Egypt, to be unto him a people of inheritance, as ye are this day. Furthermore the Lord was angry with me for your sakes, and sware that I should not go over Jordan, and that I should not go in unto that good land, which the Lord thy God giveth thee for an inheritance: But I must die in this land, I must not go over Jordan: but ye shall go over, and possess that good land. **Take heed unto yourselves, lest ye forget the covenant of the Lord your God, which he made with you, and make you a graven image, or the likeness of any thing, which the Lord thy God hath forbidden thee. For the Lord thy God is a consuming fire, even a jealous God**. KJV

Deuteronomy 27:15

'Cursed is the man who makes an idol or a molten image, an abomination to the LORD, the work of the hand of the craftsman, and sets it up in secret.' NASB

'Cursed be the man that maketh any graven or molten image, an abomination unto the LORD, the work of the hands of the craftsman, and putteth it in a secret place.' KJV

Jeremiah 25:6

"**Do not follow other gods to serve and worship them; do not provoke me to anger with what your hands have made.** Then I will not harm you." NIV

"Go not after other gods to serve them, and to worship them, and provoke me not to anger with the works of your hands; and I will do you no hurt." KJV

Revelation 21:8

But the cowardly, the unbelieving, the vile, the murderers, the sexually immoral, those who practice magic arts, **the idolaters** and all liars-their place **will be in the fiery lake of burning sulfur. This is the second death.** NIV

But the fearful, and unbelieving, and the abominable, and murderers, and whoremongers, and sorcerers, **and idolaters**, and all liars, shall have their part in the lake which burneth with fire and brimstone: which is the second death. KJV

Isaiah 31:7

For in that day **every man shall cast away**
His idols of silver, and his idols of gold,
Which your own hands have made unto you for a sin. KJV

For in that day every one of **you will reject the idols of silver and gold your sinful hands have made.** NIV

Revelation 22:15

Outside are the dogs, those who practice magic arts, the sexually immoral, the murderers, **the idolaters** and everyone who loves and practices falsehood. NIV

For without are dogs, and sorcerers, and whoremongers, and murderers**, and idolaters**, and whosoever loveth and maketh a lie. KJV

Remember…

An "idol" is something VERY important in your life … but it does not always represent a "deity". A definition you might use, "Idol": an object of worship or devotion that can be anything you spend a lot of time on or focus on to the point that the one true God is no longer a priority in your life… something like; Money, Drugs, Career, Alcohol, Social Media, etc.

Now between the First Commandment and the Second Commandment I think God makes it VERY clear that HE is to be the number one priority in your life.

THE THIRD COMMANDMENT

DO NOT MISUSE THE NAME OF THE LORD YOUR GOD.

Exodus 20:7

You shall not misuse the name of the LORD your God, for the Lord will not hold anyone guiltless who misuses his name. NIV

Thou shalt not take the name of the LORD thy God in vain: for the Lord will not hold him guiltless that taketh his name in vain. KJV

Do not misuse the name of the LORD your God. The Lord will not let you go unpunished if you misuse his name. NLT

Let us take a look at some other scriptures that support this scripture....

Exodus 22:28

"**You shall not curse God**, nor curse a ruler of your people." NASB

"**Thou shalt not revile the gods** (or judges), nor curse the ruler of thy people." KJV

Leviticus 19:12

'You shall not swear falsely by My name, so as to profane the name of your God; I am the LORD.' NASB

And ye **shall not swear by my name falsely, neither shalt thou profane the name of thy God:** I am the LORD your God. KJV

For those people who like to curse or swear a lot, especially phrases that mention God, Jesus, etc., I think you should really research this commandment more on your own time and pray for God's help.

And here are but a few of God's Names:

The Eternal God
I AM
The LORD GOD of hosts
The LORD ALMIGHTY
God of salvation
God the Lord
God of Israel
Jehovah
Him that rideth upon the heavens of heavens
The Mighty One
The blessed God/ Blessed One/the Blessed
His glorious presence (the eyes of his glory)

And this includes:

Jesus
Jesus Christ
The Christ
The Lamb of God
The Holy One
The Holy One of Israel

There are even more, so see how many you can find....

THE FOURTH COMMANDMENT

REMEMBER THE SABBATH DAY BY KEEPING IT HOLY.

Exodus 20:8-11

"**Remember the Sabbath day, to keep it holy**. Six days you shall labor and do all your work, but the seventh day is a Sabbath of the LORD your God; in it you shall not do any work, you or your son or your daughter, your male or your female servant or your cattle or your sojourner who stays with you. For in six days the LORD made the heavens and the earth, the sea and all that is in them, and rested on the seventh day; therefore the LORD blessed the Sabbath day and made it holy." NASB

Remember the Sabbath day by keeping it holy. Six days you shall labor and do all your work, but the seventh day is a Sabbath to the Lord your God. On it you shall not do any work, neither you, nor your son or daughter, nor your manservant or maidservant, nor your animals, nor the alien within your gates. For in six days the Lord made the heavens and the earth, the sea, and all that is in them, but he rested on the seventh day. Therefore the LORD blessed the Sabbath day and made it holy. NIV

"**Remember to observe the Sabbath day be keeping it holy.** Six days a week are set apart for your daily duties and regular work, but the seventh day is a day of rest dedicated to the LORD your God. On that day no one in your household may do any kind of work. This includes you, your sons and daughters, your male and female servants, your livestock, and any foreigners living among you. For in six days the LORD made the heavens, and the earth, the sea, and everything in them; then he rested on the seventh day. That is why the LORD blessed the Sabbath day and set it apart as holy." NLT

Let us take a look at some other scriptures that support this scripture....

Genesis 2:2-3

By the seventh day God completed His work which He had done, and He rested on the seventh day from all His work which He had done. **Then God blessed the seventh day and sanctified it,** because in it He rested from all His work which God had created and made. NASB

And **God blessed the seventh day and made it holy**, because on it he rested from all the work of creating that he had done. NIV

Exodus 23:12

Six days thou shalt do thy work, and on the seventh day thou shalt rest: that thine ox and thine ass may rest, and the son of thy handmaid, and the stranger, may be refreshed. KJV

"Six days do your work, but on the seventh day do not work, so that your ox and your donkey may rest and the slave born in your household, and the alien as well, may be refreshed. NIV

Isaiah 58:13-14

"If because of the Sabbath, you turn your foot from doing your own pleasure on My holy day, and call the Sabbath a delight, the holy day of the Lord honorable, and honor it, desisting from your own ways, from seeking your own pleasure and speaking your own word, then you will take delight in the LORD, and I will make you ride on the heights of the earth; and I will feed you with the heritage of Jacob your father, for the mouth of the LORD has spoken." NASB

"If you keep your feet from breaking the Sabbath and from doing as you please on my holy day, if you call the Sabbath a delight and the LORD's holy day honorable, and if you honor it by not going your own way and not doing as you please or speaking idle words, then you will find your joy in the LORD, and I will cause you to ride on the heights of the land and to feast on the inheritance of your father Jacob."

The mouth of the LORD has spoken. NIV

See also Leviticus 19:30

THE FIFTH COMMANDMENT

HONOR YOUR FATHER AND YOUR MOTHER.

Exodus 20:12

Honor your father and mother. Then you will live a long, full life in the land the Lord your God will give you. NLT

Honor your father and your mother, so that you may live long in the land the Lord your God is giving you. NIV

Honour thy father and thy mother: that thy days may be long upon the land which the LORD thy God giveth thee. KJV

Let us take a look at some other scriptures that support this scripture....

Exodus 21:15 and 17

"Anyone who attacks his father or his mother must be put to death." And **"Anyone who curses his father or mother must be put to death."** NIV

"He that smiteth his father, or his mother, shall be surely put to death." And **"he that curseth his father, or his mother, shall surely be put to death."** KJV

Leviticus 20:9

'If there is anyone who curses his father or his mother, he shall surely be put to death; he has cursed his father or his mother, his bloodguiltiness is upon him.' NASB

"All who curse their father or mother must be put to death. They are guilty of a capital offense." NLT

Deuteronomy 21:18-21

If a man has a stubborn and rebellious son who does not obey his father and mother and will not listen to them when they discipline him, his father and mother shall take hold of him and bring him to the elders at the gate of his town. They shall say to the elders, "This son of ours is stubborn and rebellious. He will not obey us. He is a profligate and a drunkard." **Then all the men of his town shall stone him to death.** You must purge the evil from among you. All Israel will hear of it and be afraid. NIV

If a man have a stubborn and rebellious son, which will not obey the voice of his father, or the voice of his mother, and that, when they have chastened him, will not hearken unto them: then shall his father and his mother lay hold on him, and bring him out unto the elders of his city, and unto the gate of his place; and they shall say unto the elders of his city, This our son is stubborn and rebellious, he will not obey our voice; he is a glutton, and a drunkard. And **all the men of his city shall stone him with stones, that he die**: so shalt thou put evil away from among you; and all Israel shall hear, and fear. KJV

Deuteronomy 27:16

'Cursed is he who dishonors his father or mother.' NASB

'Cursed is anyone who despises father or mother.' NLT

Colossians 3:20

You children must always obey your parents, for this is what pleases the Lord. NLT

Children, obey your parents in everything, for this pleases the Lord. NIV

THE SIXTH COMMANDMENT

THOU SHALT NOT KILL:

Exodus 20:13

Do not murder. NLT

Thou shalt not kill. KJV

You shall not murder. NIV and NASB

Let us take a look at some other scriptures that support this scripture....

Genesis 9:5-6

And Murder is forbidden. Animals that kill people must die, and **any person who murders must be killed. Yes, you must execute anyone who murders another person, for to kill a person is to kill a living being made in God's image.** NLT

And surely your blood of your lives will I require; at the hand of every beast will I require it, and at the hand of man; at the hand of every man's brother will I require the life of man. **Whoso sheddeth man's blood, by man shall his blood be shed**: for in the image of God made he man. KJV

Exodus 21:12-14

"Anyone who strikes a man and kills him shall surely be put to death. However, if he does not do it intentionally, but God lets it happen, he is to flee to a place I will designate. **But if a man schemes and kills another man deliberately, take him away from my altar and put him to death.** NIV

He that smiteth a man, so that he die, shall be surely put to death. And if a man lie not in wait, but God deliver him into his hand; then I will appoint thee a place whither he shall flee. But **if a man come presumptuously upon his neighbor, to slay him with guile; thou shalt take him from mine altar, that he may die**. KJV

Revelation 21:8

But the cowardly, the unbelieving, the vile, **the murderers**, the sexually immoral, those who practice magic arts, the idolaters and all liars-**their place will be in the fiery lake of burning sulfur**. This is the second death. NIV

But for the cowardly and unbelieving and abominable **and murderers** and immoral persons and sorcerers and idolaters and all liars, **their part will be in the lake that burns with fire and brimstone**, which is the second death. NASB

Numbers 35:16-21

'But **if he struck him down with an iron object, so that he died, he is a murderer; the murderer shall surely be put to death. If he struck him down with a stone in the hand, by which he will die, and as a result he died, he is a murderer; the murderer shall surely be put to death. Or if he struck him with a wooden object in the hand, by which he might die, and as a result he died, he is a murderer; the murderer shall surely be put to death.** The blood avenger himself shall put the murderer to death; he shall put him to death when he meets him. **If he pushed him of hatred or threw something at him lying in wait and as a result he died, or if he struck him down with his hand in enmity, and as a result he died, the one who struck him shall surely be put to death, he is a murderer; the blood avenger shall put the murderer to death when he meets him**.

NASB

'If a man strikes someone with an iron object so that he dies, he is a murder; the murderer shall be put to death. Or if anyone has a stone in his hand that could kill, and he strikes someone so that he dies, he is a murderer; the murderer shall be put to death. Or if anyone has a wooden object in his hand that could kill, and he hits someone so that he dies, he is a murderer; the murderer shall be put to death. The avenger of blood shall put the murderer to death; when he meets him, he shall put him to death. **If anyone with malice aforethought shoves another or throws something at him intentionally so that he dies or if in hostility he hits him with his fist so that he dies, that person shall be put to death; he is a murderer.** The avenger of blood shall put the murderer to death when he meets him. NIV

1 Timothy 1:9

Realizing the fact **that law is not made for a righteous person, but for those who are lawless** and rebellious, for the ungodly and sinners, for the unholy and profane, **for those who kill their fathers or mothers, for murderers.** NASB

But they [the Laws] were not made for people who do what is right. They are for people who are disobedient and rebellious, who are ungodly and sinful, who consider nothing sacred and defile what is holy, **who murder their father or mother or other people.** NLT

We also know that the law is made not for the righteous but for lawbreakers and rebels, the ungodly and sinful, the unholy and irreligious; **for those who kill their fathers or mothers, for murderers**. NIV

Exodus 21:22-23

"If men struggle with each other **and strike a woman with child so that she gives birth prematurely**, yet there is no injury, he shall surely be fined as the woman's husband may demand of him, and he shall pay as the judges decide. **But if there is any**

further injury, then you shall appoint as a penalty **life for life"** NASB

"If men who are fighting **hit a pregnant woman and she gives birth prematurely** but there is no serious injury, the offender must be fined whatever the woman's husband demands and the court allows. But if there is serious injury, **you are to take life for life.** NIV

THE SEVENTH COMMANDMENT

DO NOT COMMIT ADULTERY:

Exodus 20:14

Thou shalt not commit adultery. KJV

Do not commit adultery. NLT

You shall not commit adultery. NASB and NIV

Let us take a look at some other scriptures that support this scripture….

Leviticus 20:10

If a man commits adultery with another man's wife-with the wife of his neighbor-both **the adulterer and the adulteress must be put to death.** NIV

And the man that committeth adultery with another man's wife, even he that committeth adultery with his neighbour's wife, the adulterer and the adulteress shall surely be put to death. KJV

Hebrews 13:4

Marriage should be honored by all, and the marriage bed kept pure, for God will judge the adulterer and all the sexually immoral. NIV

Marriage is honourable in all, and the bed undefiled: but whoremongers and adulterers God will judge. KJV

Genesis 20:1-6

Now Abraham moved on from there into the region of Negev and lived between Kadesh and Shur. For a while he stayed in Gerar, and **there Abraham said of his wife Sarah, "She is my sister." Then Abimelech king of Gerar sent for Sarah and took her.**

But God came to Abimelech in a dream one night and said to him, "**you are as good as dead because of the woman you have taken; she is a married woman."**

Now Abimelech had not gone near her, so he said, "Lord, will you destroy an innocent nation? Did he not say to me, 'She is my sister', and didn't she also say, 'He is my brother'? I have done this with a clear conscience and clean hands."

Then God said to him in the dream, "Yes, I know you did this with a clear conscience, and so **I have kept you from sinning against me. That is why I did not let you touch her.** NIV

And Abraham journeyed from thence toward the land of the South, and dwelt between Kadesh and Shur. And he sojourned in Gerar. **And Abraham said of Sarah his wife, She is my sister. And Abimelech king of Gerar sent, and took Sarah.** But God came to Abimelech in a dream of the night, and said to him, **Behold, thou art but a dead man, because of the woman whom thou hast taken. For she is a man's wife**. Now Abimelech had not come near her. And he said, Lord, wilt thou slay even a righteous nation? Said he not himself unto me, She is my sister? And she, even she herself said, He is my brother. In the integrity of my heart and the innocency of my hands have I done this. And God said unto him in the dream, **Yea, I know that in the integrity of thy heart thou has done this, and I also withheld thee from sinning against me. Therefore suffered I thee not to touch her.** ASV

Leviticus 18:20

You shall not have intercourse with your neighbor's wife, to be defiled with her. NASB

'Do not have sexual relations with your neighbor's wife and defile yourself with her.' NIV

THE EIGHTH COMMANDMENT

THOU SHALT NOT STEAL.

Exodus 20:15

Thou shalt not steal. KJV

Do not steal. NLT

You shall not steal. NIV and NASB

Let us take a look at some other scriptures that support this scripture....

Proverbs 1:8-19

My son, hear the instruction of thy father,
and forsake not the law of thy mother:
For they shall be an ornament of grace unto thy head,
and chains about thy neck.
My son, **if sinners entice thee,**
consent thou not.
If **they say, Come with us, let us lay wait for blood,**
let us lurk privily for the innocent without cause:
Let us swallow them up alive as the grave;

and whole, as those that go down into the pit:
We shall find all precious substance,
we shall fill our houses with spoil:
Cast in thy lot among us;
let us all have one purse:
My son, walk not thou in the way with them;
refrain thy foot from their path:
For their feet run to evil,
and make haste to shed blood.
Surely in vain the net is spread in the sight of any bird.
And they lay wait for their own blood;
they lurk privily for their own lives.

So are the ways of every one that is greedy of gain; which taketh away the life of the owners thereof. KJV

My son, hear the instruction of thy father, And forsake not the law of thy mother: For they shall be a chaplet of grace unto thy head, And chains about thy neck.

My son, if sinners entice thee, **Consent thou not. If they say, Come with us, Let us lay wait for blood; Let us lurk privily for the innocent without cause; Let us swallow them up alive as Sheol, And whole, as those that go down into the pit; We shall find all precious substance; We shall fill our houses with spoil; Thou shalt cast thy lot among us; We will all have one purse**: My son, walk not thou in the way with them; Refrain thy foot from their path: **For their feet run to evil, And they make haste to shed blood**. For in vain is the net spread In the sight of any bird: **And these lay wait for their own blood; They lurk privily for their own lives. So are the ways of every one that is greedy of gain; It taketh away the life of the owners thereof.**

ASV

Matthew 19:18

"Do not steal" NLT

"Thou shalt not steal" KJV

Ezekiel 18:10-13

"But **suppose that man has a son who grows up to be a robber** or murderer and refuses to do what is right. And suppose that son does all the evil things his father would never do—worship idols on the mountains, commits adultery, oppresses the poor and helpless**, steals** from debtors by refusing to let them redeem what they have given in pledge, worships idols and takes part in loathsome practices, and lends money at interest. **Should such a sinful person live? No! He must die and must take full blame.** NLT

If he beget **a son that is a robber,** a shedder of blood, and that doeth the like to any one of these things, And that doeth not any of those duties, but even hath eaten upon the mountains, and defiled his neighbour's wife, Hath oppressed the poor and needy, hath spoiled by violence, **hath not restored the pledge**, and hath lifted up his eyes to the idols, hath committed abomination, Hath given forth upon usury, and hath taken increase: **shall he then live? he shall not live: he hath done all these abominations; he shall surely die; his blood shall be upon him.** KJV

Revelation 21:8

But the cowardly, the unbelieving, **the vile**, the murderers, the sexually immoral, those who practice magic arts, the idolaters **and all liars-their place will be in the fiery lake of burning sulfur. This is the second death.** NIV

But the fearful, and unbelieving, and **the abominable**, and murderers, and whoremongers, and sorcerers, and idolaters, **and all liars, shall have their part in the lake which burneth with fire and brimstone: which is the second death.** KJV

THE NINTH COMMANDMENT

DO NOT BEAR FALSE WITNESS:

Exodus 20:16

Do not testify falsely against your neighbor. NLT

Thou shalt not bear false witness against thy neighbour. KJV

You shall not give false testimony against your neighbor. NIV

Let us take a look at some other scriptures that support this scripture....

Exodus 23:7-8

"**Have nothing to do with a false charge** and do not put an innocent or honest person to death, **for I will not acquit the guilty.**
"**Do not accept a bribe, for a bribe blinds those who see and twists the words of the righteous.** NIV

Keep far from a false charge, and do not kill the innocent or the righteous, **for I will not acquit the guilty.**
You shall not take a bribe, for a bribe blinds the clear-sighted and subverts the cause of the just.
NASB

Jeremiah 9:3-9

And **they bend their tongues like their bow for lies;**
But they are not valiant for the truth upon the earth;

For they proceed from evil to evil.
And they know not me, saith the LORD.
And **they will deceive every one his neighbor,**
And will not speak the truth:
They have taught their tongue to speak lies,
And weary themselves to commit iniquity.
Thine habitation is in the midst of deceit;
Through deceit they refuse to know me, saith the LORD.
Therefore thus saith the Lord of hosts,
Behold, I will melt them, and try them;
For how shall I do for the daughter of my people?
Their tongue is as an arrow shot out; it speaketh deceit:
One speaketh peaceably to his neighbor with his mouth,
But in heart he layeth his wait.
Shall I not visit them for these things? Saith the LORD:
Shall not my soul be avenged on such a nation as this?

KJV

"**They make ready their tongue like a bow, to shoot lies**; it is not by truth that they triumph in the land. They go from one sin to another; they do not acknowledge me,"

declares the LORD,

"Beware of your friends; do not trust your brothers for **every brother is a deceiver, and every friend a slanderer. Friend deceives friend, and no one speaks the truth. They have taught their tongues to lie**; and weary themselves with sinning. **You live in the midst of deception; in their deceit they refuse to acknowledge me,"**

declares the LORD,

Therefore this is what the LORD Almighty says:

"See, **I will refine and test them, for what else can I do because of the sin of my people? Their tongue is a deadly arrow; it speaks with deceit. With his mouth each speaks cordially to his neighbor, but in his heart he sets a trap for him. Should I not punish them for this?"**

declares the LORD.

"Should I not avenge myself on such a nation as this?"

NIV

See also, Revelation 21:8, Revelation 22:14-15

THE TENTH COMMANDMENT:

DO NOT COVET :

Exodus 20:17

Thou shalt not covet thy neighbor's house, thou shalt not covet thy neighbor's wife, nor his manservant, nor his maidservant, nor his ox, nor his all, nor any thing that is thy neighbor's. KJV

You shall not covet your neighbor's house; you shall not covet you neighbor's wife or his male servant or his female servant or his ox or his donkey or anything that belongs to your neighbor. NASB

You shall not covet your neighbor's house. You shall not covet your neighbor's wife, or his manservant or maidservant, his ox or donkey, or anything that belongs to your neighbor. NIV

Let us take a look at some other scriptures that support this scripture....

Luke 12:15-21

And he said unto them, **Take heed, and keep yourselves from all covetousness: for a man's life consisteth not in the abundance of the things which he possesseth**. And he spake a parable unto them, saying, The ground of a certain rich man brought forth plentifully: and he reasoned within himself, saying, What shall I do, because I have not where to bestow my fruits? And he said, This will I do: I will pull down my barns, and build greater; and there will I bestow all my grain and my goods. And I will say to my soul, Soul, thou hast much goods laid up for many years; take thine ease, eat, drink, be merry. But God said unto him, Thou foolish one, this night is thy soul required of thee; and the things which thou hast prepared, whose shall they be? So is he that layeth up treasure for himself, and is not rich toward God. ASV

And he said unto them, **Take heed, and beware of covetousness: for a man's life consisteth not in the**

abundance of the things which he possesseth. And he spake a parable unto them, saying, The ground of a certain rich man brought forth plentifully: and he thought within himself, saying, What shall I do, because I have no room where to bestow my fruits? And he said, This will I do: I will pull down my barns, and build greater; and there will I bestow all my fruits and my goods. And I will say to my soul, Soul, thou hast much goods laid up for many years; take thine ease, eat, drink and be merry. But God said unto him, Thou fool, this night thy soul shall be required of thee: then whose shall those things be, which thou hast provided? So is he that layeth up treasure for himself, and is not rich towards God. KJV

Matthew 16:24-28

Then Jesus said to his disciples, "If anyone would come after me, he must deny himself and take up his cross and follow me. For whoever wants to save his life will lose it, but whoever loses his life for me will find it. **What good will it be for a man if he gains the whole world, yet forfeits his own soul?** Or what can a man give in exchange for his soul? For the Son of Man is going to come in his Father's glory with his angels, and then he will reward each person according to what he has done. I tell you the truth, some who are standing here will not taste death before they see the Son of Man coming in his kingdom" NIV

Then Jesus said to the disciples, "If any of you wants to be my follower, you must put aside your selfish ambition, shoulder your cross, and follow me. If you try to keep your life for yourself, you will lose it. But if you give up your life for me, you will find true life. **And how do you benefit if you gain the whole world but lose your own soul in the process?** Is anything worth more than your soul? For I, the Son of Man, will come in the glory of my Father with his angels and will judge all people according to their deeds. And I assure you that some of you standing here right now will not die before you see me, the Son of Man, coming in my Kingdom."

NLT

Now you know the Ten Commandments. What do you intend to do with this new knowledge? Or if you knew them before... does this refresher urge you to change anything in your life?

Chapter Four

THE COMMANDMENTS OF JESUS

Jesus also had a lot of commandments… but only a small amount compared to the "Laws of Moses" and others, so I will attempt to list them all at the end of this chapter, if I have not covered them in other areas of the chapter.

Let's start with what Jesus has to say about the original Ten Commandments given by God to Moses.

Jesus and the Ten Commandments:

Matthew 19:16-17

Now a man came up to Jesus and asked, "Teacher, what good thing must I do to get eternal life?"
"Why do you ask me about what is good?" Jesus replied. "There is only One who is good. If you want to enter life, **obey the commandments**." NIV

And someone came to Him and said, "Teacher, what good thing shall I do that I may obtain eternal life?"
And He said to him, "Why are you asking Me about what is good? There is only One who is good; but if you wish to enter into life, **keep the commandments**." NASB

Matthew 5:17-20

"**Do not think that I came to abolish the Law or the Prophets; I did not come to abolish but to fulfill.** For truly I say to you, **until heaven and earth pass away, not the smallest letter or stroke shall pass from the Law until all is accomplished. Whoever then annuls one of the least of these commandments, and teaches others to do the same, shall be called least in the kingdom of heaven; but whoever keeps and teaches them, he shall be called great in the kingdom of heaven.**

For I say to you **that unless your righteousness surpasses that of the scribes and Pharisees, you will not enter the kingdom of heaven."** NASB

"Don't misunderstand why I have come. I did not come to abolish the law of Moses or the writings of the prophets. No, I came to fulfill them. I assure you, **until heaven and earth disappear, even the smallest detail of God's law will remain until its purpose is achieved. So if you break the smallest commandment and teach others to do the same, you will be the least in the Kingdom of Heaven. But anyone who obeys God's laws and teaches them will be great in the Kingdom of Heaven.**

But I warn you---**unless you obey God better than the teachers of religious law and the Pharisees do, you can't enter the Kingdom of Heaven at all!** NLT

YOU SHALL HAVE NO OTHER GODS BEFORE ME:

Matthew 22:36-40

"Teacher, which is the most important commandment in the law of Moses?"

Jesus replied. "**'You must love the Lord your God with all your heart, all your soul, and all your mind.'**

This is the first and greatest commandment.

A second is equally important:

'Love your neighbor as yourself.'
All the other commandments and all the demands of the prophets are based on these two commandments." NLT

Master, **which is the great commandment in the law?** Jesus said unto him, **Thou shalt love the Lord thy God with all they heart, and with all thy soul, and with all thy mind.** This is the first and great commandment. And the second is like unto it. **Thou Shalt love they neighbor as thyself**. On these two commandments hang all the law and the prophets.
KJV

John 4:23-24

"But the hour cometh, and now is, when the true worshippers **shall worship the Father in spirit and in truth: for the Father seeketh such to worship him.**
God is a Spirit: and **they that worship him must worship him in spirit and in truth.** KJV

"Yet a time is coming and has now come when **the true worshipers will worship the Father in spirit and truth, for they are the kind of worshipers the Father seeks**. God is spirit, and **his worshipers must worship in spirit and in truth."** NIV

Matthew 4:10

"Thou shalt worship the Lord thy God, and him only shalt thou serve." KJV

'Worship the Lord your God, and serve him only.' NIV

This next part… while not listed in the original Ten Commandments given to Moses, is stressed so much by Jesus as being the SECOND greatest commandment that it is listed here.
The reason is probably because all of the other original Ten Commandments are based on this premise;

Matthew 19:19

"Thou shalt love thy neighbor as thyself" KJV

"Love your neighbor as yourself." NIV and NLT

John 15:12-17

This is my commandment, that ye love one another, even as I have loved you. Greater love hath no man than this, that a man lay down his life for his friends. **Ye are my friends, if ye do the things which I command you**. No longer do I call you servants; for the servant knoweth not what his lord doeth: but I have called you friends; for all things that I heard from my Father, I have made known unto you. Ye did not choose me, but I chose you, and appointed you, that ye should go and bear fruit, and that your fruit should abide: that whatsoever ye shall ask of the Father in my name, he may give it you. **These things I command you, that ye may love one another.** ASV

This is my commandment, That ye love one another, as I have loved you. Greater love hath no man than this, that a man lay down his life for his friends. **Ye are my friends, if ye do whatsoever I command you**. Henceforth I call you not servants; for the servant knoweth not what his lord doeth: but I have called you friends; for all things that I have heard of my Father I have made known unto you. Ye have not chosen me, but I have chosen you, and ordained you, that ye should go and bring forth fruit, and that your fruit should remain: that whatsoever ye shall ask of the Father in my name, he may give it you. **These things I command you, that ye love one another.** KJV

1 Peter 1:22

Now you can have sincere love for each other as brothers and sisters because you were cleansed from your sins when you accepted the truth of the Good News. **So see to it that you really do love each other intensely with all your hearts.** NLT

Seeing ye have purified your souls in obeying the truth through the Spirit unto unfeigned love of the brethren, see that ye love one another with a pure heart fervently. KJV

Luke 6:31

"Treat others the same way you want them to treat you." NASB

"As ye would that men should do to you, do ye also to them likewise" KJV

DO NOT MAKE ANY GRAVEN IMAGE OR LIKENESS:

Matthew 4:10

"YOU SHALL WORSHIP THE LORD YOUR GOD, AND SERVE HIM ONLY." NASB

"Worship the Lord your God, and serve him only" NIV

DO NOT MISUSE THE NAME OF THE LORD YOUR GOD.

I haven't found anything specific that Jesus said about this… but maybe You Can?

REMEMBER THE SABBATH DAY BY KEEPING IT HOLY:

Luke 4:16

When he came to the village of Nazareth, his boyhood home, **he went as usual to the synagogue on the Sabbath** and stood up to read the Scriptures. NLT

He went to Nazareth, where he had been brought up**, and on the Sabbath day he went into the synagogue, as was his custom.** And he stood up to read. NIV

Matthew 12:1-13

At that time Jesus went through the grainfields on the Sabbath, and His disciples became hungry and began to pick the heads of grain and eat. But when the Pharisees saw this, they said to Him, "Look, Your disciples do what is not lawful to do on the Sabbath." But He said to them, "Have you not read what David did when he became hungry, he and his companions, how he entered the house of God, and they ate the consecrated bread, which was not lawful for him to eat nor for those with him, but for the priests alone? Or have you not read the Law, that on the Sabbath the priests in the temple break the Sabbath and are innocent? But I say to you that something greater than the temple is here,

But if you had known what this means, 'I DESIRE COMPASSION, AND NOT A SACRIFICE,' you would not have condemned the innocent.

For the Son of Man is Lord of the Sabbath."

Departing from there, He went into their synagogue, and a man was there whose hand was withered. And they questioned Jesus, asking, "Is it lawful to heal on the Sabbath?"—so that they might accuse Him. And He said to them, "What man is there among you who has not sheep, and if it falls into a pit on the Sabbath, will he not take hold of it and lift it out? How much more valuable then is a man than a sheep! **So then, it is lawful to do good on the Sabbath."**

Then He said to the man, "Stretch out your hand!" He stretched it out, and it was restored to normal, like the other. NASB

At that time Jesus went on the sabbath day through the corn; and his disciples were a hungred, and began to pluck the ears of corn, and to eat. But when the Pharisees saw it, they said unto him, Behold, thy disciples do that which is not lawful to do upon the sabbath day. But he said unto them, Have ye not read what David did, when he was a hungred, and they that were with him; How he entered into the house of God, and did eat the shewbread, which was not lawful for him to eat, neither for them which were with him, but only for the priests? Or have ye not read in the law, how that on the sabbath days the priests in the temple profane the sabbath, and are blameless? But I say unto you, That in this place is one greater than the temple. But if ye had known what this meaneth**, I will have mercy, and not sacrifice, ye would not have condemned the guiltless. For the Son of man is Lord even of the sabbath day.** And when he was departed thence, he went into their synagogue: And, behold, there was a man which had his hand withered. And they asked him, saying, Is it lawful to heal on the sabbath days? that they might accuse him. And he said unto them, What man shall there be among you, that shall have one sheep, and if it fall into a pit on the sabbath day, will he not lay hold on it, and lift it out? How much then is a man better than a sheep? **Wherefore it is lawful to do well on the sabbath days**. Then saith he to the man, Stretch forth thine hand. And he stretched it forth; and it was restored whole, like as the other. KJV

Mark 2:27-28

Then he said to them, **"The Sabbath was made to benefit people, and not people to benefit the Sabbath. And I, the Son of Man, am master even of the Sabbath!"** NLT

And he said unto them, **The sabbath was made for man, and not man for the sabbath: therefore the Son of man is Lord also of the sabbath.** KJV

HONOR YOUR FATHER AND YOUR MOTHER:

Matthew 19:19

Honour thy father and thy mother: KJV

"Honor your father and mother" NIV

THOU SHALT NOT KILL:

Matthew 19:18

"Thou Shalt do no murder" KJV

"Do not murder." NLT

Matthew 5:21-22

"You have heard that the law of Moses says, '**Do not murder. If you commit murder, you are subject to judgment.'** But I say, **if you are angry with someone, you are subject to judgment! If you call someone an idiot, you are in danger of being brought before the high council. And if you curse someone, you are in danger of the fires of hell."** NLT

Ye have heard that it was said by them of old time, **Thou shalt not kill**; and whosoever shall kill shall be in danger of the judgment: but I say unto you, **That whosoever is angry with his brother without a cause shall be in danger of the judgment: and whosoever shall say to his brother, Raca, shall be in danger of the council: but whosoever shall say, Thou fool, shall be in danger of hell fire.** KJV

DO NOT COMMIT ADULTERY:

Matthew 19:18

"YOU SHALL NOT COMMIT ADULTERY" NASB

"Do not commit adultery" NIV

Matthew 5:27-32

Ye have heard that it was said, **Thou shalt not commit adultery:** but I say unto you, **that every one that looketh on a woman to lust after her hath committed adultery with her already in his heart.** And if thy right eye causeth thee to stumble, pluck it out, and cast it from thee: for it is profitable for thee that one of thy members should perish, and not thy whole body be cast into hell. And if thy right hand causeth thee to stumble, cut it off, and cast it from thee: for it is profitable for thee that one of thy members should perish, and not thy whole body go into hell. It was said also, **Whosoever shall put away his wife, let him give her a writing of divorcement**: but I say unto you, **that every one that putteth away his wife, saving for the cause of fornication, maketh her an adulteress: and whosoever shall marry her when she is put away committeth adultery.** ASV

Ye have heard that it was said by them of old time, **Thou shalt not commit adultery**: But I say unto you, **That whosoever looketh on a woman to lust after her hath committed adultery with her already in his heart.** And if thy right eye offend thee, pluck it out, and cast it from thee: for it is profitable for thee that one of thy members should perish, and not that thy whole body should be cast into hell. And if thy right hand offend thee, cut it off, and cast it from thee: for it is profitable for thee that one of thy members should perish, and not that thy whole body should be cast into hell. It hath been said, Whosoever shall put away his wife, let him give her a writing of divorcement: But I say unto you, **That whosoever shall put away his wife, saving for the cause of fornication, causeth her to commit adultery: and whosoever shall marry her that is divorced committeth adultery.** KJV

Matthew 19:9

"I tell you that anyone who divorces his wife, except for marital unfaithfulness, and marries another woman commits adultery." NIV

"And I tell you this, a man who divorces his wife and marries another commits adultery—unless his wife has been unfaithful." NLT

THOU SHALT NOT STEAL:

Matthew 19:18

"Do not steal" NLT

"Thou shalt not steal" KJV

DO NOT BEAR FALSE WITNESS:

Matthew 19:18

"Do not give false testimony" NIV

Thou shalt not bear false witness ASV

DO NOT COVET:

Luke 12:15

"Take heed, and **beware of covetousness**: for a man's life consisteth not in the abundance of the things which he possesseth." KJV

"Beware, and **be on your guard against every form of greed**; for not even when one has an abundance does his life consist of his possession." NASB

Matthew 6:19-20

"**Do not store up for yourselves treasures on earth**, where moth and rust destroy, and where thieves break in and steal. But store up for yourselves treasures in heaven, where moth and rust do not destroy, and where thieves do not break in and steal." NIV

Lay not up for yourselves treasures upon the earth, where moth and rust consume, and where thieves break through and steal: but lay up for yourselves treasures in heaven, where neither moth nor rust doth consume, and where thieves do not break through nor steal. ASV

Other Commands of Jesus...

"REPENT"

Matthew 4:17

"Jesus began to preach and say, "**Repent, for the kingdom of heaven is at hand.**" NASB

Jesus began to preach, **"Turn from your sins and turn to God, because the Kingdom of Heaven is near."** NLT

Jesus began to preach, **"Repent, for the kingdom of heaven is near**." NIV

Revelation 2:5

Remember therefore from whence thou art fallen, **and repent,** and do the first works; or else I will come unto thee quickly, and will remove thy candlestick out of his place, **except thou repent.** KJV

Look how far you have fallen from your first love! **Turn back to me again** and work as you did at first**. If you don't,** I will come and remove your lampstand from its place among the churches. NLT

"COME TO ME"

Matthew 11:28-30

Then Jesus said, **"Come to me, all of you who are weary and carry heavy burdens, and I will give you rest.**
Take my yoke upon you. Let me teach you, because I am humble and gentle, and you will find rest for your souls.
For my yoke fits perfectly, and the burden I give you is light." NLT

Come unto me, all ye that labour and are heavy laden, and I will give you rest. Take my yoke upon you, and learn of me; for I am meek and lowly in heart: and ye shall find rest unto your souls. For my yoke is easy, and my burden is light. KJV

"FOLLOW ME"

John 12:26

"**Whoever serves me must follow me;** and where I am, my servant also will be. My Father will honor the one who serves me." NIV

"If any man serve me, let him follow me; and where I am, there shall also my servant be: if any man serve me, him will my Father honour." KJV

Luke 9:23

Then he said to the crowd, **"If any of you wants to be my follower, you must put aside your selfish ambition, shoulder your cross daily, and follow me.** NLT

And he said to them all, **If any man will come after me, let him deny himself, and take up his cross daily, and follow me.** KJV

"BE BAPTIZED"

Matthew 3:13-17

Then cometh Jesus from Galilee to Jordan unto John**, to be baptized of him**. But John forbad him, **saying, I have need to be baptized of thee,** and comest thou to me?

And Jesus answering said unto him, Suffer it to be so now: **for thus it becometh us to fulfil all righteousness.**

Then he suffered him. **And Jesus, when he was baptized,** went up straightway out of the water: and lo, the heavens were opened unto him, and **he saw the Spirit of God descending like a dove, and lighting upon him: and lo a voice from heaven, saying, This is my beloved Son, in whom I am well pleased.** KJV

Then cometh Jesus from Galilee to the Jordan **unto John, to be baptized of him.** But John would have hindered him, saying, **I have need to be baptized of thee**, and comest thou to me? But Jesus answering said unto him, Suffer it now: **for thus it becometh us to fulfil all righteousness.** Then he suffereth him. **And Jesus when he was baptized,** went up straightway from the water: and lo, the heavens were opened unto him, and **he saw the Spirit of God descending as a dove, and coming upon him; and lo, a voice out of the heavens, saying, This is my beloved Son, in whom I am well pleased.** ASV

Matthew 28:19-20

Baptism and The Great Commission

"Go therefore and make disciples of all nations, **baptizing them in the name of the Father and the Son and the Holy Spirit,**

Teaching them to observe all that I commanded you; and lo, I am with you always, even to the end of the age." NASB

"Therefore, go and make disciples of all the nations, **baptizing them in the name of the Father and the Son and the Holy Spirit. Teach these new disciples to obey all commands I have given you.** And be sure of this: I am with you always, even to the end of the age." NLT

"DO THIS IN REMEMBRANCE OF ME" (COMMUNION)

Luke 22:15-20

And he said to them, "I have eagerly desired to eat this Passover with you before I suffer. For I tell you, I will not eat it again until it finds fulfillment in the kingdom of God."

After taking the cup, he gave thanks and said, "Take this and divide it among you. For I tell you I will not drink again of the fruit of the vine until the kingdom of God comes."

And he took bread, gave thanks and broke it, and gave it to them, saying, "This is my body given for you; do this in remembrance of me."

In the same way, after the supper he took the cup saying, **"This cup is the new covenant in my blood, which is poured out for you.** NIV

And he said unto them, With desire I have desired to eat this passover with you before I suffer: For I say unto you, I will not any more eat thereof, until it be fulfilled in the kingdom of God. And **he took the cup, and gave thanks, and said, Take this, and divide it among yourselves:** For I say unto you, I will not drink of the fruit of the vine, until the kingdom of God shall come. **And he took bread, and gave thanks, and brake it, and gave unto them, saying, This is my body which is given for you: this do in remembrance of me. Likewise also the cup after supper, saying, This cup is the new testament in my blood, which is shed for you.** KJV

"LOVE YOUR ENEMIES"

Luke 6:27-36

But **I say unto you that hear, Love your enemies, do good to them that hate you,** bless them that curse you, pray for them that despitefully use you. To him that smiteth thee on the one cheek offer also the other; and from him that taketh away thy cloak withhold not thy coat also. Give to every one that asketh thee; and of him that taketh away thy goods ask them not again. And as ye would that men should do to you, do ye also to them likewise. And if ye love them that love you, what thank have ye? for even sinners love those that love them. And if ye do good to them that do good to you, what thank have ye? for even sinners do the same. And if ye lend to them of whom ye hope to receive, what thank have ye? even sinners lend to sinners, to receive again as much. **But love your enemies, and do them good, and lend, never despairing**; and your reward shall be great, and ye shall be sons of the Most High: for he is kind toward the unthankful and evil. **Be ye merciful, even as your Father is merciful.** ASV

But I say unto you which hear, **Love your enemies, do good to them which hate you, Bless them that curse you, and pray for them which despitefully use you**. And unto him that smiteth thee on the one cheek offer also the other; and him that taketh away thy cloke forbid not to take thy coat also. Give to every man that asketh of thee; and of him that taketh away thy goods ask them not again. And as ye would that men should do to you, do ye also to them likewise. For if ye love them which love you, what thank have ye? for sinners also love those that love them. And if ye do good to them which do good to you, what thank have ye? for sinners also do even the same. And if ye lend to them of whom ye hope to receive, what thank have ye? for sinners also lend to sinners, to receive as much again. **But love ye your enemies, and do good, and lend, hoping for nothing again;** and your reward shall be great, and ye shall be the children of the Highest: for he is kind unto the unthankful and to the evil. **Be ye therefore merciful, as your Father also is merciful.** KJV

"DO NOT LOVE THE WORLD OR ANYTHING IN THE WORLD"

1 John 2:15-17

Do not love the world or anything in the world. If anyone loves the world, the love of the Father is not in him.

For everything in the world—the cravings of sinful man, the lust of his eyes and the boasting of what he has and does—comes not from the Father but from the world.

The world and its desires pass away, but the man who does the will of God lives forever. NIV

Love not the world, neither the things that are in the world. If any man love the world, the love of the Father is not in him. For all that is in the world, the lust of the flesh, and the lust of the eyes, and the pride of life, is not of the Father, but is of the world. And the world passeth away, and the lust thereof: but he that doeth the will of God abideth for ever.

KJV

A brief statement made to cover the Ten Commandments...

Matthew 7:12

"Do for others what you would like them to do for you. This is a summary of all that is taught in the law and the prophets. NLT

"In everything, therefore, treat people the same way you want them to treat you, for this is the Law and the Prophets."

NASB

Other Commandments of Jesus that I will let you learn about on your own...

"Learn of Me" Matthew 11:29
"Deny Yourself" Matthew 16:24
"Ask... seek...knock" Matthew 7:7
"Strive to enter in at the strait gate" Luke 13:24
"Believe the Gospel" Mark 1:15

"Let the children first be filled" Mark 7:27

"Ye believe in God, believe also in Me" John 14:1

"Believe Me that I am in the Father and the Father in Me" John 14:11

"Continue ye in My love" John 15:9

"Believe the works…I do" John 10:37-38

"While ye have light believe in the light" John 12:36

"Believe that ye receive" Mark 11:24

"Pray always" Luke 21:36

"Abide in Me and I in you" John 15:4

"Forgive if ye have ought against any" Mark 11:25

"Seek first God and His righteousness" Matthew 6:33

"Ye must be born again" John 3:7

"Cleanse first that which is within" Matthew 23:26

"Receive ye the Holy Ghost" John 20:23

"Make the tree good, and his fruit good" Matthew 12:33

"Have salt in yourselves" Mark 9:50

"Labor…for that meat which endureth unto everlasting life" John 6:27

"If any man thirst, let him come unto Me and drink" John 7:37-39

"Ye also ought to wash one another's feet" John 13:14-15

"Ask…with importunity" John 16:24; Luke 11:5-13

"Tarry…until ye be endued with power from on high" John 15:26-27

"Keep my commandments and…the Father…shall give you another Comforter" John 14:15-17

And keep looking… maybe you can find some that I missed…

Psalm 119:49-56

Remember the word unto thy servant, Because thou hast made me to hope. This is my comfort in my affliction; For thy word hath quickened me. The proud have had me greatly in derision: Yet have I not swerved from thy law. I have remembered thine ordinances of old, O Jehovah, And have comforted myself. Hot indignation hath taken hold upon me, Because of the wicked that forsake thy law. Thy statutes have been my songs In the house of my pilgrimage. I have remembered thy name, O Jehovah, in the night, And have observed thy law. This I have had, Because I have kept thy precepts. ASV

Chapter Five

Is drinking or doing drugs wrong?

In this chapter we will look at scriptures that talk about the drinking of alcohol.

You will see how you can drink alcohol and God is fine with it.

But you will also see the circumstances where God is not fine with it... and considers it a SIN.

Since Drugs were not really mentioned in the Bible you will see that I have included them here, as (judging from the scriptures) God seems very concerned when your Reason and Mental processes are impaired... which drugs do, similar to what alcohol does.

But read on, so you can understand for yourself.

John 2:1-10

And the third day there was a marriage in Cana of Galilee; and the mother of Jesus was there: And both Jesus was called, and his disciples, to the marriage. And when they wanted wine, the mother of Jesus saith unto him, They have no wine. Jesus saith unto her, Woman, what have I to do with thee? mine hour is not yet come. His mother saith unto the servants, Whatsoever he saith unto you, do it. And there were set there six waterpots of stone, after the manner of the purifying of the Jews, containing two or three firkins apiece. **Jesus saith unto them, Fill the waterpots with water. And they filled them up to the brim. And he saith unto them, Draw out now, and bear unto the governor of the feast. And they bare it. When the ruler of the feast had tasted the water that was made wine, and knew not whence it was: (but the servants which drew the water knew;) the governor of the feast called the bridegroom, And saith unto him, Every man at the beginning doth set forth good wine; and when men have well drunk,**

then that which is worse: but thou hast kept the good wine until now. KJV

On the third day there was a wedding in Cana of Galilee, and the mother of Jesus was there; and both Jesus and His disciples were invited to the wedding.

When the wine ran out, the mother of Jesus said to Him, "They have no wine." And Jesus said to her, "Woman, what does that have to do with us? My hour has not yet come." His mother said to the servants, "Whatever He says to you, do it." Now there were six stone waterpots set there for the Jewish custom of purification, containing twenty or thirty gallons each. **Jesus said to them, "Fill the waterpots with water." So they filled them up to the brim. And He said to them, "Draw some out now and take it to the headwaiter." So they took it to him. When the headwaiter tasted the water which had become wine, and did not know where it came from (but the servants who had drawn the water knew), the headwaiter called the bridegroom, and said to him, "Every man serves the good wine first, and when the people have drunk freely, then he serves the poorer wine; but you have kept the good wine until now."** NASB

Not only is God not against drinking wine… but he makes the BEST wine.

So, if God is not against drinking wine… what is all the fuss about?

Okay, let's start with how breaking Man's Laws can be **Sinning** against God.

Mark 12:14-17

"Teacher," these men said, "we know how honest you are. You are impartial and don't play favorites. You sincerely teach the ways of God. **Now tell us-is it right to pay taxes to the**

Roman government or not? Should we pay them, or should we not?"

Jesus saw through their hypocrisy and said, "Whom are you trying to fool with your trick questions? **Show me a Roman coin, and I'll tell you."**

When they handed it to him, he asked, "Whose picture and title are stamped on it?"

"Caesar's," they replied.

"Well then," Jesus said, **"give to Caesar what belongs to him. But everything that belongs to God must be given to God."** This reply completely amazed them. NLT

And when they were come, they say unto him, Master, we know that thou are true, and carest for no man: for thou regardest not the person of men, but teachest the way of God in truth: **Is it lawful to give tribute to Cesar, or not? Shall we give, or shall we not give?** But he, knowing their hypocrisy, said unto them, **Why tempt ye me? Bring me a penny, that I may see it. And they brought it. And he saith unto them, Whose is this image and superscription? And they said unto him, Cesar's. And Jesus answering said unto them, Render to Cesar the things that are Cesar's, and to God the things that are God's. And they marveled at him.** KJV

Basically God is telling you to OBEY the Laws of your country and "king".

If the Law says the Legal Age for drinking Alcohol is 21… then you are to OBEY that LAW. If the law says you are not to drink and drive, then you are NOT to drink and drive… it is the LAW.

You are also to OBEY your Parents, those in authority, etc.

ONLY if the laws or the authorities go AGAINST God's laws are you to ignore them and OBEY God's laws INSTEAD.

Let's read a few more…

Jeremiah 35:4-19

And **I brought them into the house of Jehovah**, into the chamber of the sons of Hanan the son of Igdaliah, the man of

God, which was by the chamber of the princes, which was above the chamber of Maaseiah the son of Shallum, the keeper of the threshold. **And I set before the sons of the house of the Rechabites bowls full of wine, and cups; and I said unto them, Drink ye wine. But they said, We will drink no wine; for Jonadab the son of Rechab, our father, commanded us, saying, Ye shall drink no wine, neither ye, nor your sons, for ever:** neither shall ye build house, nor sow seed, nor plant vineyard, nor have any; but all your days ye shall dwell in tents; that ye may live many days in the land wherein ye sojourn. **And we have obeyed the voice of Jonadab the son of Rechab, our father, in all that he charged us, to drink no wine all our days, we, our wives, our sons, or our daughters;** nor to build houses for us to dwell in; neither have we vineyard, nor field, nor seed: but we have dwelt in tents**, and have obeyed, and done according to all that Jonadab our father commanded us.** But it came to pass, when Nebuchadrezzar king of Babylon came up into the land, that we said, Come, and let us go to Jerusalem for fear of the army of the Chaldeans, and for fear of the army of the Syrians; so we dwell at Jerusalem.

Then came the word of Jehovah unto Jeremiah, saying, Thus saith Jehovah of hosts, the God of Israel: Go, and say to the men of Judah and the inhabitants of Jerusalem, Will ye not **receive instruction to hearken to my words? saith Jehovah. The words of Jonadab the son of Rechab, that he commanded his sons, not to drink wine, are performed; and unto this day they drink none, for they obey their father's commandment: but I have spoken unto you, rising up early and speaking; and ye have not hearkened unto me.** I have sent also unto you all my servants the prophets, rising up early and sending them, saying, Return ye now every man from his evil way, and amend your doings, and go not after other gods to serve them, and ye shall dwell in the land which I have given to you and to your fathers: but ye have not inclined your ear, nor hearkened unto me. **Forasmuch as the sons of Jonadab the son of Rechab have performed the commandment of their father which he commanded them, but this people hath not hearkened unto me; therefore thus saith Jehovah, the God of hosts, the God of Israel: Behold, I will bring upon Judah and upon all the inhabitants of Jerusalem all the evil that I have pronounced against them; because I have spoken unto them, but they**

have not heard; and I have called unto them, but they have not answered.

And Jeremiah said unto the house of the Rechabites, Thus saith Jehovah of hosts, the God of Israel: **Because ye have obeyed the commandment of Jonadab your father, and kept all his precepts, and done according unto all that he commanded you; therefore thus saith Jehovah of hosts, the God of Israel: Jonadab the son of Rechab shall not want a man to stand before me for ever.** ASV

And I brought them into the house of the Lord, into the chamber of the sons of Hanan, the son of Igdaliah, a man of God, which was by the chamber of the princes, which was above the chamber of Maaseiah the son of Shallum, the keeper of the door: **And I set before the sons of the house of the Rechabites pots full of wine, and cups, and I said unto them, Drink ye wine. But they said, We will drink no wine: for Jonadab the son of Rechab our father commanded us, saying, Ye shall drink no wine, neither ye, nor your sons for ever**: Neither shall ye build house, nor sow seed, nor plant vineyard, nor have any: but all your days ye shall dwell in tents; that ye may live many days in the land where ye be strangers. **Thus have we obeyed the voice of Jonadab the son of Rechab our father in all that he hath charged us, to drink no wine all our days, we, our wives, our sons, nor our daughters;** Nor to build houses for us to dwell in: neither have we vineyard, nor field, nor seed: But we have dwelt in tents, and have obeyed, and done according to all that Jonadab our father commanded us. But it came to pass, when Nebuchadrezzar king of Babylon came up into the land, that we said, Come, and let us go to Jerusalem for fear of the army of the Chaldeans, and for fear of the army of the Syrians: so we dwell at Jerusalem.

Then came the word of the Lord unto Jeremiah, saying, **Thus saith the Lord of hosts, the God of Israel; Go and tell the men of Judah and the inhabitants of Jerusalem, Will ye not receive instruction to hearken to my words? saith the Lord. The words of Jonadab the son of Rechab, that he commanded his sons not to drink wine, are**

performed; for unto this day they drink none, but obey their father's commandment: notwithstanding I have spoken unto you, rising early and speaking; but ye hearkened not unto me. I have sent also unto you all my servants the prophets, rising up early and sending them, saying, Return ye now every man from his evil way, and amend your doings, and go not after other gods to serve them, and ye shall dwell in the land which I have given to you and to your fathers: but ye have not inclined your ear, nor hearkened unto me. **Because the sons of Jonadab the son of Rechab have performed the commandment of their father, which he commanded them; but this people hath not hearkened unto me: Therefore thus saith the Lord God of hosts, the God of Israel; Behold, I will bring upon Judah and upon all the inhabitants of Jerusalem all the evil that I have pronounced against them:** because I have spoken unto them, but they have not heard; and I have called unto them, but they have not answered.

And Jeremiah said unto the house of the Rechabites, **Thus saith the Lord of hosts, the God of Israel; Because ye have obeyed the commandment of Jonadab your father, and kept all his precepts, and done according unto all that he hath commanded you: Therefore thus saith the Lord of hosts, the God of Israel; Jonadab the son of Rechab shall not want a man to stand before me for ever.** KJV

As you can see by this scripture... God is more concerned with people OBEYING HIM, or their PARENTS (ancestors, or the ancestor's laws) than he is about actually DRINKING Wine.

In fact, he has Jeremiah offer the Recabites wine in the Temple itself... so obviously God does not have a problem with people drinking wine. UNLESS, the person has been TOLD not to drink by someone who has authority over him/her, like a Parent, ancestor, or the Laws of the country.

Now that you know that God is not against the act of drinking wine... IF it is allowed by those in authority that is... why would God want to put a limit on how much wine (or other alcoholic beverage) you should drink?

Let us look at a few more scriptures...

Proverbs 23:20-21

Do not join those who drink too much wine or gorge themselves on meat, **for drunkards and gluttons become poor, and drowsiness clothes them in rags.** NIV

Do not be with heavy drinkers of wine,
Or with gluttonous eaters of meat;
For the heavy drinker and the glutton will come to poverty,
And drowsiness will clothe one with rags. NASB

Proverbs 23:29-35

Who has woe? Who has sorrow? Who has strife? Who has complaints? Who has needless bruises? Who has bloodshot eyes?

Those who linger over wine, who go to sample bowls of mixed wine.

Do not gaze at wine when it is red, when it sparkles in the cup, when it goes down smoothly!

In the end it bites like a snake and poisons like a viper.

Your eyes will see strange sights and your mind imagine confusing things.

You will be like one sleeping on the high seas, lying on top of the rigging.

"They hit me," you will say, "but I'm not hurt! They beat me, but I don't feel it!

When will I wake up so I can find another drink?" NIV

Who hath woe? Who hath sorrow? Who hath contentions? Who hath babbling? Who hath wounds without cause? Who hath redness of eyes?

They that tarry long at the wine; They that go to seek mixt wine.

Look not thou upon the wine when it is red, when it giveth his colour in the cup, when it moveth itself aright.
At the last it biteth like a serpent, and stingeth like an adder.
Thine eyes shall behold strange women, and thine heart shall utter perverse things.
Yea, thou shalt be as he that lieth down in the midst of the sea, or as he that lieth upon the top of a mast.
They have stricken me, shalt thou say, and I was not sick; they have beaten me, and I felt it not;
When shall I awake? I will seek it yet again. KJV

As you can see by the terms of mixed wine or trying out new drinks… God is not just speaking of wine but other types of alcoholic beverages as well.

Romans 13:13-14

We should be decent and true in everything we do, so that everyone can approve of our behavior. Don't participate in wild parties and getting drunk, or in adultery and immoral living, or in fighting and jealousy. **But let the Lord Jesus Christ take control of you, and don't think of ways to indulge your evil desires**. NLT

Let us behave decently, as in the daytime, not in orgies and **drunkenness,** not in sexual immorality and debauchery, not in dissension and jealousy. Rather, clothe yourselves with the Lord Jesus Christ, and **do not think about how to gratify the desires of the sinful nature.** NIV

1 Corinthians 5:11

But now I am writing you that **you must not associate with anyone who calls himself a brother but is** sexually immoral or greedy, an idolater or a slanderer**, a drunkard** or a swindler. **With such a man do not even eat.** NIV

What I meant was that **you are not to associate with anyone who claims to be a Christian yet** indulges in sexual sin, or is greedy, or worships idols, or **is abusive, or a drunkard,** or a swindler. **Don't even eat with such people.** NLT

Now as we can see by these scriptures God does not mind someone drinking... but He does not want them to **"drink too much"** or become a **"drunkard".**

He is not happy with people who become so out of touch with reality such that; **"eyes that see strange sights and minds that imagine confusing things."**

"Thine eyes shall behold strange women, and thine heart shall utter perverse things",

Or **"They hit me, but I didn't feel it. I didn't even know it when they beat me up."**

and especially **"When will I wake up so I can find another drink?"**

Now while the Bible doesn't really talk about DRUGS, it is clear God doesn't like people drinking too much and becoming drunk... WHY? Because it affects their MINDS (perceptions, understanding, emotions, etc.) and HEALTH. It becomes addictive and it ruins lives.

That sounds a lot like the effects that most illegal (and some questionably legal) Drugs have. So if God is against alcohol for the effects it produces... and those effects are similar to doing Drugs... then it would seem that doing Drugs is just as bad as Drinking too much Alcohol.

So to clarify again... anytime you see **"Drunkard"** or **"Drink too much"** you should include **"Do Drugs"** on that sin list.

God wants the best for us, which we cannot have if we are out of our minds, out of health, and addicted to a behavior that leads to even more sinful behaviors.

Now let's take a look at just HOW MUCH he does not like "drinking too much", "drunkard", etc....

1 Corinthians 6:9-10

Or do you not know that the unrighteous will not inherit the kingdom of God? Do not be deceived; neither fornicators, nor idolaters, nor adulterers, nor effeminate, nor homosexuals, nor thieves, nor the covetous, **nor drunkards**, nor revilers, nor swindlers, **will inherit the kingdom of God.** NASB

Don't you know that those who do wrong will have no share in the Kingdom of God? Don't fool yourselves. Those who indulge in sexual sin, who are idol worshipers, adulterers, male prostitutes, homosexuals, thieves, greedy people, **drunkards**, abusers, and swindlers-**none of these will have a share in the Kingdom of God.** NLT

Nahum 1:10

They will be entangled among thorns and **drunk from their wine; they will be consumed like dry stubble.** NIV

For while they be folden together as thorns, And **while they be drunken as drunkards, They shall be devoured as stubble fully dry.** KJV

Galatians 5:19-21

When you follow the desires of your sinful nature, your lives will produce these evil results: sexual immorality, impure thoughts, eagerness for lustful pleasure, idolatry, participation in demonic activities, hostility, quarreling, jealousy, outbursts of anger, selfish ambition, divisions, the feeling that everyone is wrong except those in your own little group, envy, **drunkenness,** wild parties, and other kinds of sin. Let me tell you again, as I have before, that **anyone living that sort of life will not inherit the Kingdom of God.** NLT

Now the deeds of the flesh are evident, which are: immorality, impurity, sensuality, idolatry, sorcery, enmities, strife, jealousy, outbursts of anger, disputes, dissensions, factions, envying**, drunkenness**, carousing, and things like these, of which I forewarn you, just as I have forewarned you, **that those who practice such things will not inherit the kingdom of God.** NASB

Many people will tell you that "Alcoholism is a disease." But to God it is NOT.

Alcoholism is SIN, pure and simple. God SPECIFICALLY states NOT to get drunk or become a Drunkard.

Those are CHOICES made by the drinker...And God is telling the drinker that they are making the WRONG CHOICES.

If it was TRULY a disease, then God would know that the drinker "Had NO choice" and would not condemn them... but God knows that it is NOT a Disease. That it is only a drunkards EXCUSE for their lack of judgment and control.

God CONDEMNS the drunkard and those who Get Drunk... because it is a SIN,

The drinker made a CHOICE to take that drink, and keep on going.

The SIN is in breaking God's Command NOT to get drunk or become a drunkard.

(If you need to know more about SIN, see the Chapter: What is SIN anyway?)

IF you are an "Alcoholic", then you need to be Praying for Forgiveness from the LORD and "PRAYING" for God to Deliver you from the "Power" of alcohol and any demons that might be keeping you a prisoner of the drink (or drugs).

(See Chapters: What is SIN anyway? and Don't know Jesus?)

There **IS HOPE** for you. Don't give up. But you must start by TAKING RESPONSIBILITY for YOUR actions and repenting.

Turn from your drink (or drugs) and PRAY fervently for help from God.

God WANTS to help you. He LOVES you… but he can't look at you when you are so full of sin. So do your best to fight the addiction and God will be there to help you do it.

He may send people to talk to you that you don't even know… DON'T DISMISS THEM OUT OF HAND… God wants you to hear what they have to say.

Ask a church to pray FOR you as well, the more people you have rooting for you the better.

1 Thessalonians 5:17

Pray without ceasing. KJV and NASB

Pray continually. NIV

And if you are reading this because you have a friend or family member that is an Alcoholic or Drug addict…

Romans 14:21

Don't eat meat or **drink wine or do anything else if it might cause another Christian to stumble.** NLT

It is good not to eat meat or **to drink wine**, **or to do anything by which your brother stumbles.** NASB

It is better not to eat meat **or drink wine or to do anything else** that will cause your brother to fall. NIV

And Pray for them: that God will deliver them from the desire, cleanse them of the need and make them whole again.

Psalm 91:15

"**He will call upon me, and I will answer him;
I will be with him in trouble,
I will deliver him** and honor him." NIV

**He shall call upon me, and I will answer him:
I will be with him in trouble;
I will deliver him,** and honour him. KJV

If you still have problems; talk with a Pastor, a Christian Therapist or therapy group. Do the AA meetings, deliberately move out of areas that help support/promote your problem (away from the local bar, the druggie hangouts, etc.).

But remember, if, after you have tried everything... you still are stricken with these sinful desires... realize that this may be something that God is not going to remove, but is actually allowing you to be tested with.

Now don't think that God is going around afflicting everyone just to test them. Those problems are usually the result of the Devil and his minions, other sinners, or our own poor judgment, etc. but God in his wisdom ALLOWS it to happen to observe your response.

God tests people regularly to help them mature in their spiritual growth.

If you are being tested, God wants you to flee from temptation and not succumb to evil/sinful ways. Every time we choose to do the right thing, God rewards us... usually when we get to heaven, but often even here on earth in unexpected ways.

When we fail our tests (give in to those temptations)... we sin.

People are tested in many ways, you are not alone. Some people are tested with handicaps (a missing leg, Down syndrome, blindness, etc.), others with diseases (Cancer, Multiple Sclerosis, Lupus, etc.).

Others face things like Clinical Depression, Schizophrenia, Bipolar disorder, past emotional or physical traumas, sexual addictions, etc.

The thing is that we all have to face tests and challenges... and it is how we handle them that God watches very closely.

2 Corinthians 12:6-10

I have plenty to boast about and would be no fool in doing it, because I would be telling the truth. But I won't do it. I don't want anyone to think more highly of me than what they can actually see in my life and my message, **even though I have received wonderful revelations from God. But to keep me from getting puffed up, I was given a thorn in my flesh, a messenger from Satan to torment me and keep me from getting proud.**

Three different times I begged the Lord to take it away. Each time he said, "My gracious favor is all you need. My power works best in your weakness." So **now I am glad to boast about my weaknesses, so that the power of Christ may work through me.** Since I know it is all for Christ's good. **I am quite content with my weaknesses and with insults, hardships, persecutions, and calamities. For when I am weak, then I am strong.** NLT

For though I would desire to glory, I shall not be a fool; for I will say the truth: but now I forbear, lest any man should think of me above that which he seeth me to be, or that he heareth of me.

And lest I should be exalted above measure through the abundance of the revelations, **there was given to me a thorn in the flesh, the messenger of Satan to buffet me, lest I should be exalted above measure.**

For this thing **I besought the Lord thrice, that it might depart from me.**

And he said unto me, "My grace is sufficient for thee: for my strength is made perfect in weakness."

Most gladly **therefore will I rather glory in my infirmities, that the power of Christ may** rest upon me.

Therefore **I take pleasure in infirmities, in reproaches, in necessities, in persecutions, in distresses for Christ's sake: for when I am weak, then am I strong.** KJV

God often lets us endure pain or "thorns" to REMIND US that we are only human and in constant need of God's help and strength, His protection... and comfort.

1 Peter 2:11

Dear friends, I urge you, as aliens and strangers in the world, to **abstain from sinful desires**, which war against your soul. NIV

Beloved, I urge you as aliens and strangers to **abstain from fleshly lusts which wage war against the soul.** NASB

Remember, every TEST is a chance for you to CHOOSE to ABSTAIN from the SIN.

Alcoholics need to Abstain from drinking alcohol, and may even need to Abstain from going to places where alcohol is available, the same for drug users.

People with Sexual Disorders need to Abstain from Sexual activities (Porn of any type, going to places where there is even a small chance of a sexual situation occurring, "thinking" and "fantasizing" about sexual activities, etc.)

Many people who have been tested with Homosexual desires/urges have chosen to live celibate lives (like many monks, some priests, etc.), to Abstain from Homosexual activities and so avoid sinning against God.

YOU ARE NOT ALONE! You are simply being tested, and hopefully refined, like everyone else God loves and wants to see in heaven with him.

Romans 6:12-14

Do not let sin control the way you live; do not give in to its lustful desires. Do not let any part of your body become a tool of wickedness**, to be used for sinning.** Instead, **give yourselves completely to God** since you have been given new life. And use your whole body as a tool **to do what is right for the glory of God**. **Sin is no longer your master, for you are no longer subject to the law, which enslaves you to sin.** Instead, **you are free by God's grace.** NLT

Therefore **do not let sin reign in your mortal body so that you obey its lusts**, and do not go on presenting the members of your body to sin as instruments of unrighteousness; but present yourselves to God as those alive from the dead, and your members as instruments of righteousness to God. **For sin shall not be master over you, for you are not under law but under grace.** NASB

Think of Alcohol (or drugs) as a TEMPTATION for you to AVOID continually (the Bible never says anything about *resisting* Temptation, only *resisting* the Devil). So remember, if you find yourself faced with Temptation... **Leave, Run away, Pray**... but GET OUT of that SITUATION!

If you are with "friends" who are drinking, and you find yourself TEMPTED to take a drink... **Leave them and go somewhere else**, drive away with other friends if necessary.

If something prevents you from actually LEAVING... Turn away and Pray! Don't LOOK at the Temptation, don't listen, etc. Pray and concentrate on something else; like God's many blessings to you, things that need to be fixed around the house, etc.

DO NOT think about HOW to avoid the Temptation; thinking about the temptation AT ALL only gives it STRENGTH and makes it HARDER to NOT think about it.

Colossians 3:1-2

Set your hearts on things above, where Christ is seated at the right hand of God.

Set your minds on things above, not on earthly things. NIV

Seek those things which are above, where Christ sitteth on the right hand of God. Set your affection on things above, **not on things on the earth.** KJV

Ephesians 6:10-11

Finally, **be strong in the Lord and in his mighty power**. **Put on the full armor of God so that you can take your stand against the devil's schemes.** NIV

Finally, my brethren, be strong in the Lord, and in the power of his might. **Put on the whole armour of God, that ye may be able to stand against the wiles of the devil.** KJV

So, if you have been living with SIN, know that it is NOT too late to change. It is NOT too late to become the person GOD wants YOU to be.

1 John 1:9

If we confess our sins, he is faithful and just and will forgive us our sins and purify us from all unrighteousness. NIV

If we confess our sins, he is faithful and just to forgive us our sins, and to cleanse us from all unrighteousness. KJV

No human being is, or was ever, Perfect (Never Sinned), except

Jesus Christ.

So, whatever the sin you may have done, or may even still be doing... You can still be forgiven.

But you must Repent (Tell God you are sorry for sinning against Him and his laws, and ask forgiveness)… and mean it, and sincerely try not to sin again.

Now that may be really hard, and you may stumble and fall many times… but if you are SINCERELY trying to stop the sin… that is what God wants from you.

But NOT SINNING, or asking forgiveness for your sins ALONE is not going to please God, save you from HELL and get you into HEAVEN and the Family of God.

For THAT you still need one VERY IMPORTANT Thing…

JESUS CHRIST

You must accept and acknowledge that Jesus Christ is the son of God. That he was born of a human woman, lived a sin-free life but willingly died on a cross (a sinners death) to save all who trust in him from their sins… and three days later he rose again (came back to life).

Don't know about Jesus Christ?

See the Chapter: **Don't know Jesus?**

Chapter Six

Is Abortion murder?

One of the biggest questions today is about Abortion. According to many of Man's Laws, it is "Legal". But is it against God's Law and a SIN in God's eyes?

Let us take a look at some scriptures that talk about this issue.

Let's start at the beginning, with Genesis...

Genesis 1:27-28

So God created man in his own image, in the image of God he created him; **male and female he created them.**

God blessed them and said to them, **"Be fruitful and increase in number**; fill the earth and subdue it. Rule over the fish of the sea and the birds of the air and over every living creature that moves on the ground." NIV

So God created man in his own image, in the image of God created he him; **male and female created he them.** And God blessed them, and God said unto them, **Be fruitful, and multiply**, and replenish the earth, and subdue it: and have dominion over the fish of the sea, and over the fowl of the air, and over every living thing that moveth upon the earth. KJV

Genesis 9:1

And God blessed Noah and his sons, and **said unto them. Be fruitful, and multiply, and replenish the earth.** KJV

And God blessed Noah and his sons and said to them, **"Be fruitful and multiply, and fill the earth."** NASB

Genesis 9:7

And you, be ye fruitful, and multiply; bring fourth abundantly in the earth, and multiply therein. KJV

"As for you, be fruitful and increase in number; multiply on the earth and increase upon it." NIV

Throughout Genesis God is stressing the importance of having children, of propagating, of perpetuating the species. He is not only stressing it... **He is COMMANDING it**. And nowhere in the scriptures does he remove or change this command.

In fact, Being Fruitful and/or Multiplying is mentioned in the Bible over **30** times.

Therefore, it stands to reason that if a person **is deliberately** seeking to avoid having a child, procreating, perpetuating the species.... **They are breaking God's commandment... they are sinning**.
But I leave it up to **you** to search the scriptures to see if you can find anything that contradicts this.

So yes, as unpleasant to some as that may seem, it would indicate that **all forms** of deliberate birth control(except to abstain before you are married), are also really **Sin** because you are not trusting the Lord to know how many children are best for you.

But let's take a look from another angle....

Genesis 4:25

And Adam knew his wife again; and she bare a son, and called his name Seth: **For God said she, had appointed me another seed** instead of Abel, whom Cain slew. KJV

Adam lay with his wife again, and she gave birth to a son and named him Seth, saying, **"God has granted me another child** in place of Abel, since Cain killed him." NIV

Genesis 15:3

And Abram said, "**You have given me no children**; so a servant in my household will be my heir." NIV

And Abram said, "**Since You have given no offspring to me**, one born in my house is my heir." NASB

Genesis 16:2

"Now behold, the LORD has prevented me from bearing children." NASB

"Behold now, the LORD hath restrained me from bearing." KJV

Genesis 29:31

When the LORD saw that Leah was not loved, **he opened her womb, but Rachel was barren**. Leah became pregnant and gave birth to a son. NIV

But because Leah was unloved, **the LORD let her have a child, while Rachel was childless.** NLT

Genesis 30:1-2

When Rachel saw that she was not bearing Jacob any children, she became jealous of her sister. So she said to Jacob. "Give me children, or I'll die!"

Jacob became angry with her and said, "**Am I in the place of God, who has kept you from having children?"** NIV

Now when Rachel saw that she bore Jacob no children, she became jealous of her sister; and she said to Jacob, "Give me children, or else I die." Then Jacob's anger burned against

Rachel, and he said, **"Am I in the place of God, who has withheld from you the fruit of the womb?"** NASB

Genesis 17:16

"I will bless her, and indeed I will give you a son by her. Then I will bless her, and she shall be a mother of nations; kings of peoples will come from her." NASB

"I will bless her and will surely give you a son by her. I will bless her so that she will be the mother of nations; kings of peoples will come from her." NIV

"And **I will bless her and give you a son from her!** Yes, I will bless her richly, and she will become the mother of many nations. Kings will be among her descendants!" NLT

Genesis 20:17-18

Then Abraham prayed to God**, and God healed Abimelech, his wife and his slave girls so they could have children again, for the LORD had closed up every womb** in Abimelech's household because of Abraham's wife Sarah. NIV

Then Abraham prayed to God, **and God healed Abimelech, his wife, and the other women of the household, so they could have children. For the LORD had stricken all the women with infertility** a warning to Abimelech for having taken Abraham's wife. NLT

Genesis 30:22-23

Then God remembered Rachel; he listened to her and **opened her womb. She became pregnant and gave birth to a son and said, "God has taken away my disgrace."** NIV

Then God remembered Rachel's plight and **answered her prayers by giving her a child. She became pregnant and gave birth to a son. "God has removed my shame."** She said. NLT

Then God remembered Rachel, and **God gave heed to her and opened her womb. So she conceived and bore a son and said, "God has taken away my reproach."** NASB

Psalm 127:3-5

Children are a gift from the LORD; they are a reward from him. Children born to a young man are like sharp arrows in a warrior's hands. **How happy is the man whose quiver is full of them!** He will not be put to shame when he confronts his accusers at the city gates. NLT

Sons are a heritage from the LORD,
Children a reward from him.
Like arrows in the hands of a warrior are sons born in one's youth.
Blessed is the man whose quiver is full of them.
They will not be put to shame when they contend with their enemies in the gate. NIV

Throughout the Bible we see that having children was not only a blessing from God, but being barren was a curse from God, and those women who were barren were thought ill of. Having children was expected... and highly desired. But more importantly...**having children was, and still is, under God's control.**

The very act of conception, of being ABLE to get pregnant is GOD'S WILL.

So having a baby is not a decision for people to make... but one that God has already made.

Remember, you are to have FAITH that GOD knows what is BEST and that HE causes everything to work together for the good of those who love Him.

Hebrews 11:6

And without faith it is impossible to please God, because anyone who comes to him must believe that he exists and that he rewards those who earnestly seek him. NIV

So, you see, **it is impossible to please God without faith**. **Anyone who wants to come to him must believe that there is a God and that he rewards those who sincerely seek him.** NLT

Romans 8:28

And we know that **in all things God works for the good of those who love him,** who have been called according to his purpose. NIV

And we know that **God causes all things to work together for the good of those who love God,** to those who are called according to His purpose. NASB

HERE ARE SOME SCRIPTURES THAT TALK ABOUT WHEN LIFE BEGINS.....

Jeremiah 1:5

"**Before I formed you in the womb I knew you,**
And before you were born I consecrated you;
I have appointed you a prophet to the nations." NASB

"**Before I formed you in the womb I knew you, before you were born** I set you apart;
I appointed you as a prophet to the nations." NIV

Psalm 139:16

"You saw me before I was born. Every day of my life was recorded in your book. Every moment was laid out before a single day had passed." NLT

"Your eyes saw my unformed body. **All the days ordained for me were written in your book before one of them came to be."** NIV

Luke 1:13-17

But the angel said unto him, **Fear not, Zacharias: for thy prayer is heard; and thy wife Elisabeth shall bear thee a son**, and thou shalt call his name John. And thou shalt have joy and gladness; and many shall rejoice at his birth. For he shall be great in the sight of the Lord, and shall drink neither wine nor strong drink; and **he shall be filled with the Holy Ghost, even from his mother's womb.** And many of the children of Israel shall he turn to the Lord their God. And he shall go before him in the spirit and power of Elias, to turn the hearts of the fathers to the children, and the disobedient to the wisdom of the just; to make ready a people prepared for the Lord." KJV

But the angel said to him: **"Do not be afraid, Zechariah; your prayer has been heard. Your wife Elizabeth will bear you a son**, and you are to give him the name John. He will be a joy and delight to you, and many will rejoice because of his birth, for he will be great in the sight of the Lord. He is never to take wine or other fermented drink, and **he will be filled with the Holy Spirit even from birth**. Many of the people of Israel will he bring back to the Lord their God. And he will go on before the Lord, in the spirit and power of Elijah, to turn the hearts of the fathers to their children and the disobedient to the wisdom of the righteous-to make ready a people prepared for the Lord." NIV

*Just one example of God having planned out an entire life, even **before it was "born"**, and how important that "life" was to be.*

Isaiah 44:2

Thus saith **the LORD that made thee, and formed thee from the womb**, KJV

This is what the LORD says-**he who made you, who formed you in the womb**, and who will help you: NIV

Luke 1:44

For behold, when the sound of your greeting reached my ears, **the baby leaped in my womb for joy.** NASB

As soon as the sound of your greeting reached my ears, **the baby in my womb leaped for joy.** NIV

Hosea 12:3

In the womb he grasped his brother's heel; as a man he struggled with God. NIV

He took his brother by the heel in the womb, and by his strength he had power with God: KJV

Job 3:16

Why was I not buried like a stillborn **child**, **like a baby who never lives to see the light?** NLT

"Or like a miscarriage which is discarded, I would not be,
As infants that never saw light." NASB

How can you "never live to see the light?" if you weren't already Alive? And you notice always the terms, infant, baby, child... never... it or thing.

So here are some things to think about:

God is your creator..."Before I formed you in the womb", "the LORD that made thee, and formed thee from the womb"**,** "you know exactly how I was made, bit by bit".
Surely, to deliberately destroy something that God has intended to exist, must be a Sin.

If **God is planning EVERYONE'S entire life... before they are even born**... **"before I began to breathe",** then God considers them alive... BEFORE THEY ARE EVEN BORN.... While they are still being made... bit by bit.

And more... **before you were born I consecrated you.** Before you were born God declared you SACRED and HONORED, Dedicated for his Service. Why would he have bothered if you weren't **meant** to have a life?

But even MORE, God says "Before I formed you in the womb **I knew you,**

And before you were born I consecrated you" That means he already knew your *spirit,* your true self... and you as a human (remember God is not bound by Time or Space) not just before you were born... But **before you were formed in the womb.**

You were ALIVE to GOD... before you were even conceived... so ANYTIME; be it during the conception, carrying, or delivering stages of pregnancy... **the BABY is ALIVE... and to take that life, to kill, to MURDER, is a Sin.**

Not only is the BABY alive... its entire Life has already been planned out by God, and for anyone to deliberately disrupt God's plan...Surely, that also is a Sin.

And what about the **SIXTH COMMANDMENT**?

THOU SHALT NOT KILL?

See Chapter Three:
What are The Ten Commandments anyway?

Or the Commands of Jesus...

Luke 6:31

"Treat others the same way you want them to treat you." NASB

"Do to others as you would have them do to you." NIV

Matthew 7:12

"**In everything, therefore, treat people the same way you want them to treat you**, for this is the Law and the Prophets. NASB

So **in everything, do to others what you would have them do to you,** for this sums up the Law and the Prophets. NIV

Would you have wanted your parents to abort/kill/murder you?

<u>Proverbs 6:16-17</u>

These six things doth **the LORD hate**:
Yea, seven are an abomination unto him;
A proud look, a lying tongue, and **hands that shed innocent blood.**
A heart that deviseth wicked imaginations, feet that be swift in running to mischief, a false witness that speaketh lies, and he that soweth discord among brethren. KJV

There are six things **the LORD hates**, seven that are detestable to him: haughty eyes, a lying tongue, **hands that shed innocent blood, a heart that devises wicked schemes, feet that are quick to rush into evil,** a false witness who pours out lies and a man who stirs up dissension among brothers. NIV

Now let's take a look at the consequences of not listening to scriptures...

<u>Exodus 21:22-23</u>

"If men struggle with each other **and strike a woman with child so that she gives birth prematurely**, yet there is no injury, he shall surely be fined as the woman's husband may demand of him, and he shall pay as the judges decide. **But if there is any further injury**, then you shall appoint as a penalty **life for life"**
NASB

"If men who are fighting **hit a pregnant woman and she gives birth prematurely** but there is no serious injury, the offender must be fined whatever the woman's husband demands and the court allows. But if there is serious injury, **you are to take life for life.** NIV

"Life for Life", "if death results"... it would seem that God is truly trying to let us see that he considers a child/infant/fetus, etc. ALIVE in the WOMB.

Deuteronomy 27:25

"Cursed is the man who accepts a bribe to kill an innocent person." NIV

Cursed be he that taketh reward to slay an innocent person. Then all the people shall say, "Amen!" KJV

He could be talking about a doctor that performs abortions with this scripture.

Exodus 21:12-14

"Anyone who strikes a man and kills him shall surely be put to death. However, if he does not do it intentionally, but God lets it happen, he is to flee to a place I will designate. **But if a man schemes and kills another man deliberately, take him away from my altar and put him to death.** NIV

"He who strikes a man so that he dies shall surely be put to death. But if he did not lie in wait for him, but God let him fall into his hand, then I will appoint you a place to which he may flee. **If, however, a man acts presumptuously toward his neighbor, so as to kill him craftily, you are to take him even from My alter, that he may die.** NASB

Abortion is a deliberate and premeditated act.

Ezekiel 33:17-20

Yet the children of thy people say, The way of the Lord is not equal: but as for them, their way is not equal. **When the righteous turneth from his righteousness, and committeth iniquity, he shall even die thereby. But if the wicked turn from his wickedness, and do that which is lawful and right, he shall live thereby.** Yet ye say, The way of the Lord is not equal. O ye house of Israel, **I will judge you every one after his ways.**
KJV

"Yet your countrymen say, 'The way of the Lord is not just.' But it is their way that is not just. **If a righteous man turns from his righteousness and does evil, he will die for it. And if a wicked man turns away from his wickedness and does what is just and right, he will live by doing so**. Yet, O house of Israel, you say, 'The way of the Lord is not just.' But **I will judge each of you according to his own ways."** NIV

Revelation 21:8

But the cowardly, the unbelieving, the vile, **the murderers**, the sexually immoral, those who practice magic arts, the idolaters and all liars-**their place will be in the fiery lake of burning sulfur. This is the second death.** NIV

But for the cowardly and unbelieving and abominable **and murderers** and immoral persons and sorcerers and idolaters and all liars, **their part will be in the lake that burns with fire and brimstone, which is the second death.** NASB

Adoption

Psalm 68:5

A Father to the fatherless, a defender of widows, is God in his holy dwelling. NIV

A father of the fatherless, and a judge of the widows, is God in his holy habitation. KJV

James 1:27

Pure and lasting religion in the sight of God our Father means that **we must care for orphans** and widows in their troubles, **and refuse to let the world corrupt us.** NLT

Religion that God our Father accepts as pure and faultless is this: **to look after orphans** and widows **in their distress and to keep oneself from being polluted by the world.** NIV

1 Corinthians 10:13

No temptation has seized you except what is common to man. And **God is faithful; he will not let you be tempted beyond what you can bear.** But **when you are tempted, he will also provide a way out so that you can stand up under it.** NIV

But remember this—the wrong desires that come into your life aren't anything new and different. Many others have faced exactly the same problems before you. And no temptation is irresistible. **You can trust God to keep the temptation from becoming so strong that you can't stand up against it**, for He has promised this and will do what He says. **He will show you how to escape temptation's power so that you can bear up patiently against it.** NLT

As you can see, God is against the murder of the unborn.

God also cares greatly for orphans… or those without parents. In the last verse you also see that God will give you a way out from the temptation to murder the child and will "provide a way out so that you can stand up under it".

That sounds a lot like helping you through the pregnancy so that you can give the baby up for adoption if you still feel the need when the baby is born.

Galatians 4:4-5

But when the fulness of the time came, God sent forth his Son, born of a woman, born under the law, that he might redeem them that were under the law**, that we might receive the adoption of sons.** ASV

But when the right time came, God sent his Son, born of a woman, subject to the law. God sent him to buy freedom for us who were slaves to the law, **so that he could adopt us as his very own children**. NLT

If anyone reading this ***has already had an abortion****, it is not too late for you to repent for your sin (see the chapter: What is sin anyway?). And if the sorrow of that lost life has already hit you...* ***do not worry; ALL things that God creates endure forever.***

Ecclesiastes 3:14-15

I know that **everything God does will remain forever; there is nothing to add to it and there is nothing to take from it**, for God has so worked that men should fear Him. That which is has been already and that which will be has already been, for God seeks what has passed by. NASB

I know that **everything God does will endure forever; nothing can be added to it and nothing taken from it**. God does it so that men will revere him.

Whatever is has already been,
And what will be has been before;
And God will call the past to account. NIV

Matthew 10:28

"Don't be afraid of those who want to kill you. **They can only kill your body; they cannot touch your soul.** Fear only God, who can destroy both soul and body in hell. NLT

Do not be afraid of those who kill the body but cannot kill the soul. Rather, be afraid of the One who can destroy both soul and body in hell. NIV

Think about this:

The child who's BODY died, DID NOT lose its SOUL.

So when you get to heaven you will be reunited with your CHILD!

But telling God that you are sorry, and asking forgiveness for your sins alone is not going to get you to heaven...

For THAT you still need one VERY IMPORTANT Thing...

JESUS CHRIST

You must accept and acknowledge that Jesus Christ is the son of God. That he was born of a human woman, lived a sin-free life but willingly died on a cross (a sinners death) to save all who trust in him from their sins... and three days later he rose again (came back to life).

Don't know about Jesus Christ?

See the Chapter: Don't know Jesus?

Need a few more scriptures to look at? Try these, but there are a lot more located throughout your Bible.

Deuteronomy 28:11, Deuteronomy 28:18, Judges 13:3-5

Chapter Seven

Is it alright if my boyfriend and I have sex if we are in love?

We are basically looking at the issue of remaining a Virgin versus becoming Promiscuous, so let's see what the scriptures have to say about these issues.

But First let us talk about the Bible Book: Song of Songs (or The Song of Solomon).

It is in the old testament and the entire book is a description of how wonderful LOVE and SEX (Yes… the Bible talks about having desired and acceptable sexual relations) are truly supposed to be: from dating, to courtship, to marriage… even into old age. When we follow Gods plan.

Now I will be the first to admit that the language used is very confusing so I would recommend reading it in an NLT (New Living Translation) or an Amplified version AND ALSO having a Study Bible that helps explain things as well.

Like; "Your teeth are like a flock of sheep just shorn, coming up from the washing. Each has its twin; not one of them is alone.
NIV

(Basically that she has all her teeth, and they are white and straight).

OR

"We have a little sister, and she hath no breasts;
What shall we do for our sister in the day when she shall be spoken for?
If she be a wall, we will build upon her a palace of silver;
And if she be a door, we will enclose her with boards of cedar.
KJV

(Basically meaning: We have a little sister too young for breasts. What will we do if [when] someone asks to marry her? If she is chaste [a virgin], we will help and encourage her. But if she is promiscuous [no longer a virgin], we will lock her away.)

[Probably so the information doesn't get around and bring shame and dishonor to the family. And so she does not continue her bad behavior.]

And the list goes on…

But believe me, a lot of the references are far more confusing and if one doesn't know how many of the sayings relate to history, customs or language translation (as I don't unless I read about it or am told about it) then it can be very intimidating to read and understand.

BUT when you **DO** get through it, and understand it, you find that God has a Wonderful plan for your love and sexuality **if you do it His way**.

We are talking about a deep, intimate, soul-mate kind of love filled with lusty, deeply satisfying, age enduring SEX.

Song of Songs (Song of Solomon) 4:16 - 5:1

Beloved
"Awake, north wind, and come, south wind!
Blow on my garden, that its fragrance may spread abroad.
Let my lover come into his garden and taste its choice fruits.

Lover
I have come into my garden, my sister, my bride;
I have gathered my myrrh with my spice.
I have eaten my honeycomb and my honey;
I have drunk my wine and my milk. NIV

Awake, O north wind; and come thou south;
Blow upon my garden, that the spices thereof may flow out.
Let my beloved come into his garden,
And eat his pleasant fruits.

I am come into my garden, my sister, my spouse;
I have gathered my myrrh with my spice;

I have eaten my honeycomb with my honey;
I have drunk my wine with my milk; KJV

Young Woman:
"Awake, north wind! Come, south wind! Blow on my garden and waft its lovely perfume to my lover. Let him come into his garden and eat its choicest fruits."
Young Man:
"I am here in my garden, my treasure, my bride! I gather my myrrh with my spices and eat my honeycomb with my honey. I drink my wine with my milk." NLT

(Of course some scriptures are a little clearer. I think most people get the gist of sexual intercourse, among other things, here. Once they know what to look for.)

Song of Solomon (Song of Songs) 3:5

Promise me, O women of Jerusalem, by the swift gazelles and the deer of the wild, **not to awaken love until the time is right**. NLT

Daughters of Jerusalem, I charge you by the gazelles and by the does of the field; **Do not arouse or awaken love** until it so desires. NIV

Song of Solomon (Song of Songs) 3:1

"On my bed night after night I sought him Whom my soul loves; I sought him but did not find him. NASB

Young Woman: "**One night as I lay in bed, I yearned deeply for my lover but he did not come**." NLT

She wants/desires to have sex with the man she loves… **but he stays strong and does not come to her room or have sex with her**. (Yet. Read after they get married).

Alright, now let's leave the Song of Solomon (Song of Songs) and see what the rest of the Bible has to say about Sex...

Exodus 22:16-17

"**If a man seduces a virgin who is not pledged to be married and sleeps with her, he must pay the bride-price, and she shall be his wife.** If her father absolutely refuses to give her to him, he must still pay the bride-price for virgins. NIV

And if a man entice a maid that is not betrothed, and lie with her, he shall surely endow her to be his wife. If her father utterly refuse to give her unto him, he shall pay money according to the dowry of virgins. KJV

Deuteronomy 22:13-21

"If any man takes a wife and goes in to her and then turns against her, and **charges her with shameful deeds and publicly defames her, and says, 'I took this woman, but when I came near her, I did not find her a virgin.'** Then the girl's father and her mother shall take and bring out the evidence of the girl's virginity to the elders of the city at the gate. The girl's father shall say to the elders, 'I gave my daughter to this man for a wife, but he turned against her; and behold, **he has charged her with shameful deeds, saying, "I did not find your daughter a virgin."** But this is the evidence of my daughter's virginity. And they shall spread the garment before the elders of the city. So the elders of that city shall take the man and chastise him, and they shall fine him a hundred shekels of silver and give it to the girl's father, because he publicly defamed a virgin of Israel. And she shall remain his wife; he cannot divorce her all his days.

"But if this charge is true, that the girl was not found a virgin, then they shall bring out the girl to the doorway of her father's house, and **the men of her city shall stone her to death because she has committed an act of folly in Israel by playing the harlot** in her father's house; thus you shall purge the evil from among you." NASB

If any man take a wife, and go in unto her, and hate her, And give occasions of speech against her, and bring up an evil name upon her, **and say, I took this woman, and when I came to her, I found her not a maid**: Then shall the father of the damsel, and her mother, take and bring forth the tokens of the damsel's virginity unto the elders of the city in the gate: And the damsel's father shall say unto the elders, I gave my daughter unto this man to wife, and he hateth her; And, lo, he hath given occasions of speech against her, **saying, I found not thy daughter a maid; and yet these are the tokens of my daughter's virginity**. And they shall spread the cloth before the elders of the city. And the elders of that city shall take that man and chastise him; And they shall amerce him in an hundred shekels of silver, and give them unto the father of the damsel, because he hath brought up an evil name upon a virgin of Israel: and she shall be his wife; he may not put her away all his days. **But if this thing be true, and the tokens of virginity be not found for the damsel**: Then they shall bring out the damsel to the door of her father's house, and **the men of her city shall stone her with stones that she die: because she hath wrought folly in Israel, to play the whore in her father's house**: so shalt thou put evil away from among you. KJV

Deuteronomy 22:23-24

"**Suppose a man meets a young woman, a virgin who is engaged to be married, and he has sexual intercourse with her**. If this happens within a town, **you must** take both of them to the gates of the town and **stone them to death.** The woman is guilty because she did not scream for help. The man must die **because he violated another man's wife**. In this way, you will cleanse the land of evil. NLT

If a man happens to meet in a town a virgin pledged to be married and he sleeps with her, you shall take both of them to the gate of that town and **stone them to death**—the girl because she was in a town and did not scream for help, and **the**

man because he violated another man's wife. You must purge the evil from among you. NIV

(It would seem that even though she was only "Engaged" and still a virgin, God still considered her already married. And so they both willingly had sexual relations with someone they were not married to, or could not marry.)

Deuteronomy 22:25-27

But if the man meets the engaged woman out in the country, and he rapes her, **then only the man should die.** Do nothing to the young woman; she has committed no crime worthy of death. This case is similar to that of someone who attacks and murders a neighbor. Since the man raped her out in the country, it must be assumed that she screamed but there was no one to rescue her. NLT

But if out in the country a man happens to meet **a girl pledged to be married** and rapes her **only the man** who has done this shall die. Do nothing to the girl; she has committed no sin deserving death. This case is like that of someone who attacks and murders his neighbor, for the man found the girl out in the country, and though the betrothed girl screamed, there was no one to rescue her. NIV

(Again it would seem, "Engaged" is already considered "Married"... or unavailable to be married to the one who forced the sexual relationship.)

Deuteronomy 22:28-29

If a man is caught in the act of raping a young woman who is not engaged, he must pay fifty pieces of silver to her father. **Then he must marry the young woman because he violated her, and he will never be allowed to divorce her.** NLT

If a man happens to meet a **virgin who is not pledged to be married** and rapes her and they are discovered, he shall pay the girl's father fifty shekels of silver. **He must marry the girl,** for he has violated her. He can never divorce her as long as he lives. NIV

(But if neither is "attached" to another, even in the case of rape, **then just by having sex** the two are to be Married and can never be divorced. It would appear God feels that if two people have sexual relations they must either BE Married… or it MAKES them Married.)

So, It would seem from these Scriptures that God is saying that yes, you need to be married before you have sex… but if you are not married, then God will consider you married to the first person you have sex with. But if you are unable to "Marry" that person (they are already married, you are already married, etc.) then it is absolutely forbidden… to the point of punishment of death.

But I would never expect you to take my word for it, so check out the scriptures for yourself…

Proverbs 5:15-23

Drink waters out of thine own cistern,
and running waters out of **thine own well.**
Let thy fountains be dispersed abroad,
and rivers of waters in the streets.
Let them be only thine own,
and not strangers' with thee.
Let thy fountain be blessed:
and **rejoice with the wife of thy youth.**
Let her be as the loving hind and pleasant roe;
let her breasts satisfy thee at all times;
and be thou ravished always with her love.
And **why wilt thou, my son, be ravished with a strange woman,**
and embrace the bosom of a stranger?
For the ways of man are before the eyes of the Lord,

and he pondereth all his goings.
His own iniquities shall take the wicked himself,
and **he shall be holden with the cords of his sins.**
He shall die without instruction;
and in the greatness of his folly he shall go astray. KJV

Drink water from your own cistern and fresh water from your own well.

Should your springs be dispersed abroad, streams of water in the streets?

Let them be yours alone and not for strangers with you.

Let your fountain be blessed, and rejoice in **the wife of your youth.**

As a loving hind and a graceful doe, **let her breasts satisfy you at all times;**

Be exhilarated always with her love.

For why should you, my son, be exhilarated with an adulteress

and embrace the bosom of a foreigner?

For the ways of a man are before the eyes of the LORD,

And He watches all his paths.

His own iniquities will capture the wicked,

and he will be held with the cords of his own sin.

He will die for lack of instruction, and in the greatness of his folly he will go astray. NASB

Ezekiel 16:30-34

"What a sick heart you have, says the Sovereign LORD, to do such things as these, **acting like a shameless prostitute**. You build your pagan shrines on every street corner and your altars to idols in every square. **You have been worse than a prostitute, so eager for sin that you have not even demanded payment for your love!** Yes, **you are an adulterous wife who takes in strangers instead of her own husband. Prostitutes charge for their services—but not you! You give gifts to your lovers, bribing them to come to you. So you are the opposite of other prostitutes. No one pays you; instead, you pay them!** NLT

How weak is thine heart, saith the Lord GOD, seeing thou doest all these things, **the work of an imperious whorish woman**; in that thou buildest thine eminent place in the head of every way, and makest thine high place in every street; **and hast not been as a harlot, in that thou scornest hire; but as a wife that committeth adultery, which taketh strangers instead of her husband. They give gifts to all whores: but thou givest thy gifts to all thy lovers, and hirest them, that they may come unto thee on every side for thy whoredom.** And the contrary is in thee from other women in thy whoredom, whereas none followeth thee to commit whoredoms; and in that **thou givest a reward, and no reward is given unto thee**, therefore thou are contrary. KJV

Now God is talking to Jerusalem at this point but you can see how passionate He is about Adultery, Prostitution and especially Promiscuity.

Judging from the Scriptures, God does NOT approve of Promiscuity… of having sex with ANYONE who is not your spouse (husband or wife).

Now let us look at some other scriptures…

Isaiah 61:6

But you will be called the priests of the LORD;
You will be spoken of as ministers of our God.
You will eat the wealth of nations,
And in their riches you will boast. NASB

But **ye shall be named the Priests of the LORD**:
Men shall call you the Ministers of our God:
Ye shall eat the riches of the Gentiles,
And in their glory shall you boast yourselves. KJV

Revelation 1:5-6

And from **Jesus Christ,** who is the faithful witness to these things**,** the first to rise from the dead, and the commander of all the rulers of the world.

All praise to him who loves us and has freed us from our sins by shedding his blood for us. He has made us his Kingdom and his priests who serve before God his Father. Give to him everlasting glory! He rules forever and ever!

Amen! NLT

And from **Jesus Christ**, the faithful witness, the firstborn of the dead, and the ruler of the kings of the earth.

To Him who loves us and released us from our sins by His blood- and **He has made us to be** a kingdom**, priests to His God and Father**-to Him be the glory and the dominion forever and ever. Amen. NASB

Since Jesus has made ALL who trust in, believe in, and obey him… **"His Priests",** then we are all EXPECTED **to live up to** the STANDARDS of a Priest of Jesus.

(This has nothing to do with the standards of "the Catholic Priesthood")

Leviticus 21:7

The Priests must not marry women defiled by prostitution or women who have been divorced, for the priests must be set apart to God as holy. NLT

They (priests) shall not take a wife that is a whore, or profane; neither shall they take a woman put away from her husband for he is holy unto his God. KJV

Leviticus 21:13-14

"**The high priest must marry a virgin. He must not marry a widow, a divorced woman, or a woman defiled by prostitution.** She must be a virgin from his own clan. NLT

"He **shall take a wife in her virginity. A widow, or a divorced woman, or one who is profaned by harlotry, these he may not take**; but rather he is to marry a virgin of his own people." NASB

In God's eyes VIRGINITY is to be honored and observed until one is married.

But IF you DO have sex with someone, then God considers THAT person to now BE YOUR SPOUSE.

Those that don't recognize this and continue to have sex with others is being Promiscuous… and may actually be committing adultery.

See the chapter: What is Adultery?

So what does all this mean?

It would seem that God wants you (male and female) to remain a virgin until you are married. If you do not you are either sinning or getting married right then in God's eyes.

You have the choice…

God condemns those that SIN; those that MAKE A CHOICE to willfully break God's Commandments.

You have a CHOICE whether to go somewhere private with someone that you know you SHOULD NOT have SEXUAL RELATIONS with. You have a CHOICE whether to make that FIRST TOUCH, take that FIRST KISS, Unbutton that FIRST button, etc.

1 Peter 2:11

Dear friends, I urge you, as aliens and strangers in the world, to **abstain from sinful desires, which war against your soul.** NIV

Beloved, I urge you as aliens and strangers to **abstain from fleshly lusts which wage war against the soul.** NASB

Romans 13:13-14

Let us behave decently, as in the daytime, not in orgies and drunkenness, not in sexual immorality and debauchery, not in dissension and jealousy. Rather, clothe yourselves with the Lord Jesus Christ, and **do not think about how to gratify the desires of the sinful nature.** NIV

We should be decent and true in everything we do, so that everyone can approve of our behavior. **Don't participate in wild parties and getting drunk, or in adultery and immoral living, or in fighting and jealousy**. But let the Lord Jesus Christ take control of you, and **don't think of ways to indulge your evil desires.** NLT

Let us behave properly as in the day, not in carousing and drunkenness, not in sexual promiscuity and sensuality, not in strife and jealousy. But put on the Lord Jesus Christ, and **make no provision for the flesh in regard to its lusts.** NASB

If you can't seem to control yourself and need HELP with your DESIRES, then remove yourself from the other person's presence, or stay always in public places and/or with other people who will basically act as "chaperones" to help the two of you control yourselves.

Don't be afraid to ask your family and friends to make sure they stay around, etc.

PRAY to God for Help, for the strength to abstain.

Pray Continually.

IN FACT, it is always recommended that dating and courting be done… in public. That way, even if desire hasn't been a problem, if it suddenly hits you or the other person hard… there is no room for mistakes.

Know that if you wait for sex until after the dating (that finding each other attractive physically/spiritually/mentally, getting to know each other, etc. Phase)… after the courtship (that getting serious, really falling in love, fighting the desire Phase)… and after the marriage (the true proof of your eternal love and commitment to each other), that God has a great personal and Sexual relationship planned out for you. You just need to be patient and chaste until that time. So yes, pray if/when you need help.

1 Thessalonians 5:17

Pray without ceasing. KJV and NASB

Pray continually; NIV

Psalm 91:15

"**He will call upon me, and I will answer him;**
I will be with him in trouble,
I will deliver him and honor him." NIV and NASB

When they call on me, I will answer;
I will be with them in trouble.
I will rescue them and honor them. NLT

Romans 6:12-14

Do not let sin control the way you live; do not give in to its lustful desires. Do not let any part of your body become a tool of wickedness**, to be used for sinning.** Instead, **give yourselves completely to God** since you have been given new life. And use your whole body as a tool **to do what is right for the glory of God**. **Sin is no longer your master, for you are**

no longer subject to the law, which enslaves you to sin. Instead, **you are free by God's grace.** NLT

Let not sin therefore reign in your mortal body, that ye should obey it in the lusts thereof. Neither yield ye your members as instruments of unrighteousness unto sin: **but yield yourselves unto God**, as those that are alive from the dead, and your members as instruments of righteousness unto God. **For sin shall not have dominion over you**: for ye are not under the law, but under grace. KJV

Think of your desire for each other as a TEMPTATION for you to AVOID continually (the Bible never says anything about *resisting* Temptation, only *resisting* the Devil). So remember, if you find yourself faced with Temptation... **Leave, Run away, Pray**... but GET OUT of that SITUATION!

If something prevents you from actually LEAVING... Turn away and Pray! Don't LOOK at the Temptation, don't listen, etc. Pray and **Focus on something else.** Like how much homework you still have to do, or what a pregnancy would do to you right now, etc.

DO NOT think about HOW to avoid the Temptation; thinking about the temptation AT ALL only gives it STRENGTH and makes it HARDER to NOT think about it.

Colossians 3:1-2

Set your hearts on things above, where Christ is seated at the right hand of God.

Set your minds on things above, not on earthly things. NIV

Seek those things which are above, where Christ sitteth on the right hand of God. Set your affection on things above, **not on things on the earth.** KJV

Ephesians 6:10-11

Finally, **be strong in the Lord and in His mighty power**. **Put on the full armor of God so that you can take your stand against the devil's schemes.** NIV

A final word: **Be strong with the Lord's mighty power.** Put on all of God's armor so that **you will be able to stand firm against all strategies and tricks of the Devil.** NLT

So, if you have been living with/in SIN, know that it is NOT too late to change. It is NOT too late to become the person GOD wants YOU to be.

1 John 1:9

If we confess our sins, he is faithful and just to forgive us our sins, and to cleanse us from all unrighteousness. KJV

If we confess our sins, he is faithful and just and will forgive us our sins and purify us from all unrighteousness. NIV

No human being is, or was ever, Perfect (Never Sinned), except

Jesus Christ.

So, whatever the sin you may have done, or may even still be doing... You can still be forgiven.

But you must Repent (Tell God you are sorry for sinning against Him and his laws, and ask forgiveness)... and mean it, and sincerely try not to sin again.

Now that may be really hard, and you may stumble and fall many times... but if you are SINCERELY trying to stop the sin... that is what God wants from you.

But NOT SINNING, or asking forgiveness for your sins ALONE is not going to please God, save you from HELL and get you into HEAVEN and the Family of God.

For THAT you still need one VERY IMPORTANT Thing...

JESUS CHRIST

You must accept and acknowledge that Jesus Christ is the son of God. That he was born of a human woman, lived a sin-free life but willingly died on a cross (a sinners death) to save all who trust in him from their sins… and three days later he rose again (came back to life).

Don't know about Jesus Christ?

See the Chapter: **Don't know Jesus?**

So I think we have all come to the same answer to the question. **NO** it is **NOT** alright if you and your boyfriend (or girlfriend if you are a boy) have sex, even if you are IN LOVE… **IF** you are **NOT MARRIED**.

OK, so really…. how does anyone ever get to the point of Marriage you might ask?

Start by "**Dating**", going out with various people, possibly in the company of groups of friends; to the movies, out to eat, amusement parks, etc. to find out if you might actually be seriously interested in someone. NO SEX or "Alone" situations.

Next is "**Courting**", dating just that person with the intention of seeing if marriage would be right for the two of you. But always in public (coffee, dinner, meet the families, etc.), never put yourself into any type of situation that could lead to either of you being comprised (NO SEX, or "Alone" situations).

Then **"Marriage"**; you have gone through the time and responsibility of choosing the right person to spend your life with… Now Get Married! Then you can have Great Sex and a wonderful, God Blessed, relationship that can stand the test of time.

Chapter Eight

Forbidden Sexual Practices:

As we have seen in previous chapters, God allows for wonderful sexual relationships... with our spouses. But Adultery, Homosexuality, Orgies, Bestiality, and other sexual practices... God has a problem with and considers them Sin.

Let us take a look at some scriptures that talk about this issue.

Galatians 5:19-21

Now the works of the flesh are manifest, which are these; **Adultery, fornication, uncleanness, lasciviousness**, idolatry, witchcraft, hatred, variance, emulations, wrath, strife, seditions, heresies, envying, murders, drunkenness, **revellings**, and such like: of the which I tell you before, as I have also told you in time past, that **they which do such things shall not inherit the kingdom of God.** KJV

The acts of the sinful nature are obvious: sexual immorality, impurity and debauchery; idolatry and witchcraft; hatred, discord, jealousy, fits of rage, selfish ambition, dissentions, factions and envy; drunkenness, **orgies**, and the like. **I warn you, as I did before, that those who live like this will not inherit the Kingdom of God.** NIV

Romans 13:13-14

Let us behave decently, as in the daytime, not in orgies and drunkenness, not in sexual immorality

and debauchery, not in dissension and jealousy. Rather, clothe yourselves with the Lord Jesus Christ, and **do not think about how to gratify the desires of the sinful nature.** NIV

Let us behave properly as in the day, not in carousing and drunkenness, not in sexual promiscuity and sensuality, not in strife and jealousy. But put on the Lord Jesus Christ, and **make no provision for the flesh in regard to its lusts.** NASB

Most of the following are from the book of Leviticus 18:4-23

For the sake of brevity I will only use two scriptures, but please, look up additional versions on your own if you feel the need.

Note: scriptures 1-5 are not sexual commands.

4-5 **"You must obey all my regulations and be careful to keep my laws**, for I, the LORD, am your God. If you obey my laws and regulations, you will find life through them. I am the LORD." NLT

"You must obey my laws and be careful to follow my decrees. I am the LORD your God. Keep my decrees and laws, for the man who obeys them will live by them. I am the LORD." NIV

6 **You must never have sexual intercourse with a close relative, for I am the Lord.** NLT

No one is to approach any close relative to have sexual relations. I am the LORD. NIV

7 **Do not** violate your father by **having sexual intercourse with your mother.** She is your mother; you must never have intercourse with her. NLT

Do not dishonor your father by **having sexual relations with your mother.** She is your mother; do not have relations with her. NIV

8 **Do not have sexual intercourse with any of you father's wives,** for this would violate your father. NLT

Do not have sexual relations with your father's wife; that would dishonor your father. NIV

9 **Do not have sexual intercourse with your sister or half sister,** whether she is your father's daughter or your mother's daughter, whether she was brought up in the same family or somewhere else. NLT

Do not have sexual relations with your sister, either your father's daughter or your mother's daughter, whether she was born in the same home or elsewhere. NIV

10 **Do not have sexual intercourse with your grand-daughter**, whether your son's daughter or your daughter's daughter; that would violate you. NLT

Do not have sexual relations with your son's daughter or your daughter's daughter; that would dishonor you. NIV

11 **Do not have sexual intercourse with the daughter of any of your father's wives; she is your half sister.** NLT

Do not have sexual relations with the daughter of your father's wife, born to your father; she is your sister. NIV

12 **Do not have intercourse with your aunt,** your father's sister, because she is your father's close relative. NLT

Do not have sexual relations with your father's sister; she is your father's close relative. NIV

13 **Do not have sexual intercourse with your aunt**, your mother's sister, because she is your mother's close relative. NLT

Do not have sexual relations with your mother's sister, because she is your mother's close relative. NIV

14 **And do not violate your uncle**, your father's brother, **by having sexual intercourse with his wife; she also is your aunt.** NLT

'Do not dishonor your father's brother by approaching his wife to have sexual relations; she is your aunt.' NIV.

15 **Do not have sexual intercourse with your daughter-in-law;** she is your son's wife. NLT

'Do not have sexual relations with your daughter-in-law. She is your son's wife; do not have relations with her.' NIV

16 **Do not have intercourse with your brother's wife**; this would violate your brother. NLT

'Do not have sexual relations with your brother's wife; that would dishonor your brother. NIV

17 **Do not have sexual intercourse with both a woman and her daughter** or marry both a woman and her grand-daughter, whether her son's daughter or her daughter's daughter. They are close relatives, and **to do this would be a horrible wickedness.** NLT

'Do not have sexual relations with both a woman and her daughter. Do not have sexual relations with either her son's daughter or her daughter's daughter; they are her close relatives. **That is wickedness.'** NIV

18 **Do not marry a woman and her sister because they will be rivals**. But if your wife dies, then it is all right to marry her sister. NLT

'Do not take your wife's sister as a rival wife and have sexual relations with her while your wife is living.' NIV

19 **Do not violate a woman by having sexual intercourse with her during her period of menstrual impurity.** NLT

'Do not approach a woman to have sexual relations during the uncleanness of her monthly period. NIV

20 **Do not defile yourself by having sexual intercourse with your neighbor's wife.** NLT

'Do not have sexual relations with your neighbor's wife and defile yourself with her. NIV

For many of these see also: Chapter Three: What are the Ten Commandments Anyway? (The Seventh Commandment: Thou Shalt Not Commit Adultery); Chapter Four: The Commandments of Jesus (Do Not Commit Adultery); and Chapter Nine: What is Adultery?

21 **Do not give any of your children as a sacrifice** to Molech, for you must not profane the name of your God. I am the Lord. NLT

'Do not give any of your children to be sacrificed to Molech, for you must not profane the name of your God. I am the LORD.' NIV

For this one, see also: Chapter Three: What are the Ten Commandments Anyway?(The First Commandment: You shall have no other gods before me. And the Fourth Commandment: Thou shalt not kill)**.**

22 **Do not practice homosexuality; it is a detestable sin.** NLT

'Do not lie with a man as one lies with a woman; that is detestable.' NIV

For this, see also Chapter Ten: Is Homosexuality a Sin? And Chapter Eleven: Is Marriage only supposed to be between a man and a woman?

23 **A man must never defile himself by having sexual intercourse with an animal, and a woman must never present herself to a male animal in order to have intercourse with it: this is a terrible perversion.** NLT

'**Do not have sexual relations with an animal** and defile yourself with it. A woman must not present herself to an animal to have sexual relations with it; **that is a perversion.'** NIV

Bestiality: Sex with Animals

Let us take a look at some other scriptures that talk about this issue.

Exodus 22:19

"Whosoever lieth with a beast shall surely be put to death." KJV

"Anyone who has sexual relations with an animal must be put to death." NIV

Leviticus 20:15-16

If a man has sexual relations with an animal, he must be put to death, and you must kill the animal. **If a woman approaches an animal to have sexual relations with it, kill both the woman** and the animal. **They must be put to death**; their blood will be on their own heads. NIV

If a man lie with a beast, he shall surely be put to death: and ye shall slay the beast. **And if a woman approach unto any beast, and lie down thereto, thou shalt kill the woman and the beast: they shall surely be put to death;** their blood shall be upon them. KJV

Deuteronomy 27:21

'Cursed be he that lieth with any manner of beast.' KJV

'Cursed is anyone who has sexual intercourse with an animal.' NLT

It appears very clear that God considers Bestiality to be a **SIN**.

Now that you've been told the Commandments (laws), what does it mean when you break them?

1 Corinthians 6:9-10

Or do you not know that the unrighteous will not inherit the kingdom of God? Do not be

deceived; neither fornicators, nor idolaters, **nor adulterers, nor effeminate, nor homosexuals**, nor thieves, nor the covetous, nor drunkards, nor revilers, nor swindlers, **will inherit the kingdom of God.** NASB

Know ye not that **the unrighteous shall not inherit the kingdom of God?** Be not deceived: **neither fornicators**, nor idolaters, **nor adulterers**, **nor effeminate**, **nor abusers of themselves with mankind,** Nor thieves, nor covetous, nor drunkards, nor revilers, nor extortioners, **shall inherit the kingdom of God**. KJV

Revelation 21:8

But the cowardly, the unbelieving, **the vile**, the murderers, **the sexually immoral**, those who practice magic arts, the idolaters and all liars-**their place will be in the fiery lake of burning sulfur. This is the second death.** NIV

But for the cowardly and unbelieving and **abominable** and murderers and **immoral persons** and sorcerers and idolaters and all liars, **their part will be in the lake that burns with fire and brimstone, which is the second death.** NASB

So what does all this mean?

The world would tell you that Alcoholism, Drug addiction, even some types of Sexual Immorality (Adultery, Homosexuality, Pedophilia, Bestiality, etc.) are Diseases, Mental/Emotional issues… or even "normal" acceptable behaviors/lifestyles.

THEY ARE NOT!

God does not condemn someone for having Cancer, or Cerebral Palsy, or some other ACTUAL Disease.

God does not condemn someone for a "normal and acceptable" behavior/lifestyle.

God condemns those that SIN; those that MAKE A CHOICE to willfully break God's Commandments.

You have a CHOICE whether to take that FIRST DRINK, or FIRST HIT of Drugs.

You have a CHOICE whether to go somewhere Private with someone, or something, that you know you SHOULD NOT have SEXUAL RELATIONS with.

You have a CHOICE whether to make that FIRST TOUCH, take that FIRST KISS, Unbutton that FIRST button, etc.

1 Peter 2:11

Dear friends, I urge you, as aliens and strangers in the world, to **abstain from sinful desires**, which war against your soul. NIV

Beloved, I urge you as aliens and strangers to **abstain from fleshly lusts which wage war against the soul.** NASB

Dear brothers and sisters, you are foreigners and aliens here. So I warn you to **keep away from evil desires because they fight against your very souls.** NLT

If you can't seem to control yourself and need HELP with these DESIRES, then PRAY to God for Help. Ask for HELP, for Deliverance from the Desire, the Craving… the Need. **Pray Continually.**

1 Thessalonians 5:17

Pray without ceasing. KJV and NASB

Pray continually; NIV

Psalm 91:15

"He will call upon me, and I will answer him;
I will be with him in trouble,
I will deliver him and honor him." NIV

He shall call upon me, and I will answer him:
I will be with him in trouble;
I will deliver him, and honour him. KJV

Talk with a Pastor, a Christian Therapist or therapy group. Deliberately move out of areas that help support/promote your problem (away from schools, farms, the Gay bar, the neighbor that keeps giving you that enticing look, etc.)

But remember, if, after you have tried everything... you still are stricken with these sinful desires... realize that this may be something that God is not going to remove, but is actually allowing you to be tested with.

Now don't think that God is going around afflicting everyone just to test them. Those problems are usually the result of the Devil and his minions (and yes, they are real but we can deal with those scriptures another time), other sinners, or our own poor judgment, etc.

But God in his wisdom ALLOWS it to happen to observe your response.

God allows people to be tested regularly to help them mature in their spiritual growth.

If you are being tested, God wants you to flee from temptation and not succumb to evil/sinful ways. Every time we choose to do the right thing, God rewards us... usually when we get to heaven, but often even here on earth in unexpected ways.

When we fail our tests (give in to those temptations)... we Sin.

People are tested in many ways, you are not alone. Some people are tested with handicaps (a missing leg, Down syndrome, blindness, etc.), others with diseases (Cancer, Multiple Sclerosis, Lupus, etc.).

Others face things like Clinical Depression, Schizophrenia, Bipolar disorder, past emotional or physical traumas, other sexual addictions, etc.

The thing is that we all have to face tests and challenges... and it is how we handle them that God watches very closely.

2 Corinthians 12:6-10

For though I would desire to glory, I shall not be a fool; for I will say the truth: but now I forbear, lest any man should think of me above that which he seeth me to be, or that he heareth of me.

And lest I should be exalted above measure through the abundance of the revelations, **there was given to me a thorn in the flesh, the messenger of Satan to buffet me, lest I should be exalted above measure.**

For this thing **I besought the Lord thrice, that it might depart from me.**

And he said unto me, "My grace is sufficient for thee: for my strength is made perfect in weakness."

Most gladly **therefore will I rather glory in my infirmities, that the power of Christ may** rest upon me.

Therefore **I take pleasure in infirmities, in reproaches, in necessities, in persecutions, in distresses for Christ's sake: for when I am weak, then am I strong.** KJV

Even **if I should choose to boast, I would not be a fool, because I would be speaking the truth. But I refrain, so no one will think more of me than is warranted by what I do or say.**

To keep me from becoming conceited because of these surpassingly great revelations, there was given me a thorn in my flesh, a messenger of Satan, to torment me.

Three times I pleaded with the Lord to take it away from me. But he said to me, "My grace is sufficient for you, for my power is made perfect in weakness." Therefore I will boast all the more gladly about my weaknesses, so that Christ's power may rest on me. That is why, for Christ's sake, I delight in weaknesses, in insults, in hardships, in persecutions, in difficulties. For when I am weak, then I am strong. NIV

God often allows pain or "thorns" to REMIND US that we are only human and in constant need of God's help, strength, protection... and comfort.

This TEST might be meant to allow a continual chance for you to CHOOSE to ABSTAIN from the SIN.

Alcoholics need to Abstain from drinking alcohol, and may even need to Abstain from going to places where alcohol is available; the same is true for drug users.

People with Sexual Disorders need to Abstain from ANY type of ungodly Sexual activities (Porn of any type, going to places where there is even a small chance of a sexual situation occurring, "thinking" and "fantasizing" about sexual activities, etc.).

God ONLY wants you to have sexual relations with your spouse (yes, AFTER you are married. And YES, your spouse must be of the opposite sex.), all else is Sin.

(But again, PLEASE read other scriptures in the Bible to see for yourself.)

Many people who have been tested with Homosexual or other sinful sexual desires/urges have chosen to live celibate lives (like many monks, priests, etc.) to Abstain from Sinful sexual activities and so avoid sinning against God.

Romans 6:12-14

Let not sin therefore reign in your mortal body, that ye should obey it in the lusts thereof. Neither yield ye your members as instruments of unrighteousness unto sin: but **yield yourselves unto God,** as those that are alive from the dead, and **your members as instruments of righteousness unto God. For sin shall not have dominion over you: for ye are not under the law, but under grace.** KJV

Therefore do not let sin reign in your mortal body so that you obey its evil desires. Do not offer the parts of your body to sin, as instruments of wickedness, but rather offer yourselves to God, as those who have been brought from death to life; and offer the parts of your body to him as instruments of righteousnesss. NIV

Think of it as a TEMPTATION for you to AVOID continually (the Bible never says anything about *resisting* Temptation, only *resisting* the Devil). So remember, if you find yourself faced with Temptation… **Leave, Run away, Pray**… but GET OUT of that SITUATION!

If you are with friends who are drinking, and you find yourself TEMPTED to take a drink… Leave them and go somewhere else, drive away with other friends if necessary.

If you find your eyes drawn to someone they shouldn't be drawn to… Go away from THAT PERSON, get out of sight of them, even the nearness of them, and **focus on something else.**

If something prevents you from actually LEAVING… Turn away and Pray! Don't LOOK at the Temptation, don't listen, etc. Pray and concentrate on something else; like God's many blessings to you, things that need to be fixed around the house, etc.

DO NOT think about HOW to avoid the Temptation; thinking about the temptation AT ALL only gives it STRENGTH and makes it HARDER to NOT think about it.

Colossians 3:1-2

Seek those things which are above, where Christ sitteth on the right hand of God. Set your affection on things above, **not on things on the earth.** KJV

Set your sights on the realities of heaven, where Christ sits at God's right hand in the place of honor and power. **Let heaven fill your thoughts. Do not think only about things down here on earth.** NLT

Ephesians 6:10-11

Finally, **be strong in the Lord and in His mighty power. Put on the full armor of God so that you can take your stand against the devil's schemes.** NIV

Finally, **my brethren, be strong in the Lord, and in the power of his might. Put on the whole armour of God, that ye may be able to stand against the wiles of the devil.** KJV

If you have been living with SIN, know that it is NOT too late to change. It is NOT too late to become the person GOD wants YOU to be. But you must be sincere in your desire to change.

1 John 1:9

If we confess our sins, he is faithful and just and will forgive us our sins and purify us from all unrighteousness. NIV

If we confess our sins, He is faithful and righteous to forgive us our sins and to cleanse us from all unrighteousness. NASB

No human being is, or was ever, Perfect (Never Sinned), except

Jesus Christ.

So, whatever the sin you may have done, or may even still be doing... You can still be forgiven.

But you must Repent (Tell God you are sorry for sinning against Him and his laws, and ask forgiveness)... and mean it, and sincerely try not to sin again.

Now that may be really hard, and you may stumble and fall many times... but if you are SINCERELY trying to stop the sin... that is what God wants from you.

But NOT SINNING, or asking forgiveness for your sins ALONE is not going to please God, save you from HELL and get you into HEAVEN and the Family of God.

For THAT you still need one VERY IMPORTANT Thing...

JESUS CHRIST

You must accept and acknowledge that Jesus Christ is the son of God. That he was born of a human woman, lived a sin-free life but willingly died on a cross (a sinners death) to save all who trust in him from their sins... and three days later he rose again (came back to life).

Don't know about Jesus Christ?

See the Chapter: Don't know Jesus?

For more to read on the subject of Sexual Immorality see: Genesis 19:4-13, Hebrews 13:4, Genesis 20:1-6. There are other scriptures as well that I am sure you will find as you work your way through your Bible.

Isaiah 66:14-16

"And the hand of the LORD will be made known to His servants,
But He will be indignant toward His enemies.
For behold, the LORD will come in fire and His chariots like the whirlwind, to render His anger with fury, and His rebuke with flames of fire.
For the LORD will execute judgment by fire and by His sword on all flesh,
And those slain by the LORD will by many." NASB

Chapter Nine

What is Adultery?

For many people "Adultery" simply means cheating on your spouse (having sex with someone other than your spouse, the person you are married to). But in Biblical, Scriptural terms… it would also seem that…

Adultery is having sex with someone who is "engaged" to another.

Adultery is having sex with someone else after you have "Divorced" your spouse… unless the divorce was because of marital unfaithfulness on THEIR part.

Adultery includes simply "Lusting" after someone who is not your spouse.

But realize also that to God, Adultery and Promiscuity are sins, and many scriptures put them together as if they almost had the same meaning… but in either case, God considers them BOTH sin.

Adultery/Promiscuity is having sex with someone who is not your spouse and who cannot become your spouse (if you are not already married).

Note: in most cases if you have sex with someone and neither is married or engaged… God will then consider you "married".

Adultery/Promiscuity is having sex with a prostitute or promiscuous woman/man… as in God's eyes they are married to their first lover who was not "unavailable" or they started out as adulterers by having sex with married people of the opposite sex.

For information on the sinfulness of Homosexual acts see the chapter "Is Homosexuality a Sin?"

But I would never expect you to take my word for any of this, so please check out the scriptures for yourself...

Proverbs 5:15-21

Drink waters out of thine own cistern,
and running waters out of **thine own well.**
Let thy fountains be dispersed abroad,
and rivers of waters in the streets.
Let them be only thine own,
and not strangers' with thee.
Let thy fountain be blessed:
and **rejoice with the wife of thy youth.**
Let her be as the loving hind and pleasant roe;
let her breasts satisfy thee at all times;
and be thou ravished always with her love.
And **why wilt thou, my son, be ravished with a strange woman,**
and embrace the bosom of a stranger?
For the ways of man are before the eyes of the Lord,
and he pondereth all his goings.
His own iniquities shall take the wicked himself,
and **he shall be holden with the cords of his sins.**
He shall die without instruction;
and in the greatness of his folly he shall go astray. KJV

Drink water from your own cistern and fresh water from your own well.

Should your springs be dispersed abroad, streams of water in the streets?

Let them be yours alone and not for strangers with you.

Let your fountain be blessed, and rejoice in **the wife of your youth.**

As a loving hind and a graceful doe, **let her breasts satisfy you at all times;**

Be exhilarated always with her love.

For why should you, my son, be exhilarated with an adulteress
and embrace the bosom of a foreigner?
For the ways of a man are before the eyes of the LORD, and He watches all his paths.
His own iniquities will capture the wicked,
and he will be held with the cords of his own sin.
He will die for lack of instruction, and in the greatness of his folly he will go astray. NASB

God seems to want us to stay loyal to our spouses and to avoid Adultery and sexual promiscuity.

Deuteronomy 22:23-24

"**Suppose a man meets a young woman, a virgin who is engaged to be married, and he has sexual intercourse with her**. If this happens within a town, **you must** take both of them to the gates of the town and **stone them to death.** The woman is guilty because she did not scream for help. The man must die **because he violated another man's wife**. In this way, you will cleanse the land of evil. NLT

If a man happens to meet in a town a virgin pledged to be married and he sleeps with her, you shall take both of them to the gate of that town and **stone them to death**—the girl because she was in a town and did not scream for help, and **the man because he violated another man's wife.** You must purge the evil from among you. NIV

(It would seem that even though she was only "Engaged" and still a virgin, God still considered her already married. And so they both willing had sexual relations with someone they were not married to, or could not marry.)

Deuteronomy 22:25-27

But if the man meets the engaged woman out in the country, and he rapes her, **then only the man should die.** Do nothing to the young woman; she has committed no crime worthy of death. This case is similar to that of someone who attacks and murders a neighbor. Since the man raped her out in the country, it must be assumed that she screamed but there was no one to rescue her. NLT

But if out in the country a man happens to meet **a girl pledged to be married** and rapes her **only the man** who has done this shall die. Do nothing to the girl; she has committed no sin deserving death. This case is like that of someone who attacks and murders his neighbor, for the man found the girl out in the country, and though the **betrothed girl** screamed, there was no one to rescue her. NIV

(Again it would seem, "Engaged" is already considered "Married"… or unavailable to be married to the one who forced the sexual relationship.)

Deuteronomy 22:13-21

If any man take a wife, and go in unto her, and hate her, And give occasions of speech against her, and bring up an evil name upon her, **and say, I took this woman, and when I came to her, I found her not a maid**: Then shall the father of the damsel, and her mother, take and bring forth the tokens of the damsel's virginity unto the elders of the city in the gate: And the damsel's father shall say unto the elders, I gave my daughter unto this man to wife, and he hateth her; And, lo, he hath given occasions of speech against her, **saying, I found not thy daughter a maid; and yet these are the tokens of my daughter's virginity**. And they shall spread the cloth before the elders of the city. And the elders of that city shall take that man and chastise him; And they shall amerce him in an hundred shekels of silver, and give them unto the father of the damsel, because he hath brought up an evil name upon a virgin of Israel: and she shall be his wife; he may not put her away all his days.

But if this thing be true, and the tokens of virginity be not found for the damsel: Then they shall bring out the damsel to the door of her father's house, and **the men of her city shall stone her with stones that she die: because she hath wrought folly in Israel, to play the whore in her father's house**: so shalt thou put evil away from among you. KJV

"If any man takes a wife and goes in to her and then turns against her, and **charges her with shameful deeds and publicly defames her, and says, 'I took this woman, but when I came near her, I did not find her a virgin.'** Then the girl's father and her mother shall take and bring out the evidence of the girl's virginity to the elders of the city at the gate. The girl's father shall say to the elders, 'I gave my daughter to this man for a wife, but he turned against her; and behold, **he has charged her with shameful deeds, saying, "I did not find your daughter a virgin."** But this is the evidence of my daughter's virginity. And they shall spread the garment before the elders of the city. So the elders of that city shall take the man and chastise him, and they shall fine him a hundred shekels of silver and give it to the girl's father, because he publicly defamed a virgin of Israel. And she shall remain his wife; he cannot divorce her all his days.

"**But if this charge is true, that the girl was not found a virgin,** then they shall bring out the girl to the doorway of her father's house, and **the men of her city shall stone her to death because she has committed an act of folly in Israel by playing the harlot** in her father's house; thus you shall purge the evil from among you." NASB

Matthew 5:27-32

"You have heard that the law of Moses says, '**Do not commit adultery.'** But I say, **anyone who even looks at a woman with lust in his eye has already committed adultery with her in his heart.** So if your eye—even if it is your good eye—causes you to lust, gouge it out and throw it away. It is better for you to lose one part of your body than for your whole body to be thrown into hell. And if your hand—even if it is your stronger hand—causes you to sin, cut it off and throw it away. It is better for you to lose one part of your body than for your whole body **to be thrown into hell.**

Your have heard that the law of Moses says, 'A man can divorce his wife by merely giving her a letter of divorce.' But I say that **a man who divorces his wife, unless she has been unfaithful, causes her to commit adultery. And anyone who marries a divorced woman commits adultery.** NLT

Ye have heard that it was said by them of old time, **Thou shalt not commit adultery**: but I say unto you, That **whosoever looketh on a woman to lust after her hath committed adultery with her already in his heart.**

And if thy right eye offend thee, pluck it out, and cast it from thee: for it is profitable for thee that one of thy members should perish, and not that thy whole body should **be cast into hell.** And if thy right hand offend thee, cut it off, and cast if from thee: for it is profitable for thee that one of thy members should perish **and not that thy whole body should be cast into hell.**

It has been said, Whosoever shall put away his wife, let him give her a writing of divorcement: but I say unto you, That **whosoever shall put away his wife, saving for the cause of fornication, causeth her to commit adultery: and whosoever shall marry her that is divorced committeth adultery.** KJV

Matthew 19:9

"I tell you that anyone who divorces his wife, except for marital unfaithfulness, and marries another woman commits adultery." NIV

"And I say to you, whoever divorces his wife, except for immorality, and marries another woman commits adultery." NASB

It would seem that even after "Divorce" the couple is still considered "Married"... unless the divorce was because of unfaithfulness.

Now let's look at a few other scriptures....

Ezekiel 16:30-33

"What a sick heart you have, says the Sovereign LORD, to do such things as these, **acting like a shameless prostitute**. You build your pagan shrines on every street corner and your altars to idols in every square. **You have been worse than a prostitute, so eager for sin that you have not even demanded payment for your love!** Yes, **you are an adulterous wife who takes in strangers instead of her own husband. Prostitutes charge for their services—but not you! You give gifts to your lovers, bribing them to come to you. So you are the opposite of other prostitutes. No one pays you; instead, you pay them!** NLT

How weak is thine heart, saith the Lord GOD, seeing thou doest all these things, the **work of an imperious whorish woman**; in that thou buildest thine eminent place in the head of every way, and makest thine high place in every street; and **hast not been as a harlot, in that thou scornest hire; but as a wife that committeth adultery**, which **taketh strangers instead of her husband. They give gifts to all whores; but thou givest thy gifts to all thy lovers**, and hirest them, that they may come unto thee on every side for **thy whoredom.** KJV

Now God is talking to Jerusalem at this point but you can see how passionate He is about Adultery, Prostitution and Promiscuity. As well as how He seems to merge them together in their Sin.

Romans 13:13-14

Let us behave properly as in the day, not in carousing and drunkenness, not in sexual promiscuity and sensuality, not in strife and jealousy. But put on the Lord Jesus Christ, and **make no provision for the flesh in regard to its lusts.** NASB

Let us behave decently, as in the daytime, not in orgies and drunkenness, not in sexual immorality and debauchery, not in dissension and jealousy. Rather, clothe yourselves with the Lord Jesus Christ, and **do not think about how to gratify the desires of the sinful nature.** NIV

Exodus 22:16-17

"**If a man seduces a virgin who is not pledged to be married and sleeps with her, he must pay the bride-price, and she shall be his wife.** If her father absolutely refuses to give her to him, he must still pay the bride-price for virgins. NIV

And if a man entice a maid that is not betrothed, and lie with her, he shall surely endow her to be his wife. If her father utterly refuse to give her unto him, he shall pay money according to the dowry of virgins. KJV

Deuteronomy 22:28-29

If a man is caught in the act of raping a young woman who is not engaged, he must pay fifty pieces of silver to her father. **Then he must marry the young woman because he violated her, and he will never be allowed to divorce her.** NLT

If a man happens to meet a **virgin who is not pledged to be married and rapes her** and they are discovered, he shall pay the girl's father fifty shekels of silver. **He must marry the girl,** for he has violated her. **He can never divorce her as long as he lives.** NIV

(But if neither is "engaged or pledged" to another, even in the case of rape, **then just by having sex** the two are to be Married and can never be divorced. So it seems God feels that if two people have sexual relations they must either BE Married... or it MAKES them Married.)

It would also seem to mean... that yes, you should be married to the person you have sex with... but if you are not, then God will consider you married to the first person you have sex with. And if you cannot become "Married" (you or they are already married, etc.) then you are committing Adultery and are being promiscuous.

Take a look at these scriptures...

Revelation 1:5-6

And from **Jesus Christ,** who is the faithful witness to these things, the first to rise from the dead, and the commander of all the rulers of the world.

All praise to him who loves us and has freed us from our sins by shedding his blood for us. He has made us his Kingdom and his priests who serve before God his Father. Give to him everlasting glory! He rules forever and ever!

Amen! NLT

And from **Jesus Christ**, the faithful witness, the firstborn of the dead, and the ruler of the kings of the earth.

To Him who loves us and released us from our sins by His blood- and **He has made us to be** a kingdom, **priests to His God and Father**-to Him be the glory and the dominion forever and ever. Amen. NASB

Since Jesus has made ALL who trust in, believe in, and obey him… **"His Priests",** then we are all EXPECTED **to live up to** the STANDARDS of a Priest of Jesus.

(This has nothing to do with the standards of "the Catholic Priesthood")

Leviticus 21:7

'They (priests) **must not marry women defiled by prostitution or divorced from their husbands**, because priests are holy to their God. NLT

They **shall not take a wife that is a whore. or profane; neither shall they take a woman put away from her husband**: for he is holy unto his God. KJV

Leviticus 21:13-14

"**The high priest must marry a virgin. He must not marry a widow, a divorced woman, or a woman defiled by prostitution. She must be a virgin** from his own clan. NLT

"'**The woman he marries must be a virgin. He must not marry a widow, a divorced woman, or a woman defiled by prostitution, but only a virgin** from his own people'." NIV

In God's eyes VIRGINITY is to be honored and observed until one is married.

IF you DO have sex with someone, then God considers THAT person to now BE YOUR SPOUSE.

Those that don't recognize this and continue to have sex with others are being Promiscuous… and actually committing Adultery.

For more scriptures dealing with Adultery, Promiscuity, etc. See also the chapters:

WHAT ARE THE TEN COMMANDMENTS ANYWAY? (THE SEVENTH COMMANDMENT: DO NOT COMMIT ADULTERY),

and

Is it alright for my boyfriend and I to have sex, if we love each other?

So what does all this mean?

It seems that God wants you (male and female) to remain a virgin until you are married and to have sex ONLY with your spouse. If you do not you are Sinning.

You have the choice…

God condemns those that SIN; those that MAKE A CHOICE to willfully break God's Commandments.

You have a CHOICE whether to go somewhere private with someone that you know you SHOULD NOT have SEXUAL RELATIONS with.

You have a CHOICE whether to make that FIRST TOUCH, take that FIRST KISS, Unbutton that FIRST button, etc.

1 Peter 2:11

Dear friends, I urge you, as aliens and strangers in the world, to **abstain from sinful desires**, which war against your soul. NIV

Beloved, I urge you as aliens and strangers to **abstain from fleshly lusts which wage war against the soul.** NASB

If you can't seem to control yourself and need HELP with your DESIRES, then remove yourself from the other person's presence, or stay always in public places and/or with other people who will basically act as "chaperones" to help you control yourself.

Don't be afraid to ask your family and friends to make sure you are never left alone with the object of your desires.

PRAY to God for Help, for the strength to abstain.

Pray Continually.

If you are still having problems; talk with a Pastor, a Christian Therapist or therapy group. Deliberately stay away from, or move out of, areas that help support/promote your problem (away from the neighbor that keeps giving you that enticing look, the co-worker that sets your mind running in bad directions, etc.)

Remember ALWAYS that God ONLY wants you to have sexual relations with your spouse! And He is there to HELP if you sincerely ask Him.

If you are not married, and have NOT committed Adultery... but might be thinking of committing it with someone that is already married...

Know that if you wait for the mate God will send you... and wait to have sex until after the dating (that finding each other attractive physically/spiritually/mentally, getting to know each other, etc. Phase)... after the courtship (that getting serious, really falling in love, fighting the desire Phase)... and after the marriage (what should be honored as the true proof of your eternal love and commitment to each other), that God has a great personal and Sexual relationship planned out for you.

You just need to be patient and chaste until that time. So yes, pray if/when you need help with any temptation that might ruin your future life with your true soul-mate.

1 Thessalonians 5:17

Pray without ceasing. KJV and NASB

Pray continually; NIV

Psalm 91:15

"He will call upon me, and I will answer him;
I will be with him in trouble,
I will deliver him and honor him." NIV and NASB

When they call on me, I will answer;
I will be with them in trouble.
I will rescue them and honor them. NLT

Romans 6:12-14

Do not let sin control the way you live; do not give in to its lustful desires. Do not let any part of your body become a tool of wickedness**, to be used for sinning.** Instead, **give yourselves completely to God** since you have been given new life. And use your whole body as a tool **to do what is right for the glory of God**. **Sin is no longer your master, for you are no longer subject to the law, which enslaves you to sin.** Instead, **you are free by God's grace.** NLT

Let not sin therefore reign in your mortal body, that ye should obey it in the lusts thereof. Neither yield ye your members as instruments of unrighteousness unto sin: **but yield yourselves unto God**, as those that are alive from the dead, and your members as instruments of righteousness unto God. **For sin shall not have dominion over you**: for ye are not under the law, but under grace. KJV

Think of your desire as a TEMPTATION for you to AVOID continually (the Bible never says anything about *resisting* Temptation, only *resisting* the Devil). So remember, if you find yourself faced with Temptation... **Leave, Run away, Pray**... but GET OUT of that SITUATION!

If something prevents you from actually LEAVING... Turn away and Pray! Don't LOOK at the Temptation, don't listen, etc. Pray and **Focus on something else.** Like how much your spouse and family mean to you, or what a pregnancy would do to you right now, etc.

DO NOT think about HOW to avoid the Temptation; thinking about the temptation AT ALL only gives it STRENGTH and makes it HARDER to NOT think about it.

Colossians 3:1-2

Set your hearts on things above, where Christ is seated at the right hand of God.

Set your minds on things above, not on earthly things. NIV

Seek those things which are above, where Christ sitteth on the right hand of God. Set your affection on things above, **not on things on the earth.** KJV

Ephesians 6:10-11

Finally, **be strong in the Lord and in His mighty power**. **Put on the full armor of God so that you can take your stand against the devil's schemes.** NIV

A final word: **Be strong with the Lord's mighty power.** Put on all of God's armor so that **you will be able to stand firm against all strategies and tricks of the Devil.** NLT

So, if you have been living with/in SIN, know that it is NOT too late to change. It is NOT too late to become the person GOD wants YOU to be.

1 John 1:9

If we confess our sins, he is faithful and just and will forgive us our sins and purify us from all unrighteousness. NIV

If we confess our sins, he is faithful and just to forgive us our sins, and to cleanse us from all unrighteousness. KJV

No human being is, or was ever, Perfect (Never Sinned), except

Jesus Christ.

So, whatever the sin you may have done, or may even still be doing… You can still be forgiven.

But you must Repent (Tell God you are sorry for sinning against Him and his laws, and ask forgiveness)… and mean it, and sincerely try not to sin again.

Now that may be really hard, and you may stumble and fall many times… but if you are SINCERELY trying to stop the sin… that is what God wants from you.

But NOT SINNING, or asking forgiveness for your sins ALONE is not going to please God, save you from HELL and get you into HEAVEN and the Family of God.

For THAT you still need one VERY IMPORTANT Thing...

JESUS CHRIST

You must accept and acknowledge that Jesus Christ is the son of God. That he was born of a virgin woman, lived a sin-free life but willingly died on a cross (a sinners death) to save all who trust in him from their sins… and three days later he rose again (came back to life).

Don't know about Jesus Christ?

See the Chapter: Don't know Jesus?

Ezekiel 16:30-34

How weak is thine heart, saith the Lord GOD, seeing thou doest all these things, the **work of an imperious whorish woman**; in that thou buildest thine eminent place in the head of every way, and makest thine high place in every street; and **hast not been as a harlot, in that thou scornest hire; but as a wife that committeth adultery**, which **taketh strangers instead of her husband. They give gifts to all whores; but thou givest thy gifts to all thy lovers**, and hirest them, that they may come unto thee on every side for **thy whoredom.**

KJV

Chapter Ten

Is Homosexuality a SIN?

Let us take a look at some scriptures that talk about this issue.

LET'S START AT THE BEGINNING, WITH GENESIS...

Genesis 1:27-28

So God created man in his own image, in the image of God **he created him; male and female** he created them.

God blessed them and said to them, "Be fruitful and increase in number; fill the earth and subdue it. Rule over the fish of the sea and the birds of the air and over every living creature that moves on the ground." NIV

So God created man in his own image, in the image of **God created he him; male and female created he them. And God blessed them, and God said unto them, Be fruitful, and multiply,** and replenish the earth, and subdue it: and have dominion over the fish of the sea, and over the fowl of the air, and over every living thing that moveth upon the earth. KJV

Genesis 2:18-24

Then the LORD God said, **"It is not good for the man to be alone; I will make him a helper suitable for him."** Out of the ground the LORD God formed every beast of the field and every bird of the sky, and brought them to the man to see what he would call them; and whatever the man called a living creature, that was its name. The man gave names to all the cattle, and to the birds of the sky, and to every beast of the field, **but for Adam there was not found a helper suitable for him. So the LORD God caused a deep sleep to fall upon the man, and he slept; then He took one of his ribs and closed up the flesh at that place. The LORD God fashioned into a woman the rib which He had taken from the man, and brought her to the man.** The man said,

"This is now bone of my bones
And flesh of my flesh;
She shall be called Woman,
Because she was taken out of Man."

For this reason a man shall leave his father and his mother, and be joined to his wife; and they shall become one flesh. NASB

And the LORD God said, **It is not good that the man should be alone; I will make him a help meet for him.** And out of the ground the LORD God formed every beast of the field, and every fowl of the air; and brought them unto Adam to see what he would call them: and whatsoever Adam called every living creature, that was the name thereof. And Adam gave names to all cattle, and to the fowl of the air, and to every beast of the field; **but for Adam there was not found a help meet for him. And the LORD God caused a deep sleep to fall upon Adam, and he slept: and he took one of his ribs, and closed up the flesh instead thereof; and the rib, which the LORD God had taken from man, made he a woman, and brought her unto the man.**

And Adam said, **This is now bone of my bones, and flesh of my flesh:** she shall be called Woman, because she was taken out of Man. **Therefore shall a man leave his father and his mother, and shall cleave unto his wife: and they shall be one flesh.** KJV

Genesis 7:2-3

Take along seven pairs of each animal that I have approved for eating and for sacrifice, and take one pair of each of the others. Then select seven pairs of every kind of bird. **There must be a male and a female in each pair to ensure that every kind of living creature will survive the flood.** NLT

Of every clean beast thou shalt take to thee by sevens, **the male and his female**: and of the beasts that are not clean by two, **the male and his female**. Of fowls also of the air by sevens, **the male and the female; to keep seed alive upon the face of all the earth.** KJV

Genesis 7:6-9

Now Noah was six hundred years old when the flood of water came upon the earth. Then **Noah and his sons and his wife and his sons' wives with him entered the ark** because of the water of the flood. Of clean animals and animals that are not clean and birds and everything that creeps on the ground, **there went into the ark to Noah by twos, male and female, as God had commanded Noah.** NASB

And Noah was six hundred years old when the flood of waters was upon the earth. **And Noah went in, and his sons, and his wife, and his sons' wives with him, into the ark,** because of the waters of the flood. Of clean beasts, and of beasts that are not clean, and of fowls, and of every thing that creepeth upon the earth, **there went in two and two unto Noah into the ark, the male and the female, as God had commanded Noah.** KJV

Genesis 8:15-17

Then God said to Noah, "**Come out of the ark,** you and your wife and your sons and their wives. Bring out every kind of living creature that is with you-the birds, the animals, and all the creatures that move along the ground-**so they can multiply on the earth and be fruitful and increase in number upon it."** NIV

Then God spoke to Noah, saying, "**Go out of the ark,** you and your wife and your sons and your sons' wives with you. Bring out with you every living thing of all flesh that is with you, birds and animals and every creeping thing that creeps on the earth, **that they may breed abundantly on the earth, and be fruitful and multiply on the earth.**" NASB

Genesis 9:1

And God blessed Noah and his sons, and said unto them. Be fruitful, and multiply, and replenish the earth. KJV

Then God blessed Noah and his sons, saying to them, "Be fruitful and increase in number and fill the earth. NIV

Genesis 9:7

"As for you, **be fruitful and increase in number; multiply on the earth and increase upon it."** NIV

"Now you must have many children and repopulate the earth. Yes, multiply and fill the earth!" NLT

Throughout Genesis God is stressing the importance of a pair being ONLY a male and a female... and of having children, of propagating, of perpetuating the species. Not only is he stressing the importance of it... **He is commanding it**. And nowhere in the scriptures does he remove or change this commandment.

Two males together or two females together, **are NOT God's definition of a PAIR**; of suitable Companions/Helpers/Help Meets... **the ones they leave their parent's for**.

And no matter how hard they try, two males or two females cannot propagate, have children or perpetuate the species (naturally, just the two of them)... therefore.... It stands to reason that homosexuals **are breaking God's commandment... they are sinning**.

But Let's take a look at some other scriptures about this issue.

Let's move on to Leviticus… To the Commandments, Laws and Statutes that God gave to Moses…

Leviticus 18:22

Do not lie with a man as one lies with a woman; that is detestable. NIV

Thou shalt not lie with mankind, as with womankind: it is abomination. KJV

Do not practice homosexuality; it is a detestable sin. NLT

Leviticus 20:13

If a man also lie with mankind, as he lieth with a woman, both of them have committed an abomination: they shall surely be put to death; their blood shall be upon them. KJV

"The penalty for homosexual acts is death to both parties. They have committed a detestable act and are guilty of a capital offense." NLT

Leviticus makes it pretty clear that **God finds homosexuality to be a detestable Sin**, a sin so bad that a blood sacrifice cannot wipe away the sin… it must be punished by death.

Now let's look at a few more scriptures…

Romans 1:25-27

They exchanged the truth of God for a lie, and worshiped and served created things rather than the Creator—who is forever praised. Amen.

Because of this, God gave them over to **shameful lusts. Even their women exchanged natural relations for unnatural ones. In the same way the men also abandoned natural relations with women and were inflamed with lust for one another. Men committed indecent acts with other men, and received in themselves the due penalty for their perversion.** NIV

Instead of believing what they knew was the truth about God, they deliberately chose to believe lies. So they worshiped the things God made but not the Creator himself, who is to be praised forever. Amen.

That is why God abandoned them **to their shameful desires. Even the women turned against the natural way to have sex and instead indulged in sex with each other. Men did shameful things with other men and, as a result, suffered within themselves the penalty they so richly deserved.**
NLT

1 Corinthians 6:9-10

Or do you not know that the unrighteous will not inherit the kingdom of God? Do not be deceived; neither fornicators, nor idolaters, nor adulterers, **nor effeminate**, **nor homosexuals**, nor thieves, nor the covetous, nor drunkards, nor revilers, nor swindlers, **will inherit the kingdom of God.** NASB

Don't you know that those who do wrong will have no share in the Kingdom of God? Don't

fool yourselves. Those who indulge in sexual sin, who are idol worshipers, adulterers, male prostitutes, **homosexuals**, thieves, greedy people, drunkards, abusers, and swindlers-**none of these will have a share in the Kingdom of God.** NLT

Revelation 21:8

But the cowardly, the unbelieving, the vile, the murderers, **the sexually immoral,** those who practice magic arts, the idolaters and all liars-**their place will be in the fiery lake of burning sulfur. This is the second death.** NIV

But for the cowardly and unbelieving and **abominable** and murderers **and immoral** persons and sorcerers and idolaters and all liars, **their part will be in the lake that burns with fire and brimstone, which is the second death**. NASB

So what does all this mean?

The world would tell you that Alcoholism, Drug addiction, even some types of Sexual Immorality (Adultery, Homosexuality, Pedophilia, Bestiality, etc.) are Diseases, Mental/Emotional issues… or even "normal" acceptable behaviors/lifestyles.

THEY ARE NOT!

God does not condemn someone for having Cancer, or Cerebral Palsy, or some other ACTUAL Disease.

God does not condemn someone for a "normal and acceptable" behavior/lifestyle.

God condemns those that SIN; those that MAKE A CHOICE to willfully break God's Commandments.

You have a CHOICE whether to take that FIRST DRINK, or FIRST HIT of Drugs.

You have a CHOICE whether to go somewhere Private with someone, or something, that you know you SHOULD NOT have SEXUAL RELATIONS with.

You have a CHOICE whether to make that FIRST TOUCH, take that FIRST KISS, Unbutton that FIRST button, etc.

1 Peter 2:11

Dear friends, I urge you, as aliens and strangers in the world, to **abstain from sinful desires**, which war against your soul. NIV

Beloved, I urge you as aliens and strangers to **abstain from fleshly lusts which wage war against the soul.** NASB

If you can't seem to control yourself and need HELP with these DESIRES, then PRAY to God for Help. Ask for HELP, for Deliverance from the Desire, the Craving… the Need. **Pray Continually.**

1 Thessalonians 5:17

Pray without ceasing. KJV and NASB

Pray continually; NIV

Psalm 91:15

"He will call upon me, and I will answer him;
I will be with him in trouble,
I will deliver him and honor him." NIV

He shall call upon me, and I will answer him:
I will be with him in trouble;
I will deliver him, and honour him. KJV

Talk with a Pastor, a Christian Therapist or therapy group. Deliberately move out of areas that help support/promote your problem (away from the Gay bar, the neighbor that keeps giving you that enticing look, etc.)

But remember, if, after you have tried everything... you still are stricken with these sinful desires... realize that this may be something that God is not going to remove, but is actually allowing you to be tested with.

Now don't think that God is going around afflicting everyone just to test them. Those problems are usually the result of the Devil and his minions, other sinners, or our own poor judgment, etc.

But God in his wisdom ALLOWS it to happen to observe your response.

God tests people regularly to help them mature in their spiritual growth.

If you are being tested, God wants you to flee from temptation and not succumb to evil/sinful ways. Every time we choose to do the right thing, God rewards us... usually when we get to heaven, but often even here on earth in unexpected ways.

When we fail our tests (give in to those temptations)... we sin.

People are tested in many ways, you are not alone. Some people are tested with handicaps (a missing leg, Down syndrome, blindness, etc.), others with diseases (Cancer, Multiple Sclerosis, Lupus, etc.).

Others face things like Clinical Depression, Schizophrenia, Bipolar disorder, past emotional or physical traumas, other sexual addictions, etc.

The thing is that we all have to face tests and challenges... and it is how we handle them that God watches very closely.

2 Corinthians 12:6-10

For though I would desire to glory, I shall not be a fool; for I will say the truth: but now I forbear, lest any man should think of me above that which he seeth me to be, or that he heareth of me.

And lest I should be exalted above measure through the abundance of the revelations, **there was given to me a thorn in the flesh, the messenger of Satan to buffet me, lest I should be exalted above measure.**

For this thing **I besought the Lord thrice, that it might depart from me.**

And he said unto me, "My grace is sufficient for thee: for my strength is made perfect in weakness."

Most gladly **therefore will I rather glory in my infirmities, that the power of Christ may** rest upon me.

Therefore **I take pleasure in infirmities, in reproaches, in necessities, in persecutions, in distresses for Christ's sake: for when I am weak, then am I strong.** KJV

Even **if I should choose to boast, I would not be a fool, because I would be speaking the truth. But I refrain, so no one will think more of me than is warranted by what I do or say.**

To keep me from becoming conceited because of these surpassingly great revelations, there was given me a thorn in my flesh, a messenger of Satan, to torment me.

Three times I pleaded with the Lord to take it away from me. But he said to me, "My grace is sufficient for you, for my power is made perfect in weakness." Therefore I will boast all the more gladly about my weaknesses, so that Christ's power may rest on me. That is why, for Christ's sake, I delight in weaknesses, in insults, in hardships, in persecutions, in difficulties. For when I am weak, then I am strong. NIV

God often allows pain or "thorns" to REMIND US that we are only human and in constant need of God's help, strength, protection... and comfort.

This TEST might be meant to allow a continual chance to CHOOSE to ABSTAIN from the SIN.

Alcoholics need to Abstain from drinking alcohol, and may even need to Abstain from going to places where alcohol is available; the same is true for drug users.

People with Sexual Disorders need to Abstain from ANY type of ungodly Sexual activities (Porn of any type, going to places where there is even a small chance of a sexual situation occurring, "thinking" and "fantasizing" about sexual activities, etc.).

God ONLY wants you to have sexual relations with your spouse (yes, AFTER you are married. And YES, your spouse must be of the opposite sex.), all else is Sin.

(But again... Please read other scriptures in the Bible to see if you find that my conclusion here is incorrect.)

Many people who have been tested with Homosexual desires/urges have chosen to live celibate lives (like many monks, priests, etc.) to Abstain from Homosexual activities and so avoid sinning against God.

Romans 6:12-14

Let not sin therefore reign in your mortal body, that ye should obey it in the lusts thereof. Neither yield ye your members as instruments of unrighteousness unto sin: but **yield yourselves unto God,** as those that are alive from the dead, and **your members as instruments of righteousness unto God. For sin shall not have dominion over you: for ye are not under the law, but under grace.** KJV

Do not let sin control the way you live; do not give in to its lustful desires. Do not let any part of your body become a tool of wickedness**, to be used for sinning.** Instead, **give yourselves completely to God** since you have been given new life. And use your whole body as a tool **to do what is right for the glory of God. Sin is no longer your master, for you are no longer subject to the law, which enslaves you to sin.** Instead, **you are free by God's grace.** NLT

Think of it as a TEMPTATION for you to AVOID continually (the Bible never says anything about *resisting* Temptation, only *resisting* the Devil). So remember, if you find yourself faced with Temptation… **Leave, Run away, Pray**… but GET OUT of that SITUATION!

If you are with friends who are drinking, and you find yourself TEMPTED to take a drink… Leave them and go somewhere else, drive away with other friends if necessary.

If you find your eyes drawn to someone they shouldn't be drawn to… Go away from THAT PERSON, get out of sight of them, even the nearness of them, and **focus on something else.**

If something prevents you from actually LEAVING… Turn away and Pray! Don't LOOK at the Temptation, don't listen, etc. Pray and concentrate on something else; like God's many blessings to you, things that need to be fixed around the house, etc.

DO NOT think about HOW to avoid the Temptation; thinking about the temptation AT ALL only gives it STRENGTH and makes it HARDER to NOT think about it.

Colossians 3:1-2

Set your hearts on things above, where Christ is seated at the right hand of God.

Set your minds on things above, not on earthly things. NIV

Seek those things which are above, where Christ sitteth on the right hand of God. Set your affection on things above, **not on things on the earth.** KJV

Ephesians 6:10-11

A final word: **Be strong with the Lord's mighty power. Put on all of God's armor so that you will be able to stand firm against all strategies and tricks of the Devil.** NLT

Finally, **my brethren, be strong in the Lord, and in the power of his might. Put on the whole armour of God, that ye may be able to stand against the wiles of the devil.** KJV

If you have been living with SIN, know that it is NOT too late to change. It is NOT too late to become the person GOD wants YOU to be. But you must be sincere in your desire to change.

1 John 1:9

If we confess our sins, he is faithful and just and will forgive us our sins and purify us from all unrighteousness. NIV

If we confess our sins, He is faithful and righteous to forgive us our sins and to cleanse us from all unrighteousness. NASB

No human being is, or was ever, Perfect (Never Sinned), except

Jesus Christ.

So, whatever the sin you may have done, or may even still be doing... You can still be forgiven.

But you must Repent (Tell God you are sorry for sinning against Him and his laws, and ask forgiveness)... and mean it, and sincerely try not to sin again.

Now that may be really hard, and you may stumble and fall many times... but if you are SINCERELY trying to stop the sin... that is what God wants from you.

But NOT SINNING, or asking forgiveness for your sins ALONE is not going to please God, save you from HELL and get you into HEAVEN and the Family of God.

For THAT you still need one VERY IMPORTANT Thing...

JESUS CHRIST

You must accept and acknowledge that Jesus Christ is the son of God. That he was born of a human woman, lived a sin-free life but willingly died on a cross (a sinners death) to save all who trust in him from their sins... and three days later he rose again (came back to life).

Don't know about Jesus Christ?

See the Chapter: **Don't know Jesus?**

For more to read on the subject of Homosexuality; Judges 19:22-24, Revelation 22:12-15, and see what else you can find.

Revelation 3:5

He who overcomes will thus be clothed in white garments; and I will not erase his name from the book of life, and I will confess his name before My Father and before His angels. NASB

Chapter Eleven

Is Marriage only supposed to be between a Man and a Woman?

This is a very controversial question across the country as some states pass laws permitting same-sex marriages while others do not. But what does God have to say about it?

Let's take a look at a few scriptures...

Genesis 2:18-24

And the LORD God said, **It is not good that the man should be alone; I will make him a help meet for him.** And out of the ground the LORD God formed every beast of the field, and every fowl of the air; and brought them unto Adam to see what he would call them: and whatsoever Adam called every living creature, that was the name thereof. And Adam gave names to all cattle, and to the fowl of the air, and to every beast of the field; **but for Adam there was not found a help meet for him. And the LORD God caused a deep sleep to fall upon Adam, and he slept: and he took one of his ribs, and closed up the flesh instead thereof; and the rib, which the LORD God had taken from man, made he a woman, and brought her unto the man.**

And Adam said, **This is now bone of my bones, and flesh of my flesh:** she shall be called Woman, because she was taken out of Man. **Therefore shall a man leave his father and his mother, and shall cleave unto his wife: and they shall be one flesh.** KJV

Then the LORD God said, "**it is not good for the man to be alone; I will make him a helper suitable for him.**" Out of the ground the LORD God formed every beast of the field and every bird of the sky, and brought them to the man to see what he would call them; and whatever the man called a living creature, that was its name. The man gave names to all the cattle, and to the birds of the sky, and to every beast of the field, **but for Adam there was not found a helper suitable for him. So the LORD God caused a deep sleep to fall upon the man, and he slept; then He took one of his ribs and closed up the flesh at that place. The LORD God fashioned into a woman the rib which He had taken from the man, and brought her to the man.** The man said,

"This is now bone of my bones
And flesh of my flesh;
She shall be called Woman,
Because she was taken out of Man."

For this reason a man shall leave his father and his mother, and be joined to his wife; and they shall become one flesh. NASB

Genesis 1:27-28

So God created man in his own image, in the image of God **he created him; male and female** he created them.

God blessed them and said to them, "Be fruitful and increase in number; fill the earth and subdue it. Rule over the fish of the sea and the birds of the air and over every living creature that moves on the ground." NIV

So God created man in his own image, in the image of **God created he him; male and female created he them. And God blessed them, and God said unto them, Be fruitful, and multiply,** and replenish the earth, and subdue it: and have dominion over the fish of the sea, and over the fowl of the air, and over every living thing that moveth upon the earth. KJV

Genesis 7:2-3

Take along seven pairs of each animal that I have approved for eating and for sacrifice, and take one pair of each of the others. Then select seven pairs of every kind of bird. **There must be a male and a female in each pair to ensure that every kind of living creature will survive the flood.** NLT

Of every clean beast thou shalt take to thee by sevens, **the male and his female**: and of the beasts that are not clean by two, **the male and his female**. Of fowls also of the air by sevens, **the male and the female; to keep seed alive upon the face of all the earth.** KJV

Genesis 7:6-9

Now Noah was six hundred years old when the flood of water came upon the earth. Then **Noah and his sons and his wife and his sons' wives with him entered the ark** because of the water of the flood. Of clean animals and animals that are not clean and birds and everything that creeps on the ground, **there went into the ark to Noah by twos, male and female, as God had commanded Noah.** NASB

And Noah was six hundred years old when the flood of waters was upon the earth. **And Noah went in, and his sons, and his wife, and his sons' wives with him, into the ark,** because of the waters of the flood. Of clean beasts, and of beasts that are not clean, and of fowls, and of every thing that creepeth upon the earth, **there went in two and two unto Noah into the ark, the male and the female, as God had commanded Noah.** KJV

Now let's look at a few scriptures of a slightly different nature...

Leviticus 18:22

Do not practice homosexuality; it is a detestable sin. NLT

You shall not lie with a male as one lies with a female; it is an abomination. NASB

Leviticus 20:13

If a man also lie with mankind, as he lieth with a woman, both of them have committed an abomination: they shall surely be put to death; their blood shall be upon them. KJV

"The penalty for homosexual acts is death to both parties. They have committed a detestable act and are guilty of a capital offense." NLT

Romans 1:25-27

They exchanged the truth of God for a lie, and worshiped and served created things rather than the Creator—who is forever praised. Amen.

Because of this, God gave them over to **shameful lusts. Even their women exchanged natural relations for unnatural ones. In the same way the men also abandoned natural relations with women and were inflamed with lust for one another. Men committed indecent acts with other men, and received in themselves the due penalty for their perversion.** NIV

Instead of believing what they knew was the truth about God, they deliberately chose to believe lies. So they worshiped the things God made but not the Creator himself, who is to be praised forever. Amen.

That is why God abandoned them **to their shameful desires. Even the women turned against the natural way to have sex and instead indulged in sex with each other. Men did shameful things with other men and, as a result, suffered within themselves the penalty they so richly deserved.** NLT

1 Corinthians 6:9-10

Or do you not know that the unrighteous will not inherit the kingdom of God? Do not be deceived; neither fornicators, nor idolaters, nor adulterers, nor effeminate, **nor homosexuals**, nor thieves, nor the covetous, nor drunkards, nor revilers, nor swindlers, **will inherit the kingdom of God.** NASB

Don't you know that those who do wrong will have no share in the Kingdom of God? Don't fool yourselves. Those who indulge in sexual sin, who are idol worshipers, adulterers, male prostitutes, **homosexuals**, thieves, greedy people, drunkards, abusers, and swindlers-**none of these will have a share in the Kingdom of God.** NLT

It would appear from Scriptures that God is against any form of homosexuality. In fact, the Bible specifically talks about God making Woman FROM and FOR Man and that ONLY these two should leave their families and marry.

It also seems God wants couples to procreate (naturally)... which two women or two men cannot do.

If God is against Homosexuality, he would NEVER approve of, or condone, same-sex marriage.

So the answer to the question would seem to be…

Yes, Marriage is only supposed to be between a Man and a Woman.

But if you still want more scriptural references; see also
Chapter Ten: Is Homosexuality a SIN? And
Chapter Eight: Forbidden Sexual Practices

Isaiah 3:10-11

Say to the righteous that it will go well with them, for they will eat the fruit of their actions. Woe to the wicked! It will go badly with him, for what he deserves will be done to him.

NASB

Chapter Twelve

BEWARE the Supernatural?

Are Witches, Astrologers, Mediums, Spiritists, Psychics, Sorcerers, etc… all SINNERS?

Are those that go to/support/believe in: Astrologers, Psychics, Witches, etc. all committing SIN?

In today's society where Horoscopes are in most Newspapers, and Psychic shops seem to be in most towns,

Where television and movies are filled with magic, witches, demons and all types of mystical and monstrous things,

It is hard to tell what is made-up nonsense, what is real, what we are allowed to do or go along with…

And what God has forbidden and considers a **SIN**.

This chapter will try to shed some light on matters. So Let's look at some scriptures that help answer these questions….

Exodus 22:18

"Do not allow a sorceress to live." NIV

Thou shalt not suffer a witch to live. KJV

Leviticus 19:26

'Do not practice divination or sorcery.' NIV

"Do not practice fortune-telling or witchcraft." NLT

"Neither shall ye use enchantment, nor observe times." KJV

"Nor practice divination or soothsaying." NASB

Leviticus 19:31

'Do not turn to mediums or seek out spiritists, for you will be defiled by them. I am the LORD.' NIV

Regard not them that have familiar spirits, neither seek after wizards, to be defiled by them: I am the LORD your God. KJV

"Do not rely on mediums and psychics, for you will be defiled by them. I, the LORD, am your God." NLT

Deuteronomy 18:9-12

"When you enter the land which the LORD your God gives you, **you shall not learn to imitate the detestable things of those nations. There shall not be found among you anyone who** makes his son or his daughter pass thought the fire, one who **uses divination, one who practices witchcraft, or one who interprets omens, or a sorcerer, or one who casts a spell, or a medium, or a spiritist, or one who calls up the dead. For whoever does these things if detestable to the LORD;** and because of these detestable things the LORD your God will drive them out before you. NASB

"When you arrive in the land the LORD your God is giving you, be very careful not to imitate the detestable customs of the nations living there. For example, never sacrifice your son or daughter as a burnt offering. And **do not let your people practice fortune-telling or sorcery, or allow them to interpret omens, or engage in witchcraft, or cast spells, or function as mediums or psychics, or call forth the spirits of the dead. Anyone who does these things is an object of horror and disgust to the LORD.** It is because the other nations have done these things that the LORD your God will drive them out ahead of you. NLT

When thou are come into the land which the LORD thy God giveth thee, **thou shalt not learn to do after the abominations of those nations. There shall not be found among you any** one that maketh his son or his daughter to pass through the fire, or **that useth divination, or an observer of times, or an enchanter, or a witch, or a charmer, or a consulter with familiar spirits, or a wizard, or a necromancer. For all that do these things are an abomination unto the LORD**: and because of these abominations the LORD thy God doth drive them out from before thee. KJV

Isaiah 8:19-20

So **why are you trying to find out the future by consulting mediums and psychics? Do not listen to their whisperings and mutterings. Can the living find out the future from the dead? Why not ask your God?**

"Check their predictions against my testimony," says the LORD. "If their predictions are different from mine, it is because there is no light or truth in them." NLT

When men tell you to consult mediums and spiritists, who whisper and mutter, should not a people inquire of

their God? Why consult the dead on behalf of the living?

To the law and to the testimony! If they do not speak according to this word, they have no light of dawn. NIV

And when they shall say unto you, Seek unto them that have familiar spirits, and unto wizards that peep, and that mutter:

Should not a people seek unto their God?
For the living to the dead?
To the law and to the testimony:
If they speak not according to this word it is because there is no light in them. KJV

Jeremiah 10:2

This is what the LORD says: **"Do not act like other nations who try to read their future in the stars. Do not be afraid of their predictions**, even though other nations are terrified by them." NLT

Thus saith the LORD,
Learn not the way of the heathen,
And be not dismayed at the signs of heaven;
For the heathen are dismayed at them. KJV

Ephesians 6:10-17

Finally, be strong in the Lord and in the strength of His might. Put on the full armor of God, **so that you will be able to stand firm against the schemes of the devil. For our struggle is not against flesh and blood, but against the rulers, against the powers, against the world forces of this darkness, against the spiritual forces of wickedness in the**

heavenly places. Therefore, take up the full armor of God, so that you will be able to resist in the evil day, and having done everything, to stand firm. Stand firm therefore, **HAVING GIRDED YOUR LOINS** WITH **TRUTH**, AND HAVING PUT ON **THE BREASTPLATE OF RIGHTEOUSNESS**, and having shod YOUR FEET WITH THE **PREPARATION OF THE GOSPEL OF PEACE**; in addition to all, taking up **the shield of faith with which you will be able to extinguish all the flaming arrows of the evil one**. And take **THE HELMET OF SALVATION, and the sword of the Spirit, which is the word of God**. NASB

Finally, my brethren, be strong in the Lord, and in the power of his might. Put on the whole armour of God**, that ye may be able to stand against the wiles of the devil. For we wrestle not against flesh and blood, but against principalities, against powers, against the rulers of the darkness of this world, against spiritual wickedness in high places.** Wherefore **take unto you the whole armour of God**, that ye may be able to withstand in the evil day, and having done all, to stand.

Stand therefore, having your loins girt about with **truth**, and having on the breastplate of **righteousness**; And your feet shod with the preparation of **the gospel of peace**; Above all, taking the shield of **faith**, wherewith ye shall be able to quench all the fiery darts of the wicked. And take the helmet of **salvation**, and the **sword of the Spirit, which is the word of God**: KJV

Revelation 21:8

But **cowards who turn away from me,** and **unbelievers**, and the corrupt, and murderers, and the immoral, and **those who practice witchcraft**, and **idol worshipers,** and all liars- **their doom is in the lake that burns with fire and sulfur.** This is the second death." NLT

But the cowardly, **the unbelieving**, the vile, the murderers, the sexually immoral, **those who practice magic arts,** the **idolaters** and all liars-**their place will be in the fiery lake of burning sulfur. This is the second death.** NIV

But for **the cowardly** and **unbelieving** and abominable and murderers and immoral persons and **sorcerers and idolaters** and all liars**, their part will be in the lake that burns with fire and brimstone, which is the second death**. NASB

What a lot of Christians do not realize is that many, if not most, of these people who deal with the "supernatural" are **NOT CHRISTIANS**. Self-proclaimed "Witches" can run the gamut from the "black" witches that **actually (and knowingly) worship SATAN (the Devil**) and seek to harm others and get as many people into Hell as possible for their "deity"... to "white" witches that are Pagans that believe in "Nature deities, nature spirits, other "gods", etc. (Unknowingly serving the Devil in disguise).

Many of these "witches" are possessed by Demons, also called "familiar spirits", and that is where they get their power.

Most of them do not realize or truly believe that they are getting their "power" or "abilities" from Demons, but that is still why God is telling people to stay away from these people as the Demons will give advice, or take actions that attempt to harm, corrupt and turn people from Jesus and God.

What the Bible called "witches", "sorcerers", "soothsayers", etc. are now going by many other names as well: Wiccans; that worship *Wicca*, Voodoo or vodun priests; that worship *gede* (spirits of the dead), and the list goes on.

But what you need to remember is: they **DO NOT believe in Jesus Christ and will never reach heaven**, if fact, the only thing they can do is TEMPT and Seduce you away from Jesus and into Sin.

Judges 2:1-4

The angel of the LORD went up from Gilgal to Bokim with a message for the Israelites. He told them, "I brought you out of Egypt into this land that I swore to give your ancestors, and I said I would never break my covenant with you. **For your part, you were not to make any covenants with the people living in this land; instead, you were to destroy their altars.** Why, then, have you disobeyed my command? Since you have done this, I will no longer drive out the people living in your land. **They will be thorns in your sides, and their gods will**

be a constant temptation to you." When the angel of the Lord finished speaking, the Israelites wept loudly. NLT

And **an angel of the LORD** came up from Gilgal to Bochim, and said, I made you to go up out of Egypt, and have brought you unto the land which I sware unto your fathers; and I said, I will never break my covenant with you. And **ye shall make no league with the inhabitants of this land; you shall throw down their altars**; but ye have not obeyed my voice: why have ye done this? Wherefore I also said, I will not drive them out from before you; but **they shall be as thorns in your sides, and their gods shall be a snare unto you.** And it came to pass, when the angel of the LORD spake these words unto all the children of Israel, that the people lift up their voice, and wept. KJV

Knowing God's commands, and reasons, against Witchcraft... If a "Witch" claims to be a "Christian" DO NOT believe them for they are actively SINNING against GOD's commandments. And while they may actually believe they are doing "good works", even that they are "Christians", they are; deceiving themselves, Sinning against God, and causing others to Sin, which God does not condone.

No Christian should ever claim to be a "witch" or any other "supernatural"-type person: sorcerer, mystic, shaman, wizard, psychic, necromancer, the list goes on.

Just as bad are people who claim to be "fortune tellers", "astrologers", "psychics", "mediums", and such that either claim to be pagan or no religion at all. Again, many of these people are knowingly or unknowingly using "familiar spirits" or Demons, to accomplish their tasks.

Others are just charlatans (scam artists) whose sole job is to make money for themselves. They have no "familiar spirits" but they have no "power" or honesty either. They simply tell people what they think will work best to bring them back again and again... and earn themselves more money.

This doesn't mean they can't put on a believable act, most are very adept at reading body language, facial clues, etc. just like the science of detecting lies only they use them to ferret out openings for their false "revelations".

Proverbs 2:12-15

Wisdom will **save you from evil people**, **from those whose speech is corrupt**. **These people turn from right ways to walk down dark and evil paths.** They rejoice in doing wrong, and **they enjoy evil** as it turns things upside down. What they do is crooked, and **their ways are wrong** NLT

To **deliver you from the way of evil, from those who leave the paths of uprightness to walk in the ways of darkness;**
Who delight in doing evil and rejoice in the perversity of evil;
Whose paths are crooked, and who are devious in their ways. NASB

These are many of the reasons GOD does NOT want people to consult or deal with people who claim to have Supernatural Powers, or access to Supernatural Powers.

Let's look at a few more slightly different scriptures...

Acts 16:16-19

And it came to pass, as we went to prayer, **a certain damsel possessed with a spirit of divination met us, which brought her masters much gain by soothsaying:**
The same followed Paul and us, and cried, saying, These men are the servants of the most high God, which show unto us the way of salvation.

And this did she many days. **But Paul**, being grieved, turned and **said to the spirit, I command thee in the name of Jesus Christ to come out of her. And he came out the same hour.**

And when **her masters saw that the hope of their gains was gone**, they caught Paul and Silas, and drew them into the marketplace unto the rulers. KJV

Once when we were going to the place of prayer, **we were met by a slave girl who had a spirit by which she predicted the future. She earned a great deal of money for her owners by fortune-telling**. This girl followed Paul and the rest of us, shouting, "These men are servants of the Most High God, who are telling you the way to be saved." She kept this up for many days. **Finally Paul became so troubled that he turned around and said to the spirit, "In the name of Jesus Christ I command you to come out of her!" At that moment the spirit left her.**

When the owners of the slave girl realized that their hope of making money was gone, they seized Paul and Silas and dragged them into the marketplace to face the authorities. NIV

1 Samuel 28:3-19

Now Samuel was dead, and all Israel had lamented him, and buried him in Ramah, even in his own city. **And Saul had put away those that had familiar spirits, and the wizards, out of the land**. And the Philistines gathered themselves together, and came and encamped in Shunem: and Saul gathered all Israel together, and they encamped in Gilboa. And when Saul saw the host of the Philistines, he was afraid, and his heart trembled greatly. And **when Saul inquired of Jehovah, Jehovah answered him not, neither by dreams, nor by Urim, nor by prophets.**

Then said Saul unto his servants, Seek me a woman that hath a familiar spirit, that I may go to her, and inquire of her. And his servants said to him, Behold, there is a woman that hath a familiar spirit at En-dor. And **Saul disguised himself**, and put on other raiment, and went, he and two men with him, **and they came to the woman by night: and he said, Divine unto me, I pray thee, by the familiar spirit, and bring me up whomsoever I shall name** unto thee. And the woman said unto him, **Behold, thou knowest what Saul hath done, how he hath cut off those that have familiar spirits, and the wizards, out of the land: wherefore then layest thou a snare for my life, to cause me to die?** And Saul sware to her by Jehovah, saying, As Jehovah liveth, there shall no punishment happen to thee for this thing. Then said the woman, Whom shall I bring up unto thee? And he said, **Bring me up Samuel.** And **when the woman saw Samuel, she cried with a loud voice; and the woman spake to Saul**, saying, **Why hast thou deceived me? for thou art Saul**. And the king said unto her, Be not afraid: for **what seest thou?** And the woman said unto Saul, **I see a god coming up out of the earth.** And he said unto her, **What form is he of? And she said, An old man cometh up; and he is covered with a robe. And Saul perceived that it was Samuel, and he bowed with his face to the ground, and did obeisance.**

And Samuel said to Saul, Why hast thou disquieted me, to bring me up? And Saul answered, I am sore distressed; for the Philistines make war against me, and **God is departed from me, and answereth me no more, neither by prophets, nor by dreams: therefore I have called thee,** that thou mayest make known unto me what I shall do. And Samuel said, Wherefore then dost thou ask of me, seeing Jehovah is departed from thee, and is become thine adversary? And Jehovah hath done unto thee, as he spake by me: and Jehovah hath rent the kingdom out of thy hand, and given it to thy neighbor, even to David. **Because thou obeyedst not the voice of Jehovah,** and didst not execute his fierce wrath upon Amalek, therefore hath Jehovah done this thing unto thee this day. Moreover Jehovah will deliver Israel also with thee into the hand of the Philistines; and **tomorrow shalt thou and thy sons be with me:** Jehovah will deliver the host of Israel also into the hand of the Philistines. ASV

Now Samuel was dead, and all Israel had lamented him, and buried him in Ramah, even in his own city. **And Saul had put away those that had familiar spirits, and the wizards, out of the land.** And the Philistines gathered themselves together, and came and pitched in Shunem: and Saul gathered all Israel together, and they pitched in Gilboa. And when Saul saw the host of the Philistines, he was afraid, and his heart greatly trembled. And when **Saul inquired of the LORD, the LORD answered him not, neither by dreams, nor by Urim, nor by prophets**. Then said Saul unto his servants, **Seek me a woman that hath a familiar spirit, that I may go to her, and inquire of her.** And his servants said to him, **Behold, there is a woman that hath a familiar spirit at En-dor**. And Saul disguised himself, and put on other raiment, and he went, and two men with him, and they came to the woman by night: and he said, **I pray three, divine unto me by the familiar spirit, and bring me him up, whom I shall name unto thee**. And the woman said unto him, Behold, thou knowest what Saul hath done, how **he hath cut off those that have familiar spirits, and the wizards, out of the land**: wherefore then layest thou a snare for my life, to cause me to die? And Saul sware to her by the LORD, saying, As the LORD liveth, there shall no punishment happen to thee for this thing. Then said the woman, **Whom shall I bring up unto thee? And he said, Bring me up Samuel. And when the woman saw Samuel, she cried with a loud voice: and the woman spake to Saul, Why hast thou deceived me: for thou art Saul.** And the king said unto her, Be not afraid: for **what sawest thou: And the woman said unto Saul, I saw gods ascending out of the earth.** And **he said unto her, What form is he of: And she said, An old man cometh up; and he is covered with a mantle. And Saul perceived that it was Samuel,** and he stooped with his face to the ground, and bowed himself.

And Samuel said to Saul, Why hast thou disquieted me, to bring me up: And Saul answered, I am sore distressed; for the Philistines make war against me, and God is departed from me, and answereth me no more, neither by prophets, nor by dreams: therefore I have called thee, that thou mayest make known unto me what I shall do.

Then said Samuel, Wherefore then dost thou ask of me, seeing the LORD is departed from thee, and is become thine enemy: And the LORD hath done to him, as he spake by me: for the LORD hath rent the kingdom out of thine hand, and given it to thy neighbor, even to David: because thou obeyest not the voice of the LORD, nor executedst his fierce wrath upon Amalek, therefore hath the LORD done this thing unto thee this day. Moreover the LORD will also deliver Israel with thee unto the hand of the Philistines: and to morrow shalt thou and thy sons be with me: the LORD also shall deliver the host of Israel into the hand of the Philistines. KJV

Mark 1:23-27

Just then a man in their synagogue **who was possessed by an evil spirit** cried out, **"What do you want with us, Jesus of Nazareth? Have you come to destroy us? I know who you are—the Holy One of God!"**

"Be quiet!" said Jesus sternly. "Come out of him!"

The evil spirit shook the man violently and came out of him with a shriek.

The people were all so amazed that they asked each other. "What is this? A new teaching—and with authority! **He even gives orders to evil spirits and they obey him."**

NIV

Just then **there was a man in their synagogue with an unclean spirit; and he cried out, saying, "What business do we have with each other, Jesus of Nazareth? Have You come to destroy us? I know who You are—the Holy One of God!" And Jesus rebuked him, saying, "Be quiet, and come out of him!" Throwing him into convulsions, the unclean spirit cried out with a loud voice and came out of him.** They were all amazed, so that they debated among themselves saying, "What is this? A new teaching with authority! **He commands even the unclean spirits, and they obey Him."** NASB

Mark 5:1-15

And they came over unto the other side of the sea, into the country of the Gadarenes. And when he was come out of the ship, **immediately there met him out of the tombs a man with an unclean spirit, Who had his dwelling among the tombs; and no man could bind him, no, not with chains: Because that he had been often bound with fetters and chains, and the chains had been plucked asunder by him, and the fetters broken in pieces: neither could any man tame him. And always, night and day, he was in the mountains, and in the tombs, crying, and cutting himself with stones.** But when **he saw Jesus afar off, he ran and worshipped him, And cried with a loud voice, and said, What have I to do with thee, Jesus, thou Son of the most high God? I adjure thee by God, that thou torment me not. For he said unto him, Come out of the man, thou unclean spirit. And he asked him, What is thy name? And he answered, saying, My name is Legion: for we are many**. And he besought him much that he would not send them away out of the country. Now there was there nigh unto the mountains a great herd of swine feeding. And **all the devils besought him, saying, Send us into the swine, that we may enter into them.** And forthwith Jesus gave them leave. **And the unclean spirits went out, and entered into the swine: and the herd ran violently down a steep place into the sea, (they were about two thousand,) and were choked in the sea.** And they that fed the swine fled, and told it in the city, and in the country. And they went out to see what it was that was done. **And they come to Jesus, and see him that was possessed with the devil, and had the legion, sitting, and clothed, and in his right mind: and they were afraid.** KJV

They came to the other side of the sea, into the country of the Gerasenes. When He got out of the boat, immediately **a man from the tombs with an unclean spirit** met Him, and he had his dwelling among the tombs. And **no one was able to bind him anymore, even with a chain; because he had often been bound with shackles and chains, and the chains had been torn apart by him and the shackles broken in pieces, and no**

one was strong enough to subdue him. Constantly, night and day, he was screaming among the tombs and in the mountains, and gashing himself with stones. Seeing Jesus from a distance, he ran up and bowed down before Him; and shouting with a loud voice, **he said, "What business do we have with each other, Jesus, Son of the Most High God? I implore You by God, do not torment me!" For He had been saying to him, "Come out of the man, you unclean spirit!"** And He was asking him, **"What is your name?" and he said to Him, "My name is Legion; for we are many."** And he began to implore Him earnestly not to send them out of the country. Now there was a large herd of swine feeding nearby on the mountain. **The demons implored Him, saying, "Send us into the swine so that we may enter them." Jesus gave them permission. And coming out, the unclean spirits entered the swine; and the herd rushed down the steep bank into the sea, about two thousand of them; and they were drowned in the sea.**

Their herdsmen ran away and reported it in the city and in the country. And the people came to see what it was that had happened. **They came to Jesus and observed the man who had been demon-possessed sitting down, clothed and in his right mind, the very man who had had the "legion"; and they became frightened.** NASB

God is not saying that mediums, spiritists, witches, etc. are NOT REAL, he is saying that of those that actually seem to have powers... those POWERS are not Really Theirs**... they come from Satan and his Demons, and these demons can even take you over (possess you).** And because of that you are NOT to GO TO THEM or seek to BECOME one of Them.

You are to Trust God for the answers you need; through his scriptures, through the dreams that he sends TO YOU, through his prophets and people God sends to you (not the other way around), etc.

You are not to turn to UNGODLY means to try to satisfy your curiosity, your own pleasure, to earn money, satisfy others desires, etc.

Some things to ask yourself before being around any of these people;

Are they claiming to be Christians or do they freely admit to worshipping pagan "gods" or dealing with "Familiar Spirits"?

If they claim to be Christians, are they prophets... or are they just people willfully sinning against God?

If they admit they worship other gods or spirits, why are you thinking about taking advice from them? If they don't have enough knowledge and wisdom to save their own souls by believing in and accepting Jesus Christ as their savior, then how can they possibly know anything that would help you and not harm you or try to corrupt you?

If they claim to be Christians, are they doing it for God's glory... or money and fame?

Are they telling you something God wants you to hear, or do, for the Glory of his kingdom... something that sounds "right" or "familiar" to you... or

Are they simply spouting things that seem "wrong" to you or giving advice or answering questions that are for YOU and not God's Glory?

And truly important: Do you go to them or does God send them to you?

The reason to ask is because GOD does have Prophets, and he does allow some of them to see the future in dreams, or visions, or such... but it is for GOD's purpose, and by GOD's acknowledged power. Such a person would never deny Jesus Christ or be allowed to use the power simply for personal gain (although when you serve God well, he often rewards his prophets and servants with wealth or power).

Numbers 12:6

"**When a prophet of the LORD is among you, I reveal myself to him in visions, I speak to him in dreams.**" NIV

If there be a prophet among you, I the LORD will make myself known unto him in a vision, and will speak unto him in a dream." KJV

"Hear now My words:
If there is a prophet among you,
I, the LORD, shall make Myself known to him in a vision.
I shall speak with him in a dream. NASB

Genesis 40 and 41

And it came to pass after these things, that the butler of the king of Egypt and his baker had offended their lord the king of Egypt. And Pharaoh was wroth against two of his officers, against the chief of the butlers, and against the chief of the bakers. And he put them in ward in the house of the captain of the guard, into the prison, the place where Joseph was bound. And the captain of the guard charged Joseph with them, and he served them: and they continued a season in ward.

And **they dreamed a dream both of them, each man his dream in one night, each man according to the interpretation of his dream, the butler and the baker of the king of Egypt, which were bound in the prison. And Joseph came in unto them in the morning, and looked upon them, and, behold, they were sad. And he asked Pharaoh's officers that were with him in the ward of his lord's house, saying, Wherefore look ye so sadly to day? And they said unto him, We have dreamed a dream, and there is no interpreter of it. And Joseph said unto them, Do not interpretations belong to God? tell me them, I pray you.** And the chief butler told his dream to Joseph, and said to him, In my dream, behold, a vine was before me; And in the vine were three branches: and it was as though it budded, and her blossoms shot forth; and the clusters thereof brought forth ripe grapes: And Pharaoh's cup was in my hand: and I took the grapes, and pressed them into Pharaoh's cup, and I gave the cup into Pharaoh's hand. And **Joseph said unto him, This is the interpretation of it: The three branches are three days: Yet within three days shall Pharaoh lift up thine head, and restore thee unto thy place: and thou shalt deliver Pharaoh's cup into his hand, after the former manner when thou wast his butler. But think on me when it shall be**

well with thee, and shew kindness, I pray thee, unto me, and make mention of me unto Pharaoh, and bring me out of this house: For indeed I was stolen away out of the land of the Hebrews: and here also have I done nothing that they should put me into the dungeon. When the chief baker saw that the interpretation was good, he said unto Joseph, I also was in my dream, and, behold, I had three white baskets on my head: And in the uppermost basket there was of all manner of bakemeats for Pharaoh; and the birds did eat them out of the basket upon my head. And Joseph answered and said, This is the interpretation thereof: The three baskets are three days: Yet within three days shall Pharaoh lift up thy head from off thee, and shall hang thee on a tree; and the birds shall eat thy flesh from off thee.

And it came to pass the third day, which was Pharaoh's birthday, that he made a feast unto all his servants: and he lifted up the head of the chief butler and of the chief baker among his servants. And he restored the chief butler unto his butlership again; and he gave the cup into Pharaoh's hand: But he hanged the chief baker: **as Joseph had interpreted to them.** Yet did not the chief butler remember Joseph, but forgat him.

And it came to pass at the end of two full years, that **Pharaoh dreamed**: and, behold, he stood by the river. And, behold, there came up out of the river seven well favoured kine and fatfleshed; and they fed in a meadow. And, behold, seven other kine came up after them out of the river, ill favoured and leanfleshed; and stood by the other kine upon the brink of the river. And the ill favoured and leanfleshed kine did eat up the seven well favoured and fat kine. So Pharaoh awoke. And he slept and **dreamed the second time**: and, behold, seven ears of corn came up upon one stalk, rank and good. And, behold, seven thin ears and blasted with the east wind sprung up after them. And the seven thin ears devoured the seven rank and full ears. And Pharaoh awoke, and, behold, it was a dream. **And it came to pass in the morning that his spirit was troubled; and he sent and called for all the magicians of Egypt, and all the wise men thereof: and Pharaoh told them his dream; but there was none that could interpret them unto Pharaoh.**

Then spake **the chief butler unto Pharaoh, saying, I do remember my faults this day**: Pharaoh was wroth with his servants, and put me in ward in the captain of the guard's house, both me and the chief baker: And we dreamed a dream in one night, I and he; we dreamed each man according to the interpretation of his dream. **And there was there with us a**

young man, a Hebrew, servant to the captain of the guard; and we told him, and he interpreted to us our dreams; to each man according to his dream he did interpret. And it came to pass, as he interpreted to us, so it was; me he restored unto mine office, and him he hanged.

Then Pharaoh sent and **called Joseph**, and they brought him hastily out of the dungeon: and he shaved himself, and changed his raiment, and came in unto Pharaoh. And Pharaoh said unto Joseph, **I have dreamed a dream, and there is none that can interpret it: and I have heard say of thee, that thou canst understand a dream to interpret it. And Joseph answered Pharaoh, saying, It is not in me: God shall give Pharaoh an answer of peace**. And Pharaoh said unto Joseph, In my dream, behold, I stood upon the bank of the river: And, behold, there came up out of the river seven kine, fatfleshed and well favoured; and they fed in a meadow: And, behold, seven other kine came up after them, poor and very ill favoured and leanfleshed, such as I never saw in all the land of Egypt for badness: And the lean and the ill favoured kine did eat up the first seven fat kine: And when they had eaten them up, it could not be known that they had eaten them; but they were still ill favoured, as at the beginning. So I awoke. And I saw in my dream, and, behold, seven ears came up in one stalk, full and good: And, behold, seven ears, withered, thin, and blasted with the east wind, sprung up after them: And the thin ears devoured the seven good ears: **and I told this unto the magicians; but there was none that could declare it to me.**

And Joseph said unto Pharaoh, **The dream of Pharaoh is one: God hath shewed Pharaoh what he is about to do. The seven good kine are seven years; and the seven good ears are seven years: the dream is one. And the seven thin and ill favoured kine that came up after them are seven years; and the seven empty ears blasted with the east wind shall be seven years of famine. This is the thing which I have spoken unto Pharaoh: What God is about to do he sheweth unto Pharaoh. Behold, there come seven years of great plenty throughout all the land of Egypt: And there shall arise after them seven years of famine; and all the plenty shall be forgotten in the land of Egypt; and the famine shall consume the land; And the plenty shall not be known in the land by reason of that famine following; for it shall be very grievous. And for that the dream was doubled unto Pharaoh twice; it is because the thing is established by God, and God will shortly**

bring it to pass. Now therefore let Pharaoh look out a man discreet and wise, and set him over the land of Egypt. Let Pharaoh do this, and let him appoint officers over the land, and take up the fifth part of the land of Egypt in the seven plenteous years. And let them gather all the food of those good years that come, and lay up corn under the hand of Pharaoh, and let them keep food in the cities. And that food shall be for store to the land against the seven years of famine, which shall be in the land of Egypt; that the land perish not through the famine.

And the thing was good in the eyes of Pharaoh, and in the eyes of all his servants. And Pharaoh said unto his servants, Can we find such a one as this is, a man in whom the Spirit of God is? And Pharaoh said unto Joseph, Forasmuch as God hath shewed thee all this, there is none so discreet and wise as thou art: Thou shalt be over my house, and according unto thy word shall all my people be ruled: only in the throne will I be greater than thou. And Pharaoh said unto Joseph, See, I have set thee over all the land of Egypt. And Pharaoh took off his ring from his hand, and put it upon Joseph's hand, and arrayed him in vestures of fine linen, and put a gold chain about his neck;

And he made him to ride in the second chariot which he had; and they cried before him, Bow the knee: and he made him ruler over all the land of Egypt. And Pharaoh said unto Joseph, I am Pharaoh, and without thee shall no man lift up his hand or foot in all the land of Egypt. And Pharaoh called Joseph's name Zaphnathpaaneah; and he gave him to wife Asenath the daughter of Potipherah priest of On. And Joseph went out over all the land of Egypt.

And Joseph was thirty years old when he stood before Pharaoh king of Egypt. And Joseph went out from the presence of Pharaoh, and went throughout all the land of Egypt. And in the seven plenteous years the earth brought forth by handfuls. And he gathered up all the food of the seven years, which were in the land of Egypt, and laid up the food in the cities: the food of the field, which was round about every city, laid he up in the same. And Joseph gathered corn as the sand of the sea, very much, until he left numbering; for it was without number. And unto Joseph were born two sons before the years of famine came, which Asenath the daughter of Potipherah priest of On bare unto him. And Joseph called the name of the firstborn Manasseh: For God, said he, hath made me forget all my toil, and all my father's house. And the name of the second called he Ephraim: For God hath caused me to be fruitful in the land of my affliction.

And the seven years of plenteousness, that was in the land of Egypt, were ended. And the seven years of dearth began to come, according as Joseph had said: and the dearth was in all lands; but in all the land of Egypt there was bread. And when all the land of Egypt was famished, the people cried to Pharaoh for bread: and Pharaoh said unto all the Egyptians, Go unto Joseph; what he saith to you, do. And the famine was over all the face of the earth: And Joseph opened all the storehouses, and sold unto the Egyptians; and the famine waxed sore in the land of Egypt. And all countries came into Egypt to Joseph for to buy corn; because that the famine was so sore in all lands. KJV

And it came to pass after these things, that the butler of the king of Egypt and his baker offended their lord the king of Egypt. And Pharaoh was wroth against his two officers, against the chief of the butlers, and against the chief of the bakers. And he put them in ward in the house of the captain of the guard, into the prison, the place where Joseph was bound. And the captain of the guard charged Joseph with them, and he ministered unto them: and they continued a season in ward.

And **they dreamed a dream both of them,** each man his dream, in one night, each man according to the interpretation of his dream, the butler and the baker of the king of Egypt, who were bound in the prison. And Joseph came in unto them in the morning, and saw them, and, behold, they were sad. And he asked Pharaoh's officers that were with him in ward in his master's house, saying, Wherefore look ye so sad to-day? And they said unto him, **We have dreamed a dream, and there is none that can interpret it. And Joseph said unto them, Do not interpretations belong to God? tell it me, I pray you.** And the chief butler told his dream to Joseph, and said to him, In my dream, behold, a vine was before me; and in the vine were three branches: and it was as though it budded, and its blossoms shot forth; and the clusters thereof brought forth ripe grapes: and Pharaoh's cup was in my hand; and I took the grapes, and pressed them into Pharaoh's cup, and I gave the cup into Pharaoh's hand. And **Joseph said unto him, This is the interpretation of it: the three branches are three days; within yet three days shall Pharaoh lift up thy head, and restore thee unto thine office: and thou shalt give Pharaoh's cup into his hand, after the former manner when thou wast his butler. But have me in thy remembrance when it shall be well with thee,**

and show kindness, I pray thee, unto me, and make mention of me unto Pharaoh, and bring me out of this house: for indeed I was stolen away out of the land of the Hebrews: and here also have I done nothing that they should put me into the dungeon. When the chief baker saw that the interpretation was good, he said unto Joseph, I also was in my dream, and, behold, three baskets of white bread were on my head: and in the uppermost basket there was of all manner of baked food for Pharaoh; and the birds did eat them out of the basket upon my head. And Joseph answered and said, This is the interpretation thereof: the three baskets are three days; within yet three days shall Pharaoh lift up thy head from off thee, and shall hang thee on a tree; and the birds shall eat thy flesh from off thee.

And it came to pass the third day, which was Pharaoh's birthday, that he made a feast unto all his servants: and he lifted up the head of the chief butler and the head of the chief baker among his servants. And he restored the chief butler unto his butlership again; and he gave the cup into Pharaoh's hand: but he hanged the chief baker: **as Joseph had interpreted to them. Yet did not the chief butler remember Joseph, but forgat him.**

And it came to pass at the end of two full years, that **Pharaoh dreamed**: and, behold, he stood by the river. And, behold, there came up out of the river seven kine, well-favored and fat-fleshed; and they fed in the reed-grass. And, behold, seven other kine came up after them out of the river, ill-favored and lean-fleshed, and stood by the other kine upon the brink of the river. And the ill-favored and lean-fleshed kine did eat up the seven well-favored and fat kine. So Pharaoh awoke. And he slept and dreamed a second time: and, behold, seven ears of grain came up upon one stalk, rank and good. And, behold, seven ears, thin and blasted with the east wind, sprung up after them. And the thin ears swallowed up the seven rank and full ears. And Pharaoh awoke, and, behold, it was a dream. And it came to pass in the morning that his spirit was troubled; **and he sent and called for all the magicians of Egypt, and all the wise men thereof: and Pharaoh told them his dream; but there was none that could interpret them unto Pharaoh.**

Then spake the chief butler unto Pharaoh, saying**, I do remember my faults this day:** Pharaoh was wroth with his servants, and put me in ward in the house of the captain of the guard, me and the chief baker: and we dreamed a dream in one night, I and he; we dreamed each man according to the interpretation of his dream. **And there was with us there a young man, a Hebrew, servant to the captain of the guard; and we told him, and he interpreted to us our dreams; to each man according to his dream he did interpret. And it came to pass, as he interpreted to us, so it was; me he restored unto mine office, and him he hanged.**

Then Pharaoh sent and called Joseph, and they brought him hastily out of the dungeon: and he shaved himself, and changed his raiment, and came in unto Pharaoh. **And Pharaoh said unto Joseph**, **I have dreamed a dream, and there is none that can interpret it: and I have heard say of thee, that when thou hearest a dream thou canst interpret it. And Joseph answered Pharaoh, saying, It is not in me: God will give Pharaoh an answer of peace**. And Pharaoh spake unto Joseph, In my dream, behold, I stood upon the brink of the river: and, behold, there came up out of the river seven kine, fat-fleshed and well-favored: and they fed in the reed-grass: and, behold, seven other kine came up after them, poor and very ill-favored and lean-fleshed, such as I never saw in all the land of Egypt for badness: and the lean and ill-favored kine did eat up the first seven fat kine: and when they had eaten them up, it could not be known that they had eaten them; but they were still ill-favored, as at the beginning. So I awoke. And I saw in my dream, and, behold, seven ears came up upon one stalk, full and good: and, behold, seven ears, withered, thin, and blasted with the east wind, sprung up after them: and the thin ears swallowed up the seven good ears: and I told it unto the magicians; but there was none that could declare it to me.

And Joseph said unto Pharaoh, **The dream of Pharaoh is one: what God is about to do he hath declared unto Pharaoh. The seven good kine are seven years; and the seven good ears are seven years: the dream is one. And the seven lean and ill-favored kine that came up after them are seven years, and also the seven empty ears blasted with the east wind; they shall be seven years of famine.** That is the thing which I spake unto Pharaoh: **what God is about to do he hath showed unto Pharaoh.** Behold, there come seven years of great plenty throughout all the land of Egypt: and there shall arise after them seven years of famine; and all the plenty shall be forgotten in the land of Egypt; and the famine shall consume the land; and the plenty shall not be known in the land by reason of that famine which followeth; for it shall be very grievous. **And for that the dream was doubled unto Pharaoh, it is because the thing is established by God, and God will shortly bring it to pass**. Now therefore let Pharaoh look out a man discreet and wise, and set him over the land of Egypt. Let Pharaoh do this, and let him appoint overseers over the land, and take up the fifth part of the land of Egypt in the seven plenteous years. And let them gather all the food of these good years that come, and lay up grain under the hand of Pharaoh for food in the cities, and let them keep it. And the food shall be for a store to the land against the seven years of famine, which shall be in the land of Egypt; that the land perish not through the famine.

And the thing was good in the eyes of Pharaoh, and in the eyes of all his servants. **And Pharaoh said unto his servants, Can we find such a one as this, a man in whom the spirit of God is? And Pharaoh said unto Joseph, Forasmuch as God hath showed thee all of this, there is none so discreet and wise as thou: thou shalt be over my house, and according unto thy word shall all my people be ruled: only in the throne will I be greater than thou**. And Pharaoh said unto Joseph, See, I have set thee over all the land of Egypt. And Pharaoh took off his signet ring from his hand, and put it upon Joseph's hand, and arrayed him in vestures of fine linen, and put a gold chain about his neck; and he made him to ride in the second chariot which he had; and they cried before him, Bow the knee: and he set him over all the land of Egypt. And Pharaoh said unto Joseph, I am Pharaoh, and without thee shall no man lift up his hand or his foot in all the land of Egypt. And Pharaoh called Joseph's name Zaphenath-paneah; and he gave him to wife Asenath, the daughter of Poti-phera priest of On. And Joseph went out over the land of Egypt.

And Joseph was thirty years old when he stood before Pharaoh king of Egypt. And Joseph went out from the presence of Pharaoh, and went throughout all the land of Egypt. And in the seven plenteous years the earth brought forth by handfuls. And he gathered up all the food of the seven years which were in the land of Egypt, and laid up the food in the cities: the food of the field, which was round about every city, laid he up in the same. And Joseph laid up grain as the sand of the sea, very much, until he left off numbering; for it was without number. And unto Joseph were born two sons before the year of famine came, whom Asenath, the daughter of Potiphera priest of On, bare unto him.

And Joseph called the name of the first-born Manasseh: For, said he, God hath made me forget all my toil, and all my father's house. And the name of the second called he Ephraim: For God hath made me fruitful in the land of my affliction.

And the seven years of plenty, that was in the land of Egypt, came to an end. And the seven years of famine began to come, according as Joseph had said: and there was famine in all lands; but in all the land of Egypt there was bread. And when all the land of Egypt was famished, the people cried to Pharaoh for bread: and Pharaoh said unto all the Egyptians, Go unto Joseph; what he saith to you, do. **And the famine was over all the face of the earth: and Joseph opened all the store-houses, and sold unto the Egyptians; and the famine was sore in the land of Egypt. And all countries came into Egypt to Joseph to buy grain, because the famine was sore in all the earth.** ASV

Daniel 2:1-49

One night during the second year of his reign, Nebuchadnezzar had a dream that disturbed him so much that he couldn't sleep. **He called in his magicians, enchanters, sorcerers, and astrologers, and he demanded that they tell him what he had dreamed.** As they stood before the king, he said, "I have had a dream that troubles me. Tell me what I dreamed, for I must know what it means."

Then **the astrologers answered the king in Aramaic, "Long live the king! Tell us the dream, and we will tell you what it means."**

But **the king said to the astrologer, "I am serious about this. If you don't tell me what my dream was and what it means, you will be torn limb from limb**, and your houses will be demolished into heaps of rubble! **But if you tell me what I dreamed and what the dream means, I will give you many wonderful gifts and honors. Just tell me the dream and what it means!"**

They said again, **"Please, Your Majesty. Tell us the dream, and we will tell you what it means."**

The king replied, **"I can see through your trick!** You are trying to stall for time because you know I am serious about what I said. If you don't tell me the dream, you will be condemned. **You have conspired to tell me lies in hopes that something will** change. **But tell me the dream, and then I will know that you can tell me what it means."**

The astrologers replied to the king. **"There isn't a man alive who can tell Your Majesty his dream! And no king, however great and powerful, has ever asked such a thing of any magician, enchanter, or astrologer! This is an impossible thing the king requires. No one except the gods can tell you your dream, and they do not live among people."**

The king was furious when he heard this, and he sent out orders to execute all the wise men of Babylon.

And because of the king's decree, **men were sent to find and kill Daniel and his friends**. When Arioch, the commander of the king's guard, came to kill them, Daniel handled the situation with wisdom and discretion. He asked Arioch, "Why has the king issued such a harsh decree?" So Arioch told him all that had happened. Daniel went at once to see the king and requested more time so he could tell the king what the dream meant.

Then **Daniel went home and told his friends Hananiah, Mishael, and Azariah what had happened. He urged them to ask the God of heaven to show them his mercy by telling them the secret, so they would not be executed along with the other wise men of Babylon. That night the secret was revealed to Daniel in a vision.** Then Daniel praised the God of heaven, saying,

"Praise the name of God forever and ever,
For he alone has all wisdom and power.
He determines the course of world events;
He removes kings and sets others on the throne.
He gives wisdom to the wise
And knowledge to the scholars.
He reveals deep and mysterious things
And knows what lies hidden in darkness,
Though he himself is surrounded by light.
I thank and praise you, God of my ancestors,
For you have given me wisdom and strength.
You have told me what we asked of you
And revealed to us what the king demanded."

Then Daniel went in to see Arioch, who had been ordered to execute the wise men of Babylon. Daniel said to him, "Don't kill the wise men. Take me to the king, and I will tell him the meaning of his dream."

Then Arioch quickly took Daniel to the king and said, "**I have found one of the captives from Judah who will tell Your Majesty the meaning of your dream!"**

The king said to Daniel (also known as Belteshazzar), "Is this true? Can you tell me what my dream was and what it means?"

Daniel replied, "There are no wise men, enchanters, magicians, or fortune-tellers who can tell the king such things. But there is a God in heaven who reveals secrets, and he has shown King Nebuchadnezzar what will happen in the future. Now I will tell you your dream and the visions you saw as you lay on your bed.

"While Your Majesty was sleeping, you dreamed about coming events. **The revealer of mysteries has shown you what is going to happen. And it is not because I am wiser than any living person that I know the secret of your dream, but because God wanted you to understand what you were thinking about.**

"Your Majesty, in your vision you saw in front of you a huge and powerful statue of a man, shining brilliantly, frightening and awesome. The head of the statue was made of fine gold, its chest and arms were of silver, its belly and thighs were of bronze, and its legs were of iron, and its feet were a combination of iron and clay. But as you watched, a rock was cut from a mountain by supernatural means. It struck the feet of iron and clay, smashing them to bits. The whole statue collapsed into a heap of iron, clay, bronze, silver, and gold. The pieces were crushed as small as chaff on a threshing floor, and the wind blew them all away without a trace. But the rock that knocked the statue down became a great mountain that covered the whole earth.

"That was the dream; now I will tell Your Majesty what it means. Your Majesty, you are a king over many kings. **The God of heaven has given you sovereignty, power, strength, and honor. He has made you the ruler over all the inhabited world**

and has put even the animals and birds under your control. You are the head of gold.

"But after your kingdom comes to an end, another great kingdom, inferior to yours, will rise to take your place. After that kingdom has fallen, yet a third great kingdom, represented by the bronze belly and thighs, will rise to rule the world. Following that kingdom, there will be a fourth great kingdom, as strong as iron. That kingdom will smash and crush all previous empires, just as iron smashes and crushes everything it strikes. The feet and toes you saw that were a combination of iron and clay show that this kingdom will be divided. Some parts of it will be as strong as iron, and others as weak as clay. This mixture of iron and clay also shows that these kingdoms will try to strengthen themselves by forming alliances with each other through intermarriage. But this will not succeed, just as iron and clay do not mix.

"**During the reign of those kings, the God of heaven will set up a kingdom that will never be destroyed; no one will ever conquer it. It will shatter all these kingdoms into nothingness, but it will stand forever. That is the meaning of the rock cut from the mountain by supernatural means, crushing to dust the statue of iron, bronze, clay, silver, and gold.**

"The great God has shown Your Majesty what will happen in the future. The dream is true, and its meaning is certain."

Then king Nebuchadnezzar bowed to the ground before Daniel and worshiped him, and he commanded his people to offer sacrifice and burn sweet incense before him. **The king said to Daniel, "Truly, your God is the God of gods, the Lord over kings, a revealer of mysteries, for you have been able to reveal this secret."**

Then the king appointed Daniel to a high position and gave him many valuable gifts. He made Daniel ruler over the whole province of Babylon, as well as chief over all his wise men. At Daniel's request, the king appointed Shadrach, Meshach, and Abednego to be in charge of all the affairs of the province of Babylon, while Daniel remained in the king's court. NLT

And in the second year of the reign of Nebuchadnezzar Nebuchadnezzar dreamed dreams, wherewith his spirit was troubled, and his sleep brake from him. **Then the king commanded to call the magicians, and the astrologers, and**

the sorcerers, and the Chaldeans, for to shew the king his dreams. So they came and stood before the king. And the king said unto them, **I have dreamed a dream, and my spirit was troubled to know the dream. Then spake the Chaldeans to the king in Syriack, O king, live for ever: tell thy servants the dream, and we will shew the interpretation. The king answered and said to the Chaldeans, The thing is gone from me: if ye will not make known unto me the dream, with the interpretation thereof, ye shall be cut in pieces, and your houses shall be made a dunghill. But if ye shew the dream, and the interpretation thereof, ye shall receive of me gifts and rewards and great honour: therefore shew me the dream, and the interpretation thereof. They answered again and said, Let the king tell his servants the dream, and we will shew the interpretation of it. The king answered and said, I know of certainty that ye would gain the time, because ye see the thing is gone from me. But if ye will not make known unto me the dream, there is but one decree for you: for ye have prepared lying and corrupt words to speak before me, till the time be changed: therefore tell me the dream, and I shall know that ye can shew me the interpretation thereof.**

The Chaldeans answered before the king, and said, There is not a man upon the earth that can shew the king's matter: therefore there is no king, lord, nor ruler, that asked such things at any magician, or astrologer, or Chaldean. And it is a rare thing that the king requireth, and there is none other that can shew it before the king, except the gods, whose dwelling is not with flesh. For this cause the king was angry and very furious, and commanded to destroy all the wise men of Babylon. And the decree went forth that the wise men should be slain; and they sought Daniel and his fellows to be slain.

Then Daniel answered with counsel and wisdom to Arioch the captain of the king's guard, which was gone forth to slay the wise men of Babylon: He answered and said to Arioch the king's captain, Why is the decree so hasty from the king? Then Arioch made the thing known to Daniel. **Then Daniel went in, and desired of the king that he would give him time, and that he would shew the king the interpretation. Then Daniel went to his house, and made the thing known to Hananiah, Mishael, and Azariah, his companions: That they would desire mercies of the God of heaven concerning this secret; that Daniel and his fellows should not perish with the rest of the wise men of Babylon.**

Then was the secret revealed unto Daniel in a night vision. Then Daniel blessed the God of heaven. Daniel answered and said, Blessed be the name of God for ever and ever: for wisdom and might are his: And he changeth the times and the seasons: he removeth kings, and setteth up kings: he giveth wisdom unto the wise, and knowledge to them that know understanding: He revealeth the deep and secret things: he knoweth what is in the darkness, and the light dwelleth with him. I thank thee, and praise thee, O thou God of my fathers, who hast given me wisdom and might, and hast made known unto me now what we desired of thee: for thou hast now made known unto us the king's matter.

Therefore Daniel went in unto Arioch, whom the king had ordained to destroy the wise men of Babylon: he went and said thus unto him; Destroy not the wise men of Babylon: **bring me in before the king, and I will shew unto the king the interpretation.** Then Arioch brought in Daniel before the king in haste, and said thus unto him, I have found a man of the captives of Judah, that will make known unto the king the interpretation. The king answered and said to Daniel, whose name was Belteshazzar, **Art thou able to make known unto me the dream which I have seen, and the interpretation thereof? Daniel answered in the presence of the king, and said, The secret which the king hath demanded cannot the wise men, the astrologers, the magicians, the soothsayers, shew unto the king; But there is a God in heaven that revealeth secrets, and maketh known to the king Nebuchadnezzar what shall be in the latter days.** Thy dream, and the visions of thy head upon thy bed, are these; As for thee, O king, thy thoughts came into thy mind upon thy bed, what should come to pass hereafter: and he that revealeth secrets maketh known to thee what shall come to pass. **But as for me, this secret is not revealed to me for any wisdom that I have more than any living, but for their sakes that shall make known the interpretation to the king, and that thou mightest know the thoughts of thy heart.**

Thou, O king, sawest, and behold a great image. This great image, whose brightness was excellent, stood before thee; and the form thereof was terrible. This image's head was of fine gold, his breast and his arms of silver, his belly and his thighs of brass, His legs of iron, his feet part of iron and part of clay. Thou sawest till that a stone was cut out without hands, which smote the image upon his feet that were of iron and clay, and brake them to pieces. Then was the iron, the clay, the brass, the silver, and the gold, broken to pieces together, and became like the chaff of the summer threshingfloors; and the wind carried them away, that no place was found for them: and the stone that smote the image became a great mountain, and filled the whole earth.

This is the dream; and we will tell the interpretation thereof before the king. Thou, O king, art a king of kings: for the God of heaven hath given thee a kingdom, power, and strength, and glory. And wheresoever the children of men dwell, the beasts of the field and the fowls of the heaven hath he given into thine hand, and hath made thee ruler over them all. Thou art this head of gold. And after thee shall arise another kingdom inferior to thee, and another third kingdom of brass, which shall bear rule over all the earth. And the fourth kingdom shall be strong as iron: forasmuch as iron breaketh in pieces and subdueth all things: and as iron that breaketh all these, shall it break in pieces and bruise. And whereas thou sawest the feet and toes, part of potter's clay, and part of iron, the kingdom shall be divided; but there shall be in it of the strength of the iron, forasmuch as thou sawest the iron mixed with miry clay. And as the toes of the feet were part of iron, and part of clay, so the kingdom shall be partly strong, and partly broken. And whereas thou sawest iron mixed with miry clay, they shall mingle themselves with the seed of men: but they shall not cleave one to another, even as iron is not mixed with clay. **And in the days of these kings shall the God of heaven set up a kingdom, which shall never be destroyed: and the kingdom shall not be left to other people, but it shall break in pieces and consume all these kingdoms, and it shall stand for ever.** Forasmuch as thou sawest that the stone was cut out of the mountain without hands, and that it brake in pieces the iron, the brass, the clay, the silver, and the gold; **the great God hath made known to the king what shall come to pass hereafter: and the dream is certain, and the interpretation thereof sure.**

Then the king Nebuchadnezzar fell upon his face, and worshipped Daniel, and commanded that they should offer an oblation and sweet odours unto him. The king answered unto Daniel, and said, **Of a truth it is, that your God is a**

God of gods, and a Lord of kings, and a revealer of secrets, seeing thou couldest reveal this secret. Then the king made Daniel a great man, and gave him many great gifts, and made him ruler over the whole province of Babylon, and chief of the governors over all the wise men of Babylon. Then Daniel requested of the king, and he set Shadrach, Meshach, and Abed–nego, over the affairs of the province of Babylon: but Daniel sat in the gate of the king. KJV

What does God do to people who do not obey him and still turn to or become involved with the Supernatural?

You've already read Revelation 21:8 earlier in the chapter. So here are a few more scriptures to look at.

Acts 13:6-12

And when they had gone through the whole island unto Paphos, they **found a certain sorcerer, a false prophet, a Jew, whose name was Bar-jesus**; who was with **the proconsul**, Sergius Paulus, a man of understanding. The same **called unto him Barnabas and Saul, and sought to hear the word of God. But Elymas the sorcerer (for so is his name by interpretation) withstood them, seeking to turn aside the proconsul from the faith**. But Saul, who is also called **Paul, filled with the Holy Spirit, fastened his eyes on him, and said, O full of all guile and all villany, thou son of the devil, thou enemy of all righteousness, wilt thou not cease to pervert the right ways of the Lord? And now, behold, the hand of the Lord is upon thee, and thou shalt be blind,** not seeing the sun for a season. And **immediately there fell on him a mist and a darkness; and he went about seeking some to lead him by the hand. Then the proconsul, when he saw what was done, believed, being astonished at the teaching of the Lord**. ASV

They traveled through the whole island until they came to Paphos. **There they met a Jewish sorcerer and false prophet named Bar-Jesus**, who was an attendant of the proconsul, Sergius Paulus. **The proconsul, an intelligent man, sent for Barnabas and Saul because he wanted to hear the word of God. But Elymas the sorcerer (for that is what his name means) opposed them and tried to turn the proconsul from the faith.** Then Saul, who was also called **Paul, filled with the Holy Spirit, looked straight at Elymas and said, "You are a child of the devil and an enemy of everything that is right! You are full of all kinds of deceit and trickery. Will you never stop perverting the right ways of the Lord? Now the hand of the Lord is against you. You are going to be blind, and for a time you will be unable to see the light of the sun."**

Immediately mist and darkness came over him, and he groped about, seeking someone to lead him by the hand. When the proconsul saw what had happened, he believed, for he was amazed at the teaching about the Lord. NIV

Isaiah 30:1

"Woe to the obstinate children."
Declares the LORD,
"to those who carry out plans that are not mine,
Forming an alliance, but not by my Spirit,
Heaping sin upon sin. NIV

Woe to the rebellious children, saith the LORD,
That take counsel, but not of me;
And that cover with a covering, but not of my Spirit,
That they may add sin to sin. KJV

Galatians 5:19-21

When you follow the desires of your sinful nature, your lives will produce these evil results: sexual immorality, impure thoughts, eagerness for lustful pleasure, **idolatry, participation in demonic activities**, hostility, quarreling, jealousy, outbursts of anger, **selfish ambition**, divisions, **the feeling that everyone is wrong except those in your own little group**, envy, drunkenness, **wild parties, and other kinds of sin. Let me tell you again, as I have before, that anyone living that sort of life will not inherit the Kingdom of God.** NLT

Now the deeds of the flesh are evident, which are: immorality, impurity, sensuality, **idolatry, sorcery**, enmities, strife, jealousy, outbursts of anger, disputes, dissensions, **factions**, envying, drunkenness, carousing, **and things like these, of which I forewarn you, just as I have forewarned you, that those who practice such things will not inherit the kingdom of God.** NASB

The acts of the sinful nature are obvious: sexual immorality, impurity and debauchery; **idolatry and witchcraft**; hatred, discord, jealousy, fits of rage, selfish ambition, dissensions, **factions** and envy; drunkenness, orgies, **and the like. I warn you, as I did before, that those who live like this will not inherit the kingdom of God.** NIV

Isaiah 66:13-16

As one whom his mother comforteth, so will I comfort you;
And ye shall be comforted in Jerusalem.
And when ye see this, your heart shall rejoice,
And your bones shall flourish like an herb:
And the hand of the LORD shall be known towards his servants,

And his indignation towards his enemies.
For behold, the LORD will come with fire,
And with his chariots like a whirlwind,
To render his anger with fury,
And his rebuke with flames of fire.
For by fire and by his sword will the LORD plead with all flesh:
And the slain of the LORD shall by many. KJV

I will comfort you there as a child is comforted by its mother.
When you see these things, your heart will rejoice.
Vigorous health will be yours! Everyone will see the good hand of the LORD on his people—**and his anger against his enemies.**
See, the LORD is coming with fire, and his swift chariots of destruction roar like a whirlwind. He will bring punishment with the fury of his anger and the flaming fire of his hot rebuke. The LORD will punish the world by fire and by his sword, and many will be killed by the LORD. NLT

Isaiah 66:22-24

"As surely as my new heavens and earth will remain, so will you always be my people, with a name that will never disappear," Says the Lord. "All humanity will come to worship me from week to week and from month to month. **And as they go out, they will see the dead bodies of those who have rebelled against me. For the worms that devour them will never die, and the fire that burns them will never go out. All who pass by will view them with utter horror."** NLT

"As the new heavens and the new earth that I make will endure before me," declared the LORD, "so will your name and descendants endure. From one New Moon to another and from one Sabbath to another, all mankind will come and bow down before me," says the LORD. **"And they will go out and look upon the dead bodies of those who rebelled against me; their worm will not die, nor will their fire be quenched, and they will be loathsome to all mankind."** NIV

But if you stay away from the Supernatural...

Psalms 1:1

Oh, the joys of those
Who do not follow the advice of the wicked,
Or stand around with sinners, or join in with scoffers. NLT

Blessed is the man
That walketh not in the counsel of the ungodly,
Nor standeth in the way of sinners,
Nor sitteth in the seat of the scornful. KJV

Jeremiah 10:2

This is what the LORD says: "**Do not act like other nations who try to read their future in the stars. Do not be afraid of their predictions, even though other nations are terrified by them.**" NLT

Thus saith the LORD,
Learn not the way of the heathen,
And be not dismayed at the signs of heaven;
For the heathen are dismayed at them. KJV

Malachi 4:1-3

"Surely **the day is coming; it will burn like a furnace**. **All the arrogant and every evildoer will be stubble, and that day that is coming will set them on fire**." Says the LORD Almighty. "Not a root or a branch will be left to them. **But for you who revere my name, the sun of**

righteousness will rise with healing in its wings. And you will go out and leap like calves released from the stall. Then you will trample down the wicked; they will be ashes under the soles of your feet on the day when I do these things," says the Lord Almighty. NIV

"For behold, **the day is coming, burning like a furnace**; and all the arrogant and every evildoer will be chaff; and the day that is coming will set them ablaze," says the LORD of hosts, "so that it will leave them neither root nor branch." **"But for you who fear My name, the sun of righteousness will rise with healing in its wings; and you will go forth and skip about like calves from the stall. You will tread down the wicked, for they will be ashes under the soles of your feet on the day which I am preparing." Says the LORD of hosts.** NASB

I think it is pretty obvious that God wants you to BEWARE of, and stay away from... the Supernatural.

And that God alone should be your "Super-Everything".

But if you need a few more scriptures about the Supernatural: Daniel (most of the book), Revelation 22:15, Acts 8:4-24, Matthew 9:32-33 and more if you go looking.

Ezekiel 33:18-19

When the righteous turneth from his righteousness, and committeth iniquity, he shall even die thereby. But if the wicked turn from his wickedness, and do that which is lawful and right, he shall live thereby. KJV

Chapter Thirteen

Are these the END TIMES, the END OF DAYS?

Is the world about to end?
Are we looking at Armageddon… or the Rapture first?
Is there Hope?

With everything happening around the world today, from earthquakes, tsunamis, rebel uprisings, military conflicts all over, financial problems and more… a lot of people are asking these questions and others.

Let's see what the Scriptures have to say….

Matthew 24:29-31

"But immediately after the tribulation of those days THE SUN WILL BE DARKENED, AND THE MOON WILL NOT GIVE ITS LIGHT, AND THE STARS WILL FALL from the sky, and the powers of the heavens will be shaken. And then the sign of the Son of Man will appear in the sky, and then all the tribes of the earth will mourn, and they will see the SON OF MAN COMING ON THE CLOUDS OF THE SKY with power and great glory. And He will send forth His angels with A GREAT TRUMPET and THEY WILL GATHER TOGETHER His elect from the four winds, from one end of the sky to the other." NASB

Immediately after the tribulation of those days shall the sun be darkened, and the moon shall not give her light, and the stars shall fall from heaven, and

the powers of the heavens shall be shaken: And then shall appear the sign of the Son of man in heaven: and then shall all the tribes of the earth mourn, and they shall see the Son of man coming in the clouds of heaven with power and great glory. And he shall send his angels with a great sound of a trumpet, and they shall gather together his elect from the four winds, from one end of heaven to the other. KJV

Matthew 24:1-14

And **Jesus** went out from the temple, and was going on his way; and his disciples came to him to show him the buildings of the temple. But he answered and said unto them, See ye not all these things? **verily I say unto you, There shall not be left here one stone upon another, that shall not be thrown down.**
And as he sat on the mount of Olives, the disciples came unto him privately, saying, Tell us, **when shall these things be? and what shall be the sign of thy coming, and of the end of the world?** And Jesus answered and said unto them, **Take heed that no man lead you astray. For many shall come in my name, saying, I am the Christ; and shall lead many astray. And ye shall hear of wars and rumors of wars; see that ye be not troubled: for these things must needs come to pass; but the end is not yet. For nation shall rise against nation, and kingdom against kingdom; and there shall be famines and earthquakes in divers places.** But all these things are the beginning of travail. **Then shall they deliver you up unto tribulation, and shall kill you: and ye shall be hated of all the nations for my name's sake.** And then shall many stumble, and shall deliver up one another, and shall hate one another. And **many false prophets shall arise, and shall lead many astray**. And because iniquity shall be multiplied, the love of the many shall wax cold. **But he that endureth to the end, the**

same shall be saved. And this gospel of the kingdom shall be preached in the whole world for a testimony unto all the nations; **and then shall the end come**. ASV

And Jesus went out, and departed from the temple: and his disciples came to him for to shew him the buildings of the temple. **And Jesus said unto them, See ye not all these things? verily I say unto you, There shall not be left here one stone upon another, that shall not be thrown down**. And as he sat upon the mount of Olives, the disciples came unto him privately, saying, **Tell us, when shall these things be? and what shall be the sign of thy coming, and of the end of the world?** And Jesus answered and said unto them, **Take heed that no man deceive you. For many shall come in my name, saying, I am Christ; and shall deceive many. And ye shall hear of wars and rumours of wars: see that ye be not troubled: for all these things must come to pass, but the end is not yet. For nation shall rise against nation, and kingdom against kingdom: and there shall be famines, and pestilences, and earthquakes, in divers places. All these are the beginning of sorrows. Then shall they deliver you up to be afflicted, and shall kill you: and ye shall be hated of all nations for my name's sake.** And then shall many be offended, and shall betray one another, and shall hate one another. And **many false prophets shall rise, and shall deceive many.** And because iniquity shall abound, the love of many shall wax cold. **But he that shall endure unto the end, the same shall be saved**. **And this gospel of the kingdom shall be preached in all the world for a witness unto all nations; and then shall the end come.** KJV

Beware the Anti-Christ and False Prophets during these times.

Matthew 24:21-27

For then **there will be a great tribulation, such as has not occurred since the beginning of the world until now, nor ever will.** Unless those days had been cut short, no life would have been saved: but for the sake of the elect those days will be cut short. **Then if anyone says to you. 'Behold, here is the Christ,' or 'There He is,' do not believe him. For false Christs and false prophets will arise and will show great signs and wonders, so as to mislead, if possible, even the elect. Behold, I have told you in advance. So if they say to you 'Behold, He is in the wilderness,' do not go out, or, 'Behold, He is in the inner rooms,' do not believe them.**
For just as the lightning comes from the east and flashes even to the west, so will the coming of the Son of Man be. NASB

For **then shall be great tribulation, such as was not since the beginning of the world to this time, no, nor ever shall be. And except those days should be shortened, there should no flesh be saved:** but for the elect's sake those days shall be shortened. Then **if any man shall say unto you, Lo, here is Christ, or there; believe it not. For there shall arise false Christs, and false prophets, and shall shew great signs and wonders; insomuch that, if it were possible, they shall deceive the very elect. Behold, I have told you before. Wherefore if they shall say unto you, Behold, he is in the desert; go not forth: behold, he is in the secret chambers; believe it not. For as the lightning cometh out of the east, and shineth even unto the west; so shall also the coming of the Son of man be.**
KJV

For a more complete understanding read All of Matthew 24:1-35

2 Thessalonians 2:1-13

Now we beseech you, brethren, **touching the coming of our Lord Jesus Christ, and our gathering together unto him**; to the end that ye **be not quickly shaken from your mind, nor yet be troubled, either by spirit**, or by word, or by epistle as from us, as that the day of the Lord is just at hand; let no man beguile you in any wise: for it will not be, except the falling away come first, **and the man of sin be revealed, the son of perdition, he that opposeth and exalteth himself against all that is called God or that is worshipped; so that he sitteth in the temple of God, setting himself forth as God.**
Remember ye not, that, when I was yet with you, I told you these things? And now ye know that which restraineth, to the end that he may be revealed in his own season. **For the mystery of lawlessness doth already work:** only there is one that restraineth now, until he be taken out of the way. **And then shall be revealed the lawless one, whom the Lord Jesus shall slay with the breath of his mouth, and bring to nought by the manifestation of his coming;** even he, **whose coming is according to the working of Satan with all power and signs and lying wonders, and with all deceit of unrighteousness for them that perish; because they received not the love of the truth, that they might be saved.** And for this cause God sendeth them a working of error, that they should believe a lie: that they all might be judged who believed not the truth, but had pleasure in unrighteousness.
But we are bound to give thanks to God always for you, brethren beloved of the Lord, for that God chose you from the beginning unto salvation in sanctification of the Spirit and belief of the truth:

ASV

Now we beseech you, brethren, **by the coming of our Lord Jesus Christ, and by our gathering together unto him**, That ye **be not soon shaken** in mind, or be troubled, neither by spirit, nor **by word, nor by letter as from us, as that the day of Christ is at hand. Let no man deceive you by any means: for that day shall not come, except there come a falling away first, and that man of sin be revealed,**

the son of perdition; Who opposeth and exalteth himself above all that is called God, or that is worshipped; so that he as God sitteth in the temple of God, shewing himself that he is God. Remember ye not, that, when I was yet with you, I told you these things? And now ye know what withholdeth that he might be revealed in his time. For the mystery of iniquity doth already work: only he who now letteth will let, until he be taken out of the way. **And then shall that Wicked be revealed, whom the Lord shall consume with the spirit of his mouth, and shall destroy with the brightness of his coming: Even him, whose coming is after the working of Satan with all power and signs and lying wonders, And with all deceivableness of unrighteousness in them that perish; because they received not the love of the truth, that they might be saved.** And for this cause God shall send them strong delusion, that they should believe a lie: **That they all might be damned who believed not the truth, but had pleasure in unrighteousness.** But we are bound to **give thanks always to God for you, brethren beloved of the Lord, because God hath from the beginning chosen you to salvation through sanctification of the Spirit and belief of the truth:** KJV

Daniel 12:1-4

"At that time Michael, the archangel who stands guard over your nation, will arise. **Then there will be a time of anguish greater than any since nations first came into existence. But at that time every one of your people whose name is written in the book will be rescued.**
Many of those whose bodies lie dead and buried will rise up, some to everlasting life and some to shame and everlasting contempt.
Those who are wise will shine as bright as the sky, and those who turn many to righteousness will shine like stars forever.
But you, Daniel, keep this prophecy a secret; seal up the book until **the time of the end.** NLT

And at that time shall Michael stand up, the great prince which standeth for the children of thy people: and **there shall be a time of trouble, such as never was since there was a nation even to that same time: and at that time thy people shall be delivered, every one that shall be found written in the book**.
And many of them that sleep in the dust of the earth shall awake, some to everlasting life, and some to shame and everlasting contempt. And they that be wise shall shine as the brightness of the firmament; and they that turn many to righteousness as the stars for ever and ever.
But thou, O Daniel, shut up the words, and seal the book, **even to the time of the end.** KJV

Daniel 7:9-10

"I kept looking
Until thrones were set up,
And the Ancient of Days took His seat;
His vesture was like white snow
And the hair of His head like pure wool.
His throne was ablaze with flames,
Its wheels were a burning fire.
"A river of fire was flowing
And coming out from before Him;
Thousands upon thousands were attending Him,
And myriads upon myriads were standing before Him;
The court sat,
And the books were opened." NASB

I beheld till the thrones were cast down, and **the Ancient of days did sit,** whose garment was white as snow, and the hair of his head like the pure wool: his throne was like the fiery flame, and his wheels as burning fire. A fiery stream issued and came forth from before him: thousand thousands ministered unto him, and ten thousand times ten thousand stood before him: **the judgment was set, and the books were opened.**
KJV

Daniel 7:2-8

In my vision that night, I, Daniel, **saw a great storm churning the surface of a great sea, with strong winds blowing from every direction. Then four huge beasts came up out of the water, each different from the others.**
The first beast was like a lion with eagles' wings. As I watched, its wings were pulled off, and it was left standing with its two hind feet on the ground, like a human being. **And a human mind was given to it.**
Then I saw a second beast, and it looked like a bear. It was rearing up on one side, and it had three ribs in its mouth between its teeth. And I heard a voice saying to it, **"Get up! Devour many people!"**
Then the third of these strange beasts appeared, and it looked like a leopard. It had four wings like birds' wings on its back, and it had four heads. **Great authority was given to this beast.**
Then in my vision that night, I saw a fourth beast, terrifying, dreadful, and very strong. It devoured and crushed its victims with huge iron teeth and trampled what was left beneath its feet. It was different from any of the other beasts, and it had ten horns. As I was looking at the horns, suddenly another small horn appeared among them. Three of the first horns wrenched out, roots and all, to make room for it. **This little horn had eyes like human eyes and a mouth that was boasting arrogantly.** NLT

Daniel spake and said, I saw in my vision by night, and, behold, **the four winds of the heaven strove upon the great sea. And four great beasts came up from the sea, diverse one from another**. The first was like a lion, and had eagle's wings: I beheld till the wings thereof were plucked, and it was lifted up from the earth, and made stand upon the feet as a man, **and a man's heart was given to it**. And behold another beast, a second, like to a bear, and it raised up itself on one side, and it had three ribs in the mouth of it between the teeth of it: and they said thus unto it, **Arise, devour much flesh.** After this I beheld, and lo another, like a leopard, which had upon the back of it four wings of a fowl; the beast had also four heads; and dominion was given to it. After this I saw in the night visions, and behold a fourth beast, dreadful and terrible, and strong exceedingly; and it had great iron teeth: it devoured and brake in pieces, and stamped the residue with the feet of it: and it was diverse from all the beasts that were before it; and it **had ten horns. I considered the horns, and, behold, there came up among them another little horn, before whom there were three of the first horns plucked up by the roots:**

and, behold, in this horn were eyes like the eyes of man, and a mouth speaking great things. KJV

To help you better understand all these 'Beast' references it might be good to look at some of today's many books, or television specials about The End Times, or even attend a Revelation seminar at church.

In most of these, the "beasts" are considered to be Nations or the Rulers of such nations or some other powerful force. Many even say the Pope of the Catholic Church will be the beast that is the antichrist... But please, the debates are everywhere...

Check all of these things out for yourself as I also take insight from many different sources to try to understand many of these scriptures.

Daniel 7:19-27

"Then **I desired to know the exact meaning of the fourth beast, which was different from all the others, exceedingly dreadful, with its teeth of iron and its claws of bronze, and which devoured, crushed and trampled down the remainder with its feet,** and the meaning of the ten horns that were on its head and the other horn which came up, and before which three of them fell, namely, that horn which had eyes and a mouth uttering great boasts and which was larger in appearance than its associates.

I kept looking, and that horn was waging war with the saints and overpowering them **until the Ancient of Days came and judgment was passed in favor of the saints of the Highest One, and the time arrived when the saints took possession of the kingdom.**

"Thus he said: '**The fourth beast will be a fourth kingdom on the earth**, which will be different from all the other kingdoms and **will devour the whole earth and tread it down and crush it.** As for the ten horns, out of this kingdom ten kings will arise; and another will arise after them, and he will be different from the previous ones and will subdue three kings. **He will speak out against the most High and wear down the saints of the Highest**

One, and he will intend to make alterations in times and in law; and they will be given into his hand for a time, times, and half a time. **But the court will sit for judgment, and his domination will be taken away, annihilated and destroyed forever**. Then the sovereignty, the dominion and the greatness of all the kingdoms under the whole heaven will be given to the people of the saints of **the Highest One; His kingdom will be an everlasting kingdom, and all the dominions will serve and obey Him.'** NASB

Then I would know the truth of the fourth beast, which was diverse from all the others, exceeding dreadful, whose teeth were of iron, and his nails of brass; which devoured, brake in pieces, and stamped the residue with his feet; And of the ten horns that were in his head, and of the other which came up, and before whom three fell; even of that horn that had eyes, and a mouth that spake very great things, whose look was more stout than his fellows. I beheld, and the same horn made war with the saints, and prevailed against them; **Until the Ancient of days came, and judgment was given to the saints of the most High; and the time came that the saints possessed the kingdom.** Thus he said, **The fourth beast shall be the fourth kingdom upon earth,** which shall be diverse from all kingdoms, and **shall devour the whole earth, and shall tread it down, and break it in pieces.** And the ten horns out of this kingdom are ten kings that shall arise: and another shall rise after them; and **he shall be diverse from the first, and he shall subdue three kings. And he shall speak great words against the most High, and shall wear out the saints of the most High, and think to change times and laws:** and they shall be given into his hand until a time and times and the dividing of time. **But the judgment shall sit, and they shall take away his dominion, to consume and to destroy it unto the end.** And the kingdom and dominion, and the greatness of the kingdom under the whole heaven, shall be given to the people of the saints of the **most High, whose kingdom is an everlasting kingdom, and all dominions shall serve and obey him.** KJV (time, times, and half a time is generally agreed to mean a year, 2 years and half a year... so 3½ years total.) Check your Bible footnotes to confirm as that is where my information comes from.)

The Book of Daniel 7-12 speaks more thoroughly of the End Times or the End of Days.

Revelation 20:1-6

And I saw an angel come down from heaven, having the key of the bottomless pit and a great chain in his hand. And he laid hold on the dragon, that old serpent, which is the devil, and Satan, and bound him a thousand years, and cast him into the bottomless pit, and shut him up, and set a seal upon him, that he should deceive the nations no more, till the thousand years should be fulfilled: and after that he must be loosed a little season.
And I saw thrones, and they sat upon them, and judgment was given unto them; **and I saw the souls of them that were beheaded for the witness of Jesus, and for the word of God, and which had not worshipped the beast, neither his image, neither had received his mark upon their foreheads, or in their hands; and they lived and reigned with Christ a thousand years. But the rest of the dead lived not again until the thousand years were finished. This is the first resurrection**. Blessed and holy is he that hath part in the first resurrection: on such the second death hath no power, but they shall be priests of God and of Christ, **and shall reign with him a thousand years.** KJV

And I saw an angel coming down out of heaven, having the key of the abyss and a great chain in his hand. And **he laid hold of the dragon, the old serpent, which is the Devil and Satan, and bound him for a thousand years, and cast him into the abyss, and shut it, and sealed it over him, that he should deceive the nations no more**, until the thousand years should be finished: after this he must be loosed for a little time. **And I saw thrones, and they sat upon them, and judgment was given unto them: and I saw the souls of them that had been beheaded for the testimony of Jesus, and for the word of God, and such as worshipped not the beast, neither his image, and received not the mark upon their forehead and upon their hand; and they lived, and reigned with Christ a thousand years. The rest of the dead lived not until the thousand years should be finished. This is the first resurrection.** Blessed and holy is he that hath part in the first resurrection: over these the second death hath no power; **but they shall be priests of God and of Christ, and shall reign with him a thousand years.** ASV

1 Thessalonians 4:16-17

For the Lord himself will come down from heaven with a commanding shout, with the call of the archangel, and with the trumpet call of God. First all the Christians who have died will rise from their graves. Then, together with them, we who are still alive and remain on the earth will be caught up in the clouds to meet the Lord in the air and remain with him forever. NLT

For the Lord himself shall descend from heaven with a shout, with the voice of the archangel, and with the trump of God: and the dead in Christ shall rise first: Then we which are alive and remain shall be caught up together with them in the clouds, to meet the Lord in the air: and so shall we ever be with the Lord. ASV

Many people debate on when the “Rapture” (when those who believe in Christ, the saints, will be ‘caught up’ to him) takes place verses the “Resurrection” (or the raising of the dead). But according to this scripture they BOTH seem to happen at the same time.

Revelation 11:15

Then the seventh angel blew his trumpet, and there were loud voices shouting in heaven: **"The whole world has now become the Kingdom of our Lord and of his Christ, and he will reign forever and ever."** NLT

And the seventh angel sounded; and there were great voices in heaven, saying, **The kingdoms of this world are become the kingdoms of our Lord, and of his Christ; and he shall reign for ever and ever.** KJV

1 Corinthians 15:51-52

But let me tell you a wonderful secret God has revealed to us. Not all of us will die, but we will all be transformed. **It will happen in a moment, in the blinking of an eye, when the last trumpet is blown. For when the trumpet sounds, the Christians who have died will be raised with transformed bodies. And then we who are living will be transformed so that we will never die.** NLT

Behold, I shew you a mystery; **We shall not all sleep, but we shall all be changed, In a moment, in the twinkling of an eye, at the last trump:** for the trumpet shall sound, **and the dead shall be raised** incorruptible, and we shall be changed. KJV

Let us look at something more in the news…

Psalms 83:4-5

"Come," they say, **"Let us wipe out Israel as a nation. We will destroy the very memory of its existence." This was their unanimous decision. They signed a treaty as allies against you.** NLT

They have said, **Come, and let us cut them off from being a nation**
That the name of Israel may be no more in remembrance.
For they have consulted together with one consent:
They are confederate against thee. KJV

Israel is always on the defensive from the Muslim countries who vow to destroy it... but now even the U.N. is aligning against Israel in favor of the Palestinians. And for the first time... AMERICA is not supporting Israel as it has always done! Woe to the countries that attack... or turn their backs on... Israel.

Isaiah 54:9-15

"Just as I swore in the time of Noah that I would never again let flood cover the earth and destroy its life, so now I swear that I will never again pour out my anger on you. **For the mountains may depart and the hills disappear, but even then I will remain loyal to you.** My covenant of blessing will never be broken," says the LORD, who has mercy on you. **O storm-battered city, troubled and desolate!** I will rebuild you on a foundation of sapphires and make the walls of your houses from precious jewels. I will make your towers of sparkling rubies and your gates and walls of singing gems. **I will teach all your citizens, and their prosperity will be great.** You will live under a government that is just and fair. Your enemies will stay far away; you will live in peace. Terror will not come near. **If any nation comes to fight you it will not be because I sent them to punish you. Your enemies will always be defeated because I am on your side.** NLT

For this is as the waters of Noah unto me: for as I have sworn that the waters of Noah should no more go over the earth; so have I sworn that I would not be wroth with thee, nor rebuke thee. **For the mountains shall depart, and the hills be removed; but my kindness shall not depart from thee, neither shall the covenant of my peace be removed, saith the LORD that hath mercy on thee**. O thou afflicted, tossed with tempest, and not comforted, behold, I will lay thy stones with fair colours, and lay thy foundations with sapphires. And I will make thy windows of agates, and thy gates of carbuncles, and all thy borders of pleasant stones. **And all thy children shall be taught of the LORD; and great shall be the peace of thy children**. In righteousness shalt thou be established: thou shalt be far from oppression; for thou shalt not fear: and from terror; for it shall not come near thee. **Behold, they shall surely gather together, but not by me: whosoever shall gather together against thee shall fall for thy sake.** KJV

Isaiah 66:22-24

"**As surely as my new heavens and earth will remain, so will you always be my people, with a name that will never disappear**." says the LORD. "**All humanity will come to worship me** from week to week and from month to month. **And as they go out, they will see the dead bodies of those who have rebelled against me. For the worms that devour them will never die, and the fire that burns them will never go out. All who pass by will view them with utter horror.**" NLT

For as the new heavens and the new earth, which I will make, shall remain before me, saith the LORD, so shall your seed and your name remain. And it shall come to pass, that from one new moon to another, and from one sabbath to another, **shall all flesh come to worship before me**, saith the LORD. **And they shall go forth, and look upon the carcasses of the men that have**

transgressed against me: for their worm shall not die, neither shall their fire be quenched; and they shall be an abhorring unto all flesh. KJV

Matthew 28:19-20

"Therefore go and make disciples of all nations, baptizing them in the name of the Father and of the Son and of the Holy Spirit, and **teaching them to obey everything I have commanded you. And surely I am with you always, to the very end of the age."** NIV

Go ye therefore, and teach all nations, baptizing them in the name of the Father, and of the Son, and of the Holy Ghost: Teaching them to observe all things whatsoever I have commanded you: and, lo, **I am with you always, even unto the end of the world. Amen.** KJV

For more information about the End Times (or End of Days): Read ALL of the book of REVELATION; a lot from the book of Isaiah; again, much of Daniel; and as you read your Bible you will be surprised at where, and how many, references you will find...

Matthew 9:37

Then He said to His disciples, "The harvest is plentiful, but the workers are few. Therefore beseech the Lord of the harvest to send out workers into His harvest." NASB

Chapter Fourteen

Why should I go to church?

How do you really learn about God?
How and when do you unashamedly show your Worship to God?
How can you love your brothers and sisters in Christ... as you are supposed to do... if you never meet them or get to know them?
How can you fulfill your part in the body of Christ (the Church), as God wants you to do... if you never go?

Here are some scriptures that mention how God feels about you going to church.

Hebrews 10:24-25

Let us consider how we may spur one another on toward love and good deeds. **Let us not give up meeting together, as some are in the habit of doing, but let us encourage one another**—and all the more as you see the Day approaching. NIV

Think of ways to encourage one another to outbursts of love and good deeds. And **let us not neglect our meeting together, as some people do, but encourage and warn each other, especially now that the day of his coming back again is drawing near.** NLT

Ephesians 4:11-13

He is the one who **gave these gifts to the church**; the apostles, the prophets, the evangelists, and the pastors and teachers. **Their responsibility is to equip God's people to do his work and build up the church,**

the body of Christ, until we come to such **unity in our faith and knowledge of God's Son that we will be mature and full grown in the Lord, measuring up to the full stature of Christ.** NLT

It was **he who gave** some to be apostles, some to be prophets, some to be evangelists, and some to be pastors and teachers, **to prepare God's people for works of service, so that the body of Christ may be built up until we all reach unity in the faith and in the knowledge of the Son of God and become mature, attaining to the whole measure of the fullness of Christ**. NIV

Psalm 149:1

Praise the LORD!
Sing to the LORD a new song,
Sing his praises in the assembly of the faithful. NLT

Praise the LORD.
Sing to the LORD a new song, **his praise in the assembly of the saints**. NIV

1 Corinthians 12:4-7

"Now there are different kinds of spiritual gifts, but it is the same Holy Spirit who is the source of them all. **There are different kinds of service in the church**, **but it is the same Lord we are serving**. There are different ways God works in our lives, but it is the same God who does the work through all of us. **A spiritual gift is given to each of us as a means of helping the entire church."** NLT

Now there are varieties of gifts, but the same Spirit. And **there are varieties of ministries, and the same Lord**. There are varieties of effects, but the same God who works all things in all persons. **But to each one is given the manifestation of the Spirit for the common good**. NASB

Luke 4:16

When he (Jesus) came to the village of Nazareth, his boyhood home, **he went as usual to the synagogue on the Sabbath** and stood up to read the Scriptures. NLT

And he came to Nazareth, where he had been brought up: and, **as his custom was, he went into the synagogue on the sabbath day**, and stood up for to read. KJV

(The synagogue was the "church" in Jesus' time, and He went AS USUAL. If it was important to Jesus, then it should be important to all of us.)

Acts 12:5-12

Peter therefore was kept in prison: but **prayer was made without ceasing of the church unto God for him**. And when Herod would have brought him forth, the same night Peter was sleeping between two soldiers, bound with two chains: and the keepers before the door kept the prison. **And, behold, the angel of the Lord came upon him, and a light shined in the prison: and he smote Peter on the side, and raised him up, saying, Arise up quickly. And his chains fell off from his hands. And the angel said unto him, Gird thyself, and bind on thy sandals. And so he did. And he saith unto him, Cast thy garment about thee, and follow me. And he went out, and followed him; and wist not that it was true which was done by the angel; but thought he saw a vision. When they were past the first and the second ward, they came unto the iron gate that leadeth unto the city; which opened to them of his own accord: and they went out, and passed on through one street; and forthwith the angel departed from him.** And when Peter was come to himself, he said, **Now I know of a surety, that the Lord hath sent his angel, and hath delivered me out of the hand of Herod,** and from all the expectation of the people of the Jews. And when he had considered the thing, he came to the house of Mary the mother of John, whose surname was Mark; **where many were gathered together praying.** KJV

So Peter was kept in prison, but **the church was earnestly praying to God for him.**

The night before Herod was to bring him to trial, Peter was sleeping between two soldiers, bound with two chains, and sentries stood guard at the entrance. **Suddenly an angel of the Lord appeared and a light shone in the cell. He struck Peter on the side and woke him up. "Quick, get up!" he said, and the chains fell off Peter's wrists.**

Then the angel said to him, "Put on your clothes and sandals." And Peter did so. "Wrap your cloak around you and follow me." the angel told him. Peter followed him out of the prison, but he had no idea that what the angel was doing was really happening; he thought he was seeing a vision. They passed the first and second guards and came to the iron gate leading to the city. It opened for them by itself, and they went through it. When they had walked the length of one street, suddenly the angel left him.

Then Peter came to himself and said, **"Now I know without a doubt that the Lord sent his angel and rescued me from Herod's clutches** and from everything the Jewish people were anticipating."

When this had dawned on him, **he went to the house of Mary the mother of John, also called Mark, where many people had gathered and were praying.** NIV

Psalm 22:22

I will declare your name to my brothers;
In the congregation I will praise you. NIV

I will tell of Your name to my brethren;
In the midst of the assembly I will praise You.
NASB

Acts 20:28-32

"And now beware! **Be sure that you feed and shepherd God's flock-his church, purchased with his blood-over who the Holy Spirit has appointed you as elders.**

I know full well that **false teachers, like vicious wolves, will come in among you after I leave**, not sparing the flock.

Even some of you will distort the truth in order to draw a following. Watch out! Remember the three years I was with you-my constant watch and care over you night and day, and my many tears for you.

And now I **entrust you to God and the word of his grace-his message that is able to build you up and give you an inheritance with all those he has set apart for himself."** NLT

Take heed unto yourselves, and to all the flock, in which the Holy Spirit hath made you bishops, to feed the church of the Lord which he purchased with his own blood. I know that after my departing grievous wolves shall enter in among you, not sparing the flock; and **from among your own selves shall men arise, speaking perverse things, to draw away the disciples after them.** Wherefore watch ye, remembering that by the space of three years I ceased not to admonish every one night and day with tears. And now **I commend you to God, and to the word of his grace, which is able to build you up, and to give you the inheritance among all them that are sanctified**. ASV

Hebrews 3:12-13

See to it, brothers, that none of you has a sinful, unbelieving heart that turns away from the living God. But **encourage one another daily, as long as it is called Today, so that none of you may be hardened by sin's deceitfulness.** NIV

Be careful then, dear brothers and sisters. Make sure that your own hearts are not evil and unbelieving, turning you away from the living God. **You must warn each other every day, as long as it is called "today," so that none of you will be deceived by sin and hardened against God**. NLT

Colossians 3:16

Let the words of Christ, in all their richness, live in your hearts and make you wise. **Use his words to teach and**

counsel each other. Sing psalms and hymns and spiritual songs to God with thankful hearts. NLT

Let the word of Christ dwell in you richly in all wisdom; **teaching and admonishing one another in psalms and hymns and spiritual songs, singing with grace in your hearts to the Lord.** KJV

Matthew 18:20

"**For where two or three come together in my name, there am I with them**." NIV

For where two or three are gathered together in my name, there am I in the midst of them. KJV

There are a lot more scriptures about this subject... but why don't you check out a local church... or two.

Any church that believes that Jesus Christ is the son of God and man, and lived and died for our sins... and rose again on the third day, is a Christian Church. But from there they vary greatly: Baptist, Non-Denominational, Lutheran, Pentecostal, Catholic... and yes, the list goes on.

If you went to a church before that you were unhappy with... try a different one! You may not have liked it because that was God's way of moving you to a Church where they really need your help, or where they have the ability to really help YOU.

If you haven't really been to a Church before... please try a few out. Sometimes one church will actually have more than one type of service: Classical, Modern, etc.

And just changing services, rather than Churches will put you where God is trying to lead you.

Only God knows who you will meet, what you will hear or see, and what kind of impact it may have on your life. Or what kind of impact you may have on another's.

I hope I bump into a few of you at Church!

Chapter Fifteen

OTHER QUESTIONS OR SUNDRY COMMANDMENTS:

The following are questions or commandments that either have a connection of some kind to previous questions… or I felt the Holy Spirit guiding me to list them here.

I will not list very many, but please look these up on your own and try to find more if the question/commandment interests you.

What does the Bible say about…

Can I lose my salvation?

Revelation 21:8

"**But cowards who turn from me**, and unbelievers, and the corrupt, and murderers, and the immoral, and those who practice witchcraft, and idol worshippers, and all liars—**their doom is in the lake that burns with fire and sulfur. This is the second death."** NLT

But **the fearful,** and unbelieving, and the abominable, and murderers, and whoremongers, and sorcerers, and idolaters, and all liars, **shall have their part in the lake which burneth with fire and brimstone: which is the second death.** KJV

Deuteronomy 30:17-18

But if your heart turns away and you are not obedient, and if you are drawn away to bow down to other gods and worship them. I declare to you this day that you will certainly be

destroyed. You will not live long in the land you are crossing the Jordan to enter and possess. NIV

But if your heart turns away and you refuse to listen, and if you are drawn away to serve and worship other gods, then I warn you now that you will certainly be destroyed. You will not live a long, good life in the land you are crossing the Jordan to occupy. NLT

Hebrews 10:39

But **we are not like those who turn their backs on God and seal their fate**. We have faith that assures our salvation. NLT

But **we are not of them who draw back unto perdition;** but of them that believe to the saving of the soul. KJV

Matthew 10:16-22

Behold, I send you forth as sheep in the midst of wolves: **be ye therefore wise as serpents, and harmless as doves. But beware of men: for they will deliver you up to the councils, and they will scourge you in their synagogues; And ye shall be brought before governors and kings for my sake, for a testimony against them and the Gentiles. But when they deliver you up, take no thought how or what ye shall speak: for it shall be given you in that same hour what ye shall speak. For it is not ye that speak, but the Spirit of your Father which speaketh in you. And the brother shall deliver up the brother to death, and the father the child: and the children shall rise up against their parents, and cause them to be put to death. And ye shall be hated of all men for my name's sake: but he that endureth to the end shall be saved**. KJV

"I am sending you out like sheep among wolves. **Therefore be as shrewd as snakes and as innocent as doves.**

"Be on your guard against men; they will hand you over to the local councils and flog you in their synagogues. On my account you

will be brought before governors and kings as witnesses to them and to the Gentiles. But when they arrest you, do not worry about what to say or how to say it. At that time you will be given what to say, for it will not be you speaking, but the Spirit of your Father speaking through you.

"Brother will betray brother to death, and a father his child; children will rebel against their parents and have them put to death. All men will hate you because of me, but he who stands firm to the end will be saved. NIV

Revelation 2:10

Fear none of those things which thou shalt suffer: behold, the devil shall cast some of you into prison, that ye may be tried; and ye shall have tribulation ten days: be thou faithful unto death, and I will give thee a crown of life. KJV

Don't be afraid of what you are about to suffer. The Devil will throw some of you into prison and put you to the test. You will be persecuted for 'ten days.' **Remain faithful even when facing death, and I will give you the crown of life.** NLT

1 Peter 2:11

Dear friends, I urge you, as aliens and strangers in the world, to **abstain from sinful desires**, **which war against your soul**. NIV

Beloved, I urge you as aliens and strangers to **abstain from fleshly lusts which wage war against the soul.** NASB

Galatians 5:19-21

When you follow the desires of your sinful nature, your lives will produce these evil results: sexual immorality, impure thoughts, eagerness for lustful pleasure, idolatry, participation in demonic activities, hostility, quarreling, jealousy, outbursts of anger, selfish ambition, divisions, the feeling that everyone is wrong except those in your own little group, envy, drunkenness, **wild parties, and other kinds of sin. Let me tell you again, as I have before, that anyone living that sort of life will not inherit the Kingdom of God.** NLT

Now the works of the flesh are manifest, which are these; **Adultery, fornication, uncleanness, lasciviousness**, idolatry, witchcraft, hatred, variance, emulations, wrath, strife, seditions, heresies, envying, murders, drunkenness, **revellings**, and such like: of the which I tell you before, as I have also told you in time past, that **they which do such things shall not inherit the kingdom of God.**
KJV

Malachi 3:10

Even now **the ax of God's judgment is poised, ready to sever your roots.** Yes, **every tree that does not produce good fruit will be chopped down and thrown into the fire.** NLT

The axe is already laid at the root of the trees; therefore every tree that does not bear good fruit is cut down and thrown into the fire. NASB

Hebrews 3:15-19

Whilst it is said, **To day if ye will hear his voice, harden not your hearts, as in the provocation. For some, when they had heard, did provoke: howbeit not all that came out of Egypt by Moses. But with whom was he grieved forty years**? **was it not with them that had sinned,** whose carcases fell in the wilderness? **And to whom sware he that they should not**

enter into his rest, but to them that believed not? So we see that they could not enter in because of unbelief. KJV

As has just been said:
**"Today, if you hear his voice,
Do not harden your hearts
As you did in the rebellion."**
Who were they who heard and rebelled? Were they not all those Moses led out of Egypt? And with whom was he angry for forty years? Was it not with those who sinned, whose bodies fell in the desert? And to whom did God swear that they would never enter his rest if not to those who disobeyed? So we see that they were not able to enter, because of their unbelief. NIV

Revelation 3:5

He who overcomes will thus be clothed in white garments; and **I will not erase his name from the book of life**, and I will confess his name before My Father and before His angels. NASB

All who are victorious will be clothed in white. **I will never erase their names from the Book of Life,** but I will announce before my Father and his angels that they are mine. NLT

If we are already Christians, already saved just by knowing Jesus, then…
What/why do we have to "overcome"?
Why so much talk about "the war for your soul"? And "Being faithful until the end"?
Or even talk of "Cowards WHO TURN AWAY FROM ME"?

Could it be God is warning you that while HE is faithful and will stand by YOU… IF you let SIN (and Satan) win its war with you, it causes YOU to Turn Away from God (reject his commandments, values… HIM) and hence it is YOU who throws away your salvation?

I cannot say for sure with so many scriptures that seem vague on the issue. But if you are concerned you may want to read more Bible scriptures, other books on the topic, or ask your church pastor/preacher/etc. their opinion.

Circumcision?

Genesis 17:10-14

"This is the covenant that you and your descendants must keep: Each male among you must be circumcised; the flesh of his foreskin must be cut off. This will be a sign that you and they have accepted this covenant. Every male child must be circumcised on the eighth day after his birth. This applies not only to members of your family, but also to the servants born in your household and the foreign-born servants whom you have purchased. **All must be circumcised**. Your bodies will thus bear the mark of my everlasting covenant. **Anyone who refuses to be circumcised will be cut off from the covenant family for violating the covenant."** NLT

This is my covenant, which ye shall keep, between me and you and thy seed after thee; Every man child among you shall be circumcised. And ye shall circumcise the flesh of your foreskin; and it shall be a token of the covenant betwixt me and you. And he that is eight days old shall be circumcised among you, every man child in your generations, he that is born in the house, or bought with money of any stranger, which is not of thy seed. He that is born in thy house, and he that is bought with thy money, **must needs be circumcised: and my covenant shall be in your flesh for an everlasting covenant. And the uncircumcised man child**

whose flesh of his foreskin is not circumcised, that soul shall be cut off from his people; he hath broken my covenant. KJV

Genesis 21:4

Then Abraham circumcised his son Isaac when he was eight days old, as God had commanded him. NASB

Eight days after Isaac was born, Abraham circumcised him as God had commanded. NLT

Leviticus 12:2-3

When a woman becomes pregnant and gives birth to a son, she will be ceremonially unclean for seven days, just as she is defiled during her menstrual period. **On the eight day, the boy must be circumcised.** NLT

Speak unto the children of Israel, saying, If a woman have conceived seed, and born a man child: then she shall be unclean seven days; according to the days of the separation for her infirmity shall she be unclean. **And in the eighth day the flesh of his foreskin shall be circumcised.** KJV

Cross-dressing?

Deuteronomy 22:5

A woman must not wear men's clothing, nor a man wear women's clothing, for the Lord your God detests anyone who does this. NIV

"A woman shall not wear man's clothing, nor shall a man put on a woman's clothing; for whoever does these things is an abomination to the LORD your God. NASB

Since cross-dressing has all the appearance of men or women wanting to be the opposite sex there are a couple of things going on here that would upset God.

The first of course, is the predominance of homosexuals that are cross-dressers. Or the many people on the verge of deciding, or announcing, that they are homosexuals.

See the chapters: Is Homosexuality a Sin? and Is Marriage only supposed to be between a Man and a Woman?

Also, even if the person is not a homosexual...(or transsexual) the person is still showing signs of wanting to be the opposite sex.

Which is a non-verbal (and sometimes verbal) way of telling God that YOU think HE was Wrong in the choices He made when He formed you and created you. God is NEVER wrong.

Cuttings, Tattoos and other body markings?

Leviticus 19:28

Do not cut your bodies for the dead **or put tattoo marks on yourselves**. I am the Lord. NIV

Never cut your bodies in mourning for the dead **or mark your skin with tattoos**, for I am the LORD. NLT

You shall not make any cuts in your body for the dead **nor** make **any tattoo marks on yourselves**: I am the LORD. NASB

1 Kings 18:26-29

Then they took the ox which was given them and **they** prepared it and **called on the name of Baal** from morning until noon **saying, "O Baal, answer us."** But there was no voice and no one answered. And they leaped about the altar which they made. It came about at noon, that Elijah mocked them and said, "Call out with a loud voice, for he is a god; either he is occupied or gone aside, or is on a journey, or perhaps he is asleep and needs to be awakened."

So they cried with a loud voice and cut themselves according to their custom with swords and lances until the blood gushed out on them. When midday was past, they raved until the time of the offering of the evening sacrifice; but there was no voice, no one answered, and no one paid attention. NASB

And they took the bullock which was given them, and they dressed it, **and called on the name of Baal from morning even until noon,** saying, **O Baal, hear us.** But there was no voice, nor any that answered. And they leaped upon the altar which was made. And it came to pass at noon, that Elijah mocked them, and said, Cry aloud: for he is a god; either he is talking, or he is pursuing, or he is in a journey, or peradventure he sleepeth, and must be awaked. And **they cried aloud, and cut themselves after their manner with knives and lancets, till the blood gushed out upon them**. And it came to pass, when midday was past, and they prophesied until the time of the offering of the evening sacrifice, that there was neither voice, nor any to answer, nor any that regarded. KJV

Deuteronomy 14:1-2

"Since you are the people of the LORD your God, never cut yourselves or shave the hair above your foreheads for the sake of the dead. You have been set apart as holy to the LORD your God, and he has chosen you to be his own special treasure from all the nations of the earth." NLT

Ye are the children of the LORD your God: ye shall not cut yourselves, nor make any baldness between your eyes for the dead. For thou art an holy people unto the LORD thy God, and the LORD hath chosen thee to be a peculiar people unto himself, above all the nations that are upon the earth. KJV

Some people cut or even mutilated themselves over lost loved ones.

But Baal worshippers, witches, and other pagans and idol worshippers marked their bodies with tattoos, scars, cut their hair in certain ways and such for their deities, or for presumed magical power...

Remember, God does not want you to act like those of the world around you. To do something that others did, especially as for another god or such... was to desecrate themselves.

1 Corinthians 3:16-17

Know ye not that ye are the temple of God, and that the Spirit of God dwelleth in you? If any man defile the temple of God, him shall God destroy; for the temple of God is holy, which temple ye are. KJV

Don't you realize that all of you together are the temple of God and that the Spirit of God lives in you? God will bring ruin upon anyone who ruins this temple. For God's temple is holy, and you Christians are that temple. NLT

So according to the scriptures, Christians are to treat their bodies as temples to God. I personally, find it hard to believe he would want you to treat it badly, damage it, or put graffiti all over it. But again, that is how I see the scriptures I have read. Please look and find the answers for yourself.

Husband as the Head of the Household?

Genesis 3:16

Then he said to the woman, "You will bear children with intense pain and suffering. And though your desire will be **for your husband, he will be your master."** NLT

Unto the woman he said, I will greatly multiply thy sorrow and thy conception; in sorrow thou shalt bring forth children; **and thy desire shall be to thy husband, and he shall rule over thee.** KJV

1 Corinthians 11:3

But I would have you know, that the head of every man is Christ; and **the head of the woman is the man**; and the head of Christ is God. KJV

Now I want you to realize that the head of every man is Christ, **and the head of the woman is man,** and the head of Christ is God. NIV

Ephesians 6:1-4

Children, obey your parents because you belong to the Lord, for this is the right thing to do. **"Honor your father and mother."** This is the first of the Ten Commandments that ends with a promise: **If you honor your father and mother, "you will live a long life, full of blessing."**

And now a word to you fathers. Don't make your children angry by the way you treat them. Rather, bring them up with the discipline and instruction approved by the Lord. NLT

Children, obey your parents in the Lord: for this is right. Honour thy father and mother; (which is the first commandment with promise;) That it may be well with thee, and thou mayest live long on the earth. **And, ye fathers, provoke not your children to wrath: but bring them up in the nurture and admonition of the Lord.** KJV

Ephesians 5:25-28

Husbands, love your wives, just as Christ loved the church and gave himself up for her to make her holy, cleansing her by the washing with water through the word, and to present her to himself as a radiant church, without stain or wrinkle or any other blemish, but holy and blameless. In this same way**, husbands ought to love their wives as their own bodies. He who loves his wife loves himself.** NIV

Husbands, love your wives, even as Christ also loved the church, and gave himself for it; That he might sanctify and cleanse it with the washing of water by the word, That he might present it to himself a glorious church, not having spot, or wrinkle, or any such thing; but that it should be holy and without blemish. **So ought men to love their wives as their own bodies. He that loveth his wife loveth himself.** KJV

Ephesians 5:33

So again I say, **each man must love his wife as he loves himself, and the wife must respect her husband.** NLT

Nevertheless **let every one of you in particular so love his wife even as himself; and the wife see that she reverence her husband.** KJV

Respect your Elders?

Leviticus 19:32

Show your fear of God by **standing up in the presence of elderly people and showing respect for the aged.** I am the LORD. NLT

'Rise in the presence of the aged, show respect for the elderly and revere your God. I am the Lord.' NIV

1 Timothy 5:8

But if any provide not for his own, and specially for those of his own house, he hath denied the faith, and is worse than an infidel. KJV

If anyone does not provide for his relatives, especially for his immediate family, he has denied the faith and is worse than an unbeliever. NIV

2 Samuel 19:31-38

And Barzillai the Gileadite came down from Rogelim, and went over Jordan with the king, to conduct him over Jordan. **Now Barzillai was a very aged man, even fourscore years old:** and he had provided the king of sustenance while he lay at Mahanaim; for he was a very great man. **And the king said unto Barzillai, Come thou over with me, and I will feed thee with me in Jerusalem.** And Barzillai said unto the king, How long have I to live, that I should go up with the king unto Jerusalem? I am this day fourscore years old: and can I discern between good and evil? can thy servant taste what I eat or what I drink? can I hear any more the voice of singing men and singing women? wherefore then should thy servant be yet a burden unto my lord the king? Thy servant will go a little way over Jordan with the king: and **why should the king recompense it me with such a reward?** Let thy servant, I pray thee, turn back again, that I may die in mine own city, and be buried by the grave of my father and of my mother. But behold thy servant Chimham; let him go over with my lord the king; and do to him what shall seem good unto thee. **And the king answered,** Chimham shall go over with me, **and I will do to him that which shall seem good unto thee: and whatsoever thou shalt require of me, that will I do for thee.** KJV

And Barzillai the Gileadite came down from Rogelim; and he went over the Jordan with the king, to conduct him over the Jordan. **Now Barzillai was a very aged man, even fourscore years old:** and he had provided the king with sustenance while he lay at Mahanaim; for he was a very great man. **And the king said unto Barzillai, Come thou over with me, and I will sustain thee with me in Jerusalem**. And Barzillai said unto the king, How many are the days of the years of my life, that I should go up with the king unto Jerusalem? I am this day fourscore years old: can I discern between good and bad? can thy servant taste what I eat or what I drink? can I hear any more the voice of singing men and singing women? wherefore then should thy servant be yet a burden unto my lord the king? Thy servant would but just go over the Jordan with the king: and why should the king recompense it me with such a reward? Let thy servant, I pray thee, turn back again, that I may die in mine own city, by the grave of my father and my mother. But behold, thy servant Chimham; let him go over with my lord the king; and do to him what shall seem good unto thee. **And the king answered,** Chimham shall go over with me, and **I will do to him that which shall seem good unto thee: and whatsoever thou shalt require of me, that will I do for thee.** ASV

Psalm 71:9

Cast me not off in the time of old age; forsake me not when my strength faileth. KJV

And now, in my old age, don't set me aside.
Don't abandon me when my strength is failing. NLT

See also the chapter: What are the Ten Commandments anyway? (the 5th Commandment: Honor your Father and Mother.)

Tithing?

Deuteronomy 14:22-23

Be sure to set aside a tenth of all that your fields produce each year. Eat the tithe of your grain, new wine and oil, and the firstborn of your herds and flocks in the presence of the LORD your God at the place he will choose as a dwelling for his Name, so that you may learn to revere the LORD your God always.
NIV

Thou shalt truly tithe all the increase of thy seed, that the field bringeth forth year by year. And thou shalt eat before the LORD thy God, in the place which he shall choose to place his name there, the tithe of thy corn, of thy wine, and of thine oil, and the firstlings of thy herds and of thy flocks; that thou mayest learn to fear the LORD thy God always. KJV

Luke 11:42

"But how terrible it will be for you Pharisees! **For you are careful to tithe even the tiniest part of your income,** but you completely forget about justice and the love of God. **You should tithe, yes,** but you should not leave undone the more important things." NLT

"Woe to you Pharisees, because **you give God a tenth of your mint, rue and all other kinds of garden herbs,** but you neglect justice and the love of God. **You should have practiced the latter without leaving the former undone."** NIV

1 Corinthians 16:1-2

Now about the money being collected for the Christians in Jerusalem: you should follow the same procedures I gave to the churches in Galatia. **On every Lord's Day, each of you should put aside some amount of money in relation to what you have earned and save it for this offering**. NLT

Now concerning the collection for the saints, as I have given order to the churches of Galatia, even so do ye. **Upon the first day of the week let every one of you lay by him in store, as God hath prospered him, that there be no gatherings when I come**. KJV

2 Corinthians 9:7-8

You must **each make up your own mind as to how much you should give. Don't give reluctantly or in response to pressure. For God loves the person who gives cheerfully. And God will generously provide all you need.** Then you will always have everything you need and plenty left over to share with others. NLT

Every man according as he purposeth in his heart, so let him give; not grudgingly, or of necessity: for God loveth a cheerful giver. And God is able to make all grace abound toward you; that ye, always having all sufficiency in all things, may abound to every good work: KJV

Leviticus 27:30

And **all the tithe of the land,** whether of the seed of the land, or of the fruit of the tree, **is the LORD's**: it is holy unto the LORD. KJV

And **all the tithe of the land, whether of the seed of the land, or of the fruit of the tree, is Jehovah's: it is holy unto Jehovah.** ASV

Deuteronomy 14:22

Thou shalt truly tithe all the increase of thy seed, that the field bringeth forth year by year. KJV

Thou shalt surely tithe all the increase of thy seed, that which cometh forth from the field year by year. ASV

Cruelty to Animals?

Proverbs 12:10

A righteous man regardeth the life of his beast: **but the tender mercies of the wicked are cruel.** KJV

The godly are concerned for the welfare of their animals, but even the kindness of the wicked is cruel. NLT

Exodus 23:4-5

"**If you come across** your enemy's **ox or donkey wandering off, be sure to take it back** to him. **If you see**

the donkey of someone who hates you **fallen down under its load, do not leave it there; be sure you help** him with it. NIV

If thou meet thine enemy's **ox or his ass going astray, thou shalt surely bring it back** to him again. **If thou see the ass** of him that hateth thee **lying under his burden and wouldest forbear to help him, thou shalt surely help with him**. KJV

Isaiah 66:2-3

Has not my hand made all these things, and so they came into being?" declares the Lord,

"This is the one I esteem:

He who is humble and contrite in spirit, and trembles at my word.

But whoever sacrifices a bull is like one who kills a man,

And whoever offers a lamb, like one who breaks a dog's neck; Whoever makes a grain offering is like one who presents pig's blood, and whoever burns memorial incense, like one who worships an idol. They have chosen their own ways, and **their souls delight in their abominations;** NIV

For all those things hath mine hand made, and all those things have been, saith the LORD: but to this man will I look, even to him that is poor and of a contrite spirit, and trembleth at my word. **He that killeth an ox is as if he slew a man; he that sacrificeth a lamb, as if he cut off a dog's neck; he that offereth an oblation, as if he offered swine's blood;** he that burneth incense, as if he blessed an idol. **Yea, they have chosen their own ways, and their soul delighteth in their abominations.** KJV

Luke 12:6

Are not five sparrows sold for two farthings, and not one of them is forgotten before God? KJV

Are not five sparrows sold for two pennies? Yet not one of them is forgotten by God. NIV

Deuteronomy 25:4

"Do not keep an ox from eating as it treads out the grain." NLT

Thou shalt not muzzle the ox when he treadeth out the corn. KJV

Do these scriptures seem to indicate that in the past it was necessary for animals to be sacrificed, or killed for food, but that HARMING an animal when it was not necessary was... and still would be... an ABOMINATION?

If that is the case then humanely killing animals for food today is acceptable. And since Jesus saved us we no longer need to make animal sacrifices.

But CRUELTY to animals is NOT acceptable to God as all animals are also God's creations and HE is concerned for their welfare and HE expects US to be concerned with their welfare.

Besides cruelty to an animal itself, another thing to consider is this:

It has been proven that people (adults and children) that are cruel to animals (even insects), if left unchecked, tend to escalate their cruelty until you get: bullies, spouse and child abusers, murderers... and yes, even serial killers. The information, studies, documentaries are all over, research it for yourself.

John 17:15

I do not ask You to take them out of the world, **but to keep them from the evil one.** NASB

I hope you found the answers to the questions you were looking into, and if not, I hope you will open up your Bible and start searching for yourself. Good Searching!

And Remember

1 Corinthians 2:9

"No eye has seen, no ear has heard, and no mind has imagined what God has prepared for those who love him." NLT

Hebrew 13:8

Jesus Christ the same yesterday,
and to day, and for ever. KJV

Matthew 28:19-20

"Therefore go and make disciples of all nations, baptizing them in the name of the Father and of the Son and of the Holy Spirit, and teaching them to obey everything I have commanded you. And surely I am with you always, to the very end of the age." NIV

About the Author

A.G. TERRILL is a Wife, Mother, Stepmother, and Grandmother.

She has Multiple Sclerosis, Asthma, Carpel Tunnel, Planar Fasciitis, and several other "thorns" that she deals with on a daily basis with God's help.

She enjoys spending time with her family, helping out at church, reading, and yes, watching movies and television.

But the most important thing that she has to say about herself is that she strives daily, with the help of The Holy Spirit, to become a more devoted and willing servant of God.

References

KJV - Scriptures quoted from The Holy Bible, King James Version, public domain
ASV - Scripture quoted from the American Standard Version of 1901, public domain.
NASB – New American Standard Bible
NLT- New Living Translation
NIV- New International Version

"Scripture taken from the NEW AMERICAN STANDARD BIBLE®, *NASB*®,
© Copyright 1960, 1962, 1963, 1968, 1971, 1972, 1973, 1975, 1977, 1995 by The Lockman Foundation
All rights reserved. Used by permission. (www.Lockman.org)

Scripture quotations marked (NLT) are taken from the *Holy Bible,* New Living Translation, copyright © 1996, 2004, 2007 by Tyndale House Foundation. Used by permission of Tyndale House Publishers, Inc., Carol Stream, Illinois 60188. All rights reserved.

Unless otherwise indicated, all Scripture quotations are taken from the *Holy Bible,* New Living Translation, copyright © 1996, 2004, 2007 by Tyndale House Foundation. Used by permission of Tyndale House Publishers, Inc., Carol Stream, Illinois 60188. All rights reserved.

Scripture taken from the Holy Bible, NEW INTERNATIONAL VERSION®. Copyright © 1973, 1978, 1984, 2011 by Biblica, Inc. All rights reserved worldwide. Used by permission.

NEW INTERNATIONAL VERSION® and NIV® are registered trademarks of Biblica, Inc. Use of either trademark for the offering of goods or services requires the prior written consent of Biblica US, Inc.

Definitions taken from Dictionary.com. LLC. Copyright © 2012. All rights reserved.

American Psychological Association (APA):

sin. (n.d.). *Dictionary.com Unabridged..* Retrieved December 03, 2012, from Dictionary.com website: http://dictionary.reference.com/browse/sin

Chicago Manual Style (CMS):

sin. Dictionary.com. Dictionary.com Unabridged. Random House, Inc. http://dictionary.reference.com/browse/sin (accessed: December 03, 2012).

Modern Language Association (MLA):

"sin." *Dictionary.com Unabridged.* Random House, Inc. 03 Dec. 2012. <Dictionary.com http://dictionary.reference.com/browse/sin>.

Institute of Electrical and Electronics Engineers (IEEE):

Dictionary.com, "sin," in *Dictionary.com Unabridged.* Source location: Random House Inc. http://dictionary.reference.com/browse/sin. Available: http://dictionary.reference.com. Accessed: December 03, 2012.

BibTeX Bibliography Style (BibTeX)

```
@article {Dictionary.com2012,
    title = {Dictionary.com Unabridged},
    month = {Dec},day = {03},year = {2012},
    url = {http://dictionary.reference.com/browse/sin},}
```

Definitions taken from WEBSTER'S ENCYCLOPEDIC UNABRIDGED DICTIONARY of the ENGLISH LANGUAGE

Acknowledgments and Permissions

The "A Dictionary of the English Language" portion of *Webster's Encyclopedic Unabridged Dictionary* is based on the second edition of *The Random House Dictionary of the English Language, the Unabridged Edition*, copyright © 1993,1987

Copyright © 1996 by Random House Value Publishing, Inc.

All rights reserved under International and Pan-American Copyright Conventions.

The 1996 edition is published by Gramercy Books, a division of Random House Value Publishing Inc.

www.ingramcontent.com/pod-product-compliance
Lightning Source LLC
Chambersburg PA
CBHW022116080426
42734CB00006B/156
* 9 7 8 1 3 1 2 1 4 5 4 0 5 *